ACADEMIC QUALITY RANKINGS
OF
AMERICAN COLLEGES AND UNIVERSITIES

ACADEMIC QUALITY RANKINGS
OF
AMERICAN COLLEGES AND UNIVERSITIES

By

DAVID S. WEBSTER, Ph.D.

Assistant Professor of Education
Graduate School of Education
University of Pennsylvania
Philadelphia, Pennsylvania

CHARLES C THOMAS • PUBLISHER
Springfield • Illinois • U.S.A.

Published and Distributed Throughout the World by

CHARLES C THOMAS • PUBLISHER
2600 South First Street
Springfield, Illinois 62717

ISBN 0-398-05212-3
Library of Congress Catalog Card Number: 85-28932

With THOMAS BOOKS *careful attention is given to all details of manufacturing and design. It is the Publisher's desire to present books that are satisfactory as to their physical qualities and artistic possibilities and appropriate for their particular use.* THOMAS BOOKS *will be true to those laws of quality that assure a good name and good will.*

Printed in the United States of America
SC-R-3

Library of Congress Cataloging-in-Publication Data

Webster, David S.
    Academic quality rankings of American colleges and
universities.

    Bibliography: p.
    Includes index.
    1. Universities and colleges—United States—
Evaluation.   I. Title.
LB2331.63.W43   1986   378.73   85-28932
ISBN 0-398-05212-3

To my mother and the memory of my father

ON ACADEMIC QUALITY

Christ, a superior-being type! The kind who think since the ratio of Radcliffe to Harvard is five to one, the girls must be five times as smart.

Erich Segal, *Love Story*

                                    I could not print
Ground where the grass had yielded to the steps
Of generations of illustrious men,
Unmoved. I could not always lightly pass
Through the same gateways, sleep where they had slept,
Wake where they waked, range that inclosure old,
That garden of great intellects, undisturbed.

William Wordsworth, *The Prelude*

Yes, certainly, it is this mild, miasmal air, not less than the grey beauty and gravity of the buildings, that has helped Oxford to produce, and foster eternally, her peculiar race of artist-scholars, scholar-artists.

Max Beerbohm, *Zuleika Dobson*

The local situation of the college, so far secluded from the sight and sound of the busy world, is peculiarly favorable to the moral, if not to the literary, habits of its students.

Nathaniel Hawthorne, *Fanshawe*

The contests were to take place on a Wednesday evening. On the Monday previous all the Yale athletes went to New York.

Special permission from the faculty had to be obtained for this absence from the college, but there was no difficulty in getting that, as there is hardly a professor at Yale who does not have a strong interest in athletic events.

Burt L. Standish (pseud.), *Frank Merriwell's Return to Yale*

For there is nothing in England to be matched with what lurks in the vapours of these meadows, and in the shadows of these spires—that mysterious, inenubilable spirit, spirit of Oxford, Oxford! The very sight of the word printed, or sound of it spoken, is fraught for me with most actual magic.

Max Beerbohm, *Zuleika Dobson*

"Don't send my son to Harvard," the dying mother said,
"Don't send him to Michigan, I'd rather see him dead . . . "

Anonymous song

Pencey Prep is this school that's in Agerstown, Pennsylvania. You probably heard of it. You've probably seen the ads, anyway. They advertise in about a thousand magazines, always showing some hotshot guy on a horse jumping over a fence. Like as if all you ever did at Pencey was play polo all the time. I never even saw a horse anywhere *near* the place. And underneath the guy on the horse's picture, it always says: "Since 1888 we have been molding boys into splendid, clear-thinking young men." Strictly for the birds. They don't do any damn more *molding* at Pencey than they do at any other school. And I didn't know anybody there that was splended and clear-thinking and all. Maybe two guys. If that many. And they probably *came* to Pencey that way.

J.D. Salinger, *The Catcher in the Rye*

" . . . the trouble with Harvard," he told Bessie in the kitchen, "is that all the instructors are guys from Tufts, and Clark, and Oberlin, and all dinky colleges like that, and they mark hard because they're jealous."

Myron S. Kaufmann, *Remember Me to God*

I nearly petrified! By some celestial coincidence your friend and mine, Merritt of the U, had been radared upon the beach in Fort Lauderdale, Florida, beside an Ivy Leaguer!

Glendon Swarthout, *Where the Boys Are*

. . . where *I* come from, a section man's a person that takes over a class when the professor isn't there or is busy having a nervous breakdown or is at the dentist or something. He's usually a graduate student or something. Anyway, if it's a course in Russian Literature, say, he comes in, in his little button-down collar shirt and striped tie, and starts knocking Turgenev for about a half hour. Then, when he's finished, when he's completely *ruined* Turgenev for you, he starts talking about Stendahl. . . .

J.D. Salinger, *Franny and Zooey*

To the University of Oxford *I* acknowledged no obligation; and she will as cheerfully renounce me for a son as I am willing to discard her for a mother. I spent fourteen months at Magdalen College; they proved the fourteen months, the most idle and unprofitable of my whole life.

Edward Gibbon, *Autobiography*

In these colleges the professors contrive new rules and methods of agriculture and building, and new instruments and tools for all trades and manufactures, whereby, as they undertake, one man shall do the work of ten; a palace may be built in a week, of materials so durable as to last for ever without repairing. All the fruits of the earth shall come to maturity at whatever season we think fit to choose, and increase an hundred fold more than they do at present with innumerable other happy proposals. The only inconvenience is, that none of these projects are yet brought to perfection, and in the mean time the whole country lies miserably waste, the houses in ruins, and the people without food or clothes.

Jonathan Swift, *Gulliver's Travels*

Since talking with you I have confidence in your ability to do a good job. As I said, we're looking for people who can hold up their end of it and keep the department running smoothly. This is a fine place to start your college teaching, and if you're our type, it's a good place to stay. We don't pretend we're anything more than a typical American state college. The atmosphere is relaxed. There's no "publish or perish" hanging over everybody's head. There are no geniuses around to make you uncomfortable. Life is peaceful here. . . .

Bernard Malamud, *A New Life*

"Yes," picked up Fargo. "We on the Student Council feel that however rich Harvard may be, however 'wide her title and proud her name,' she still has failed if in these cold halls there reigns no comradely feeling of good fellowship. In this very entry there are men who put book-learning above comradeship."

George Weller, *Not to Eat, Not for Love*

Kay suspected that he was angry because Helena had failed to get *magna cum laude,* when a lot of the Jewish girls had. Mrs. Davison evidently had the same thought, because she now cleared her throat and remarked that the simple *cum laude,* Helena's meed, was the sign of a real student as opposed to what, in *her* day, had been called "a greasy grind." "I *watched* those *magnas* go up for their diplomas," she announced, "and I didn't like the look of them at all; they smelled of the lamp. . . . "

Mary McCarthy, The Group

The tower that in view of his window sprang upward, grew into a spire, yearning higher until its uppermost tip was half invisible against the morning skies, gave him the first sense of the transiency and unimportance of the campus figures except as holders of the apostolic succession. He liked knowing that Gothic architecture, with its upward trend, was peculiarly appropriate to universities, and the idea became personal to him. The silent stretches of green, the quiet halls with an occasional late-burning scholastic light held his imagination in a strong grasp, and the chastity of the spire became a symbol of this perception.

"Damn it all," he whispered aloud, wetting his hands in the damp and running them through his hair. "Next year I work!"

F. Scott Fitzgerald, This Side of Paradise

PREFACE

PLAN OF THE BOOK

The plan of this book is as follows. Chapter One briefly discusses surveys of the literature on academic quality rankings; Chapter Two makes comparisons of early (pre-1959) with modern quality rankings, showing the similarities and differences between them; Chapter Three examines the European debate, during the last third of the 19th century and the early years of the 20th century, over whether geniuses were the product of heredity or environment; it then shows the importance of this debate in the pre-history of academic quality rankings.

Chapters Four through Six can be considered as a group. They all look at the efforts of organizations that classified colleges, universities, professional schools, or some combination of these, based on criteria which these organizations thought reflected academic quality. These groups then stratified institutions and professional schools into broad quality levels, the number of levels they employed generally ranging from two to six. The organizations discussed are as follows.

Chapter Four—The United States Bureau of Education

Chapter Five—The American Medical Association's Council on Medical Education and the work, following its methods, of several other professional associations and organizations accrediting professional fields

Chapter Six—The stratification efforts of the Methodist Episcopal Church, South and various state agencies

Chapters Seven through Twelve can be considered as a group, as well. They discuss the work of organizations that seldom (there were a few exceptions) attempted to stratify colleges and universities into levels according to their "quality." They did, though, all publish undifferentiated lists of colleges and universities that they thought excelled most others, or at least most others of the same type. (A "type" of school could be a university, for example, as opposed to a college, or an institution that enrolled women as undergraduates.)

Chapter Thirteen discusses Abraham Flexner's landmark study of the quality of medical schools, *Medical Education in the United States and Canada*, and three works which, using some of Flexner's techniques, studied the quality of education provided by dental schools, law schools, and schools for blacks. Chapter Fourteen shows how James McKeen Cattell "invented" academic quality rankings in 1910.

The next three chapters focus on modern academic quality rankings. Chapter Fifteen discusses in detail the best multidisciplinary ranking ever done, the National Academy of Sciences' *Assessment of Research-Doctorate Programs in the United States* (1982); it then determines America's highest-ranked institutions for graduate education in the arts, sciences, and engineering, from 1925 to 1982. Chapter Sixteen discusses the six methods most often used today to rank institutions according to their academic quality, examining the advantages and disadvantages of each method. Chapter Seventeen enumerates the minimal requirements that an ideal academic quality ranking should meet.

PREVIOUSLY PUBLISHED MATERIAL

Parts of this book have been published elsewhere in different form. Chapter Three, "European Studies of the Backgrounds of Eminent People," appeared in slightly different form under the title "Academic Quality Rankings: Why They Developed in the United States and Not Europe," in the *History of Higher Education Annual*, vol. 2, 1982, pp. 102–127.

Chapter Four, "The United States Bureau of Education's Stratifications," appeared in somewhat different form in the *History of Education Quarterly*, vol. 24, no. 4, winter, 1984, pp. 499–511.

Part of Chapter Five, "Classification Efforts by the Council on Medical Education and Similar Groups," appeared in different form in *Focus on Learning*, vol. 11, no. 1, February, 1985, pp. 81–85.

Chapter Fourteen, "James McKeen Cattell and the Invention of Academic Quality Rankings," appeared in different form in the *Review of Higher Education*, vol. 8, no. 2, winter, 1985, pp. 107–121. Part of the same chapter appeared in different form as "A Note on a Very Early Academic Quality Ranking by James McKeen Cattell," in the *Journal of the History of the Behavioral Sciences*, vol. 20, no. 2, April, 1984, pp. 180–183.

Chapter Fifteen, "The National Academy of Sciences' Ranking of 1982 and America's Best Graduate Schools, 1925–1982," appeared in somewhat different form in *Change*, vol. 15, no. 4, May/June, 1983, pp. 14–24.

Chapter Sixteen, "Contemporary Methods of Assessing College and University Quality," appeared in slightly altered form in *Change*, vol. 13, no. 7, October, 1981, pp. 20–24.

ACKNOWLEDGMENTS

In studying the history of efforts to compare the quality of colleges and universities, I have been helped by many people. I want to thank collectively the dozens of people who have sent me academic quality rankings or information about them. Of these, a few have given me materials so valuable that I must thank them individually. They are Mrs. Allan M. Cartter of Beverly Hills, California; Theodora Kalikow of the University of Northern Colorado; Mary Langenfeld of the University of Wisconsin at Madison, who has helped me greatly on many occasions over several years; Toby Fishbein Murray of the University of Tulsa; Emery R. Walker of Claremont, California; Claude Welch of the Graduate Theological Union, Berkeley, California; and Logan Wilson of Austin, Texas.

Fourteen people received chapters of this book. These chapters and their reviewers are as follows: Chapter Three, on studies of the backgrounds of eminent people, by George Becker of Vanderbilt University and Marion White McPherson of the Archives of the History of American Psychology at the University of Akron; Chapter Four, on the United States Bureau of Education, by Michael Katz of the University of Pennsylvania and Richard Wayne Lykes of George Mason University; the part of Chapter Five on the American Medical Association's Council on Medical Education, by Richard Egan, M.D., of that organization; the part of Chapter Six on state accrediting organizations and all of Chapter Twelve, on regional accrediting agencies, by Frank Dickey of Lexington, Kentucky; Fred Harcleroad of Tucson, Arizona; James Phillips of the Association of Independent Colleges and Schools; and William Selden of Princeton, New Jersey; Chapter Nine, on the General Education Board, by J. William Hess of the Rockefeller Archive Center and Flora Rhind of Kennett Square, Pennsylvania; Chapter Ten, on the Carnegie Foundation for the Advancement of Teaching, by Florence Anderson of the Carnegie Corporation of New York and Ellen Condliffe Lagemann of Columbia University Teachers College; and Chapter Fourteen, on James McKeen Cattell, by Michael Sokal of Worcester Polytechnic Institute, who helped me repeatedly, in many ways, over several years. All of them improved the chapters they reviewed; responsibility for any faults that remain is mine alone.

I am grateful to Helen Astin, Gordon Kipling, Melvin Pollner, Richard Shavelson, and Peter Thorslev, all of UCLA, for their help with this book when it was in its early stages. Others have helped me, too. Dr. Lorraine Mathies, Librarian of UCLA's Education/Psychology Library, extended many courtesies to me while I was doing research. I greatly appreciate the two grants given to me by the University of Pennsylvania's Research Foundation; they enabled me to complete this book faster than I would have been able to otherwise. At Penn's Graduate School of Education, I thank my colleague Ruth Ebert for her superb editorial and clerical work on the manuscript, and Martha Fitzgerald, a doctoral candidate, for her fine work in proofreading it. I also thank my colleagues Dell Hymes, Ed Boe, and Allan Glatthorn for helping make GSE a stimulating setting in which to teach and write.

I want to thank the three mentor-friends I've been lucky to have: Tom McKnight, professor of geography at UCLA, for his continuing guidance, advice, and support on countless occasions; Alexander Astin, professor of education at UCLA and Director of the Higher Education Research Institute, for the huge amount of help he has given me on this book and in my fledgling career as a scholar and teacher of American higher education; and Irving Louis Horowitz, Hannah Arendt Distinguished Professor of Sociology and Political Science at Livingston College, Rutgers—the State University of New Jersey, for all he has taught me about the publishing industry, academic life, and how to play basketball.

My greatest debts are to my wife, Sandrel, for the joy, contentment, and fulfillment that she has brought me, and to my mother, father, and stepfather for their financial sacrifices, over many years, to pay for my long and expensive education.

LIST OF TABLES

CONTENTS

ACADEMIC QUALITY RANKINGS
OF
AMERICAN COLLEGES AND UNIVERSITIES

Chapter One

INTRODUCTION

This book examines attempts to measure and compare American colleges' and universities' academic quality. It concentrates on efforts to rank institutions in order of their excellence and on those projects that bore the promise of evolving into such rankings, even if they did not ultimately do so. It concentrates on efforts beginning in the late 19th century, when several different lines of work purporting to measure college and university quality all developed more or less independently of each other. It shows who were the people and organizations that wanted to measure college and university quality, why they wanted to do so, how well they succeeded, and why some of them did not have more success than they did.

It focuses on the years before 1925, with only the last three chapters devoted to contemporary academic quality rankings. The year 1925 provides a useful stopping point, because that is when academic quality rankings are almost universally—although quite wrongly—thought to have begun. The history of rankings of colleges, universities, and individual departments according to their quality is a subject that, for reasons worthy of study in themselves, has very seldom been investigated. The evolution of these rankings before 1925 has been almost entirely unknown.

PREVIOUS WORK ON QUALITY RANKINGS

Only one, very brief history of academic quality rankings has ever been written, and it was never published. Although three literature reviews of rankings have been published, none contains so much as one reference to anything published before 1925.

The source that tells most about the early history of academic quality rankings is one chapter of an unpublished Ed.D. dissertation, Arthur Higgins' "Rating of Selected Fields of Doctoral Study in the Graduate Schools of Education: An Opinion Survey" (1968).[1] Its bibliography lists some 190 items, 48 of them published before 1950, by far the largest number of pre-1950 items ever included in a review of rankings. Higgins' work is the only one that mentions rankings done before the 1925 reputational ranking of graduate school departments by Raymond Hughes.[2] He refers very briefly to three studies by James McKeen Cattell on the academic origins of American scientists without, however, discussing these works' significance in the development of academic quality rankings.[3] Thereafter, his chapter examines the history of efforts to judge the quality of graduate schools and graduate school departments, from Hughes's reputational rankings of 1925 to Allan Cartter's *Assessment of Quality in Graduate Education* (1966).[4]

In addition to Higgins' historical sketch, three more or less comprehensive reviews of the literature of academic quality rankings have been published. Higgins' dissertation, remaining unpublished as it did, scarcely influenced them. Of the three, only one so much as mentioned it. The first of these reviews was Richard Smith and Fred Fiedler's "Measurement of Scholarly Work: A Critical Review of the Literature" (1971).[5] The authors cited only three items published before 1950, of which two are by Hughes and the other is a 1949 article on the publication productivity of social scientists.

The next was Robert Blackburn and Paul Lingenfelter's *Assessing Quality in Doctoral Programs: Criteria and Correlates of Excellence* (1973).[6] It was a monograph commissioned by the New York State Board of Regents, which had been "examining the rate of production of students in that state."[7] The Regents apparently wanted information about what criteria should be used to judge which departments to support and which to phase out. This monograph was the only review to cite Higgins's dissertation, giving it exactly one sentence, as follows: "Higgins (1968: 8–55) effectively summarizes the history of graduate school assessment in his unpublished rating of doctoral programs in education" (p. 4). Blackburn and Lingenfelter cited only four items published before 1950, three by Hughes and the other a book on the professoriate published in 1942.

The most recent and comprehensive review of the literature of academic quality rankings is Lawrence and Green's monograph, *A Question of Quality: The Higher Education Ratings Game* (1980).[8] Its bibliography lists some 220 items, of which about 50 bear not on the subject of academic quality rankings per se but rather on accreditation, so about 170 of its sources focus more or less directly on the subject of academic quality rankings. Of these, only two were published before 1950, both of them by Hughes.

So, with the exception of Higgins's unpublished dissertation chapter, no review of the literature of academic quality rankings so much as mentions any work about the study of academic quality rankings before Hughes's 1925 study. They cite, as a group, exactly two items published before 1950 other than the work of Hughes.

Not only do these three literature reviews fail to cite or discuss anything before Hughes's 1925 study, but it is clear that they are not simply using 1925 as a convenient starting point for their literature reviews. Their authors, to the extent that they discuss the matter at all, believe that the first significant academic quality rankings of graduate schools, and, for all practical purposes, academic quality rankings in general, began with Hughes's 1925 study.[9]

Even Logan Wilson, former President of the American Council on Education, implied that Hughes's ranking was the first one published for graduate education. He wrote, concerning studies of graduate school quality, that "Raymond Hughes made the first published appraisal in 1924...."[10] One purpose of this book is thus to show that academic quality rankings originated before 1925.

ACADEMIC QUALITY RANKINGS—A DEFINITION

Only some of the work discussed in this book can be considered academic quality rankings. An academic quality ranking, as defined here, meets both these criteria:

1. It must be arranged according to some criterion or set of criteria which the compiler(s) of the list believed measured or reflected academic quality.

2. It must be a list of the best colleges, universities, or departments in a field of study, in numerical order according to their supposed quality, with each school or department having its own individual rank, not just lumped together with other schools into a handful of quality classes, groups, or levels.

Therefore, the many classifications of all the schools in a field—for example, medical schools—into several levels of quality are not quality rankings because schools were grouped into only a few strata according to their presumed quality, with several and sometimes dozens of schools at each level. Similarly, many organizations that devoted great amounts of time and effort to deciding which institutions to admit to membership did not produce quality rankings. That is because these organizations generally divided all the schools they considered into two groups—those that qualified for membership and those that did not. They seldom tried to differentiate further among the schools in either group.

Most early efforts to measure academic quality are thus precursors or forerunners of academic quality rankings. Even so, academic quality rankings meeting both criteria stated above were invented years before Raymond Hughes's reputational ranking of 1925.

THE USEFULNESS OF QUALITY RANKINGS

Quality rankings have been criticized often and for many reasons. A whole book has even been published which vigorously attacks rankings that are based on scholars' research reputations in the eyes of other scholars.[11] Nonetheless, just as democracy, according to Winston Churchill, is the worst form of government except for all the others, so quality rankings are the worst device for comparing the quality of American colleges and universities, except for all the others.

Accrediting agencies, both the ones responsible for geographical regions and those that assess programs in particular fields of study, are of little use in showing the comparative quality of American colleges and universities. The information they reveal to the public is usually that a particular institution is or is not accredited or a candidate for accreditation. They generally release no more detailed information about the quality of the schools which they accredit or, for that matter, fail to accredit.

College catalogs are not much help on the subject of comparative quality. They seldom contain much information on a school's quality, either relative to American colleges and universities as a whole or to comparable institutions.

The commercial guidebooks to colleges and universities which sell, in aggregate, by the hundreds of thousands each year, do not help much. Though they are gold mines of facts and statistics concerning the institutions they list, most of them make no attempt to compare directly the quality of the schools they cover. The few that do, like *Barron's Profiles of American Colleges* and Cass and Birnbaum's *Comparative Guide to American Colleges*, stratify institutions into several levels.

These groupings are not intended to be quality rankings, and they have two characteristics which prevent them from being used as such.

First, institutions are placed into levels based on how "selective" they were in admitting a recent freshman class, and the relationship between admissions selectivity and overall institutional quality is far from clear. Second, there are only a few "selectivity" strata—*Comparative Guide to American Colleges* used eight in its 1983 edition—and consequently dozens or even hundreds of schools are lumped together on the same level.

Other sources are of no more help concerning comparative college quality. Arthur Levine, President of Bradford College in Massachusetts, has written of his despair when, after writing to 20 different organizations, agencies, and public officials, he could not find out even the most basic information about the academic reputation of one particular institution.[12]

Every day, material that makes claims for which there is little convincing evidence is published about American colleges and universities. Some of it is promulgated by the institutions themselves in the form of advertising. Here are some typical examples.

Blackburn College in Carlinville, Illinois ran a classified ad that called it "one of America's finest liberal-arts colleges."[13] The College of Idaho in Caldwell referred in a classified ad to its "ninety year history of academic distinction."[14] A display ad placed by Mercy College of Dobbs Ferry, New York said that "Mercy College has an outstanding faculty with the highest credentials."[15] A display ad for the University of San Francisco referred to it as a "great university," although it offers the doctorate in only the field of education.[16] An ad for Slippery Rock State College (now Slippery Rock University) in Slippery Rock, Pennsylvania said that this school was "acclaimed by many as the nation's best-known small college," despite the possibility that Slippery Rock is widely known at least as much for its charming name as for any academic feature that people would "acclaim."[17]

Statements that might prove hard to substantiate appear elsewhere than in advertisements. They are often made by officials of colleges and universities themselves and reported in the metropolitan press. So, for example, the administrator for financial and business matters of the Community College of Philadelphia (CCP) said the following:

> [The Community College of Philadelphia's] tuition rate, the best bargain in all of education, is just $456 a semester, or $912 a year, for full-time students.[18]

At the time, though, CCP's yearly tuition for full-time students was higher than that, for in-state residents, of the University of Texas at

Austin, the University of Arizona, Arizona State University, Louisiana State University, San Francisco State University, and San Jose State University, among others. These institutions have at least as much claim to academic excellence as has CCP. Therefore, the college's tuition might not necessarily have been the best bargain in "all of education," or even all of higher education.

The president of Rutgers University recently said that the English department of Rutgers' New Brunswick campus ranked "second or third — maybe . . . first" in the United States.[19] But the last four multidisciplinary academic quality rankings rate this department, at least its Ph.D. program, somewhat differently. The *Cartter Report* of 1966 ranked it at some unspecified point in a group of 13, below the top 29 English departments;[20] the Roose-Andersen study ranked it somewhere in a group of 11, below the top 23 English departments;[21] the Ladd and Lipset study ranked only the top 11 English departments, a group that did not include Rutgers.[22]

The National Academy of Sciences (NAS) used twelve different criteria to rate English departments. Rutgers did not rank first, second, or third in any of them. To consider the two NAS criteria that have been used most often, over the years, to assess academic quality, in reputation for its faculty's scholarly quality Rutgers' English department ranked 15th; in reputation for its Ph.D. program's effectiveness, it ranked 18th.[23]

The president-elect of Temple University said this to a reporter:

> We're not going to make Temple into a Harvard — and that's not because we're not as good as Harvard, but because Harvard hasn't done as well as Temple has at this social role.[24]

College and university officials are not the only ones who make statements about institutions which it might be hard to corroborate. For example, a newspaper reporter wrote this about the University of Southern California (USC):

> Overall, USC has not been able to climb into the small circle of the nation's highest-ranked universities. It is on everybody's list of the 20 best universities but seldom on a list of the 10 best.[25]

This comment overlooks the reality that in none of the seven major, multidisciplinary academic quality rankings published from 1925 to 1982 has USC ever ranked among the top 25 schools, much less the top 20.[26]

A student at Howard University's College of Medicine was quoted in one of the nation's most respected newspapers as follows: "Howard University has always ranked with the top medical schools in the nation.

That's why I came here."[27] This remark ignores the fact that in a very carefully done reputational ranking of American medical schools published three years before the student spoke, of the 94 American medical schools that had been approved by the American Medical Association in 1971–72, Howard ranked 89th.[28]

All things considered, academic quality rankings are needed. They provide evidence against which claims like those cited above, and hundreds more like them spoken and published every day, can be tested. Academic quality rankings, despite all their faults, have nevertheless been useful, from their beginnings, in providing more accurate information about the comparative quality of American colleges, universities, and individual departments and professional fields of study than any other source. They still fulfill this useful role today.

Chapter Two

COMPARISON OF EARLY WITH MODERN ACADEMIC QUALITY RANKINGS

There are both important similarities and major differences between early—those published before 1959[1]—and modern academic quality rankings. Their similarities will be discussed first.

SIMILARITIES

Academic quality rankings, both early and modern, have been very much influenced by the kinds of general reference works that were available at the time they were produced. It is no coincidence that the origin of academic quality rankings occurred very shortly after the publication of the first editions of *Who's Who in America* (1899) and James McKeen Cattell's *American Men of Science* (1906).[2]

These reference works, originally intended for very different uses than to serve as a basis for academic quality rankings, were nonetheless very useful sources for those who wished to use them as such. And, as the historian and sociologist of science Arnold Thackray has pointed out, because Cattell's *American Men of Science* was available more than 20 years before the first volumes of the *Dictionary of American Biography* began to appear, *American Men of Science* was probably used more often as source material for academic quality rankings than it otherwise would have been.

The kinds of available reference works have strongly influenced the development of modern academic quality rankings, too. For example, the publication of the *Science Citation Index* (which appeared first in 1961 and annually thereafter) and the *Social Sciences Citation Index* (which appeared first in 1966 and yearly afterwards), two reference works that also were intended for very different purposes than serving as source material for quality rankings, stimulated dozens of academic quality rankings using the number of "citations" an academic department's faculty had achieved as the basis for the ranking.

Academic quality rankings, almost since their inception, have been the target for cries of outrage from administrators unhappy with their institutions' ranking.[3] Such a great uproar greeted a classification, even before it was officially released, made by the Bureau of Education in 1911, that two successive United States presidents suppressed it. Many modern academic quality rankings have provoked storms of protest, too. For example, in 1971 Claude Welch, Dean of the Graduate Theological Union in Berkeley, California, published *Graduate Education in Religion: A Critical Appraisal,* which classified theological schools and seminaries into six groups according to their academic "quality."[4] Officials of many institutions assigned to the two lowest categories were incensed, some of them threatening to sue him.

Both early and recent academic quality rankings have very seldom ranked institutions by *type.* While many applicants to college may only wish, or at least strongly prefer, to attend a Catholic institution, an historically black college,[5] or a Protestant fundamentalist college, few rankings of schools in these categories have been made. Similarly, very few academic quality rankings have ever rated only women's colleges, private junior colleges, or public community colleges. This situation is unfortunate.

The high school senior in the Texas panhandle who belongs to the Church of Christ and who wishes to attend a college sponsored by, or at least maintaining ties with, that church will find little or no information in the form of academic quality rankings to inform him about these schools. Are nearby Lubbock Christian College, Oklahoma Christian College, and Abilene Christian University about as good academically as any college in the country related to the Church of Christ? Or is it worthwhile, on academic grounds, to travel to far-off David Lipscomb College (Tennessee) or Pepperdine University (California)? Quality rankings are very little help.

Similarly, the female high school senior who wishes to attend a private junior college for women in the Northeast has virtually no information in the form of quality rankings about which school—Bay Path, Endicott, Fisher, or Lasell (all in Massachusetts) or Harcum (in Pennsylvania)—would be better academically, either overall or in any particular field of study.

This absence of quality rankings for types of colleges is lamentable. For although there is no shortage of folklore about what are the academically best historically black institutions—according to folklore, Howard University, Morehouse College, and Hampton Institute are a few of them—there is very little objective evidence available about their relative quality. The black high school senior in Louisiana who wishes to attend an historically black institution in his home state will find very little in the way of academic quality rankings to apprise him or her of the differences in academic quality, overall or in any individual field of study, among Grambling, Dillard, Xavier, and Southern University's campuses in Baton Rouge and New Orleans.

Academic quality rankings, then, both early and modern, in listing mainly the better institutions and the better departments within a discipline, have failed to provide for the needs of students and others who wish to make choices only within a particular type of institution.[6]

Those who have published academic quality rankings, both early and modern ones, have usually been social scientists. That is not surprising, for it is social scientists who generally have the greatest professional interest in such concepts as prestige, status, recognition, and mobility that the rankings reflect. There have been a few exceptions, of course. Raymond Hughes, for example, was a chemist and Hayward Keniston a Romance philologist.

Both early and modern academic quality rankings, at least the best-known, multidisciplinary ones, have generally been done by people at highly-regarded research universities. Cattell established the pattern by inventing academic quality rankings while he was at Columbia. Some of the single-discipline quality rankings that have appeared in the *American Psychologist* since at least 1960 and were published in the *American Sociologist* from shortly after it was founded in 1965 until it stopped publishing them in 1975 have been done by people at very obscure colleges. The major multidisciplinary studies, though, both old and recent, have generally been done by researchers at highly-regarded universities, such as Peter Blau and Rebecca Zames Margulies (Columbia), and Allan Cartter, Alexander Astin, and Lewis Solmon (UCLA).

There has always been enormous disparity among the academic disciplines and professional fields of study in terms of how often they were the subject of academic quality rankings. A disproportionately large number of early efforts to group colleges, universities, and fields of study into classes or strata were done for professional fields of study, especially for the major professions, such as medicine and law. A large percentage of the modern ones have been done for social science disciplines, especially psychology, sociology, and economics. (Several rankings have been done of subfields of these three disciplines, such as counseling psychology, rural sociology, and agricultural economics.) Both early and modern academic quality rankings, though, have slighted the natural sciences (Cattell's work was an exception); most of the minor professions, such as library science, nursing, optometry, and social work; and, especially, all the humanities.

Many academic quality rankings, early and recent, have been based upon students' success in later life, as measured by such criteria as how many of them go on to earn a Ph.D., win a fellowship of one type or another, or enter a prestigious occupation. Those who do these rankings usually ignore the possibility that colleges and universities may simply "pass along" students to the kinds of careers for which their abilities and aspirations destine them, no matter where they attend college. Many colleges and universities consider it important for their students to achieve other goals as well—to become concerned, responsible members of their local communities, for example, or remain devout members of their church. Yet no academic quality ranking, old or new, has ever been based upon how well graduates of various colleges achieve these goals.

The academic pecking order of the best American research universities, as measured by the most commonly done types of academic quality rankings, has remained remarkably stable throughout the 20th century. In Cattell's first academic quality ranking (1910), which showed the "scientific strength" of leading universities based upon the research reputations of their faculty members in twelve science and social science disciplines, the fifteen leading universities, in order, were as follows: Harvard, Chicago, Columbia, Johns Hopkins, Yale, Cornell, Wisconsin, MIT, Michigan, California, Stanford, Princeton, Illinois, Pennsylvania, and Clark.

In the multidimensional ranking published by the National Academy of Sciences of doctoral programs in the arts, sciences, and engineering published in 1982,[7] 13 of these 15 universities—all but Johns Hopkins and Clark—ranked among the top 14 for doctoral work when their program scores were combined.[8] It is extremely unlikely that there would be such stability from 1910 to 1982 in the leaders, no matter how leadership was measured, of most other American institutions—for example, corporations, newspapers, banks, or hospitals.

Both old and recent academic quality rankings have very seldom been based upon *what actually happens* to students during their years in college. Those who compile them have a penchant for measuring students' abilities *when the students arrive* at college, as in early classifications and stratifications of institutions according to their academic quality, the number of years of high school or the number of Carnegie units they had completed, and, in recent rankings, their freshmen's combined SAT or ACT scores.

They have frequently measured the achievements of students *after they graduated*—for example, by their success in the nation's leading graduate schools, their earning Ph.D.s, winning prestigious fellowships and awards, and becoming scholars or scientists.

They have measured the academic resources available to students on campus, such as the ratio of instructors to students and the number of volumes in the library. However, they have made very little effort to determine how much colleges and universities actually *teach* their students. They have very seldom tried to find out how much students actually learn from their instructors, how often and how rewardingly they actually read the volumes in their campus libraries, and to rank colleges and universities according to these criteria.

Besides these similarities, there have been several important differences between early and modern academic quality rankings.

DIFFERENCES

Early efforts to classify and stratify colleges and universities into groups according to their quality or to form lists of the best colleges and universities were often multidimensional. That is, in assessing the quality of institutions, they often used several dimensions of quality, averaging them to obtain an overall score.

By contrast, modern academic quality rankings are much more likely to use only a single criterion, such as faculty publication productivity or faculty scholarly "reputation" as a basis for measuring academic quality. The National Academy of Sciences' recent multidimensional rating is a prominent exception to this rule.

Most early attempts to classify, stratify, and admit to membership institutions according to their academic quality used "whole" institutions as their unit of measurement. Modern academic quality rankings, on the other hand, are almost always arranged by academic field or discipline. They rank economics, geography, or sociology departments—or all three of them—but very seldom entire institutions. Almost all the modern researchers who have compiled multidisciplinary rankings have refrained from aggregating their departmental scores to obtain institution-wide scores.

Many early attempts to classify and stratify colleges and universities, based as they were on "whole" institutions, were inevitably based largely or entirely on the quality of undergraduate education. That was because most of the schools included in these studies were institutions either exclusively for undergraduates or ones with small graduate programs. The great majority of modern academic quality rankings, on the other hand, have been done for Ph.D.-granting departments and professional schools. Consequently, quality rankings of undergraduate education, either by "whole" institutions or disaggregated by department, are badly needed. Rankings of graduate-level programs offering the master's as the highest degree are needed, too.[9]

Early academic quality rankings, from the evidence that is available, affected colleges and universities differently from the way that modern ones do. Their impact was greater, primarily because rankings, classifications, and stratifications were usually organized by whole institutions, not by discipline. Consequently, the reputation and well-being of a whole institution, not just a department or professional field, depended on its position in some classification system or upon whether or not it was admitted to some organization.

Today's academic quality rankings, however, probably affect student applications, especially applications to graduate and professional school, far more than did early rankings, classifications, and stratifications. Early academic classifications and stratifications were generally published in obscure sources, sources that a high school senior or even a college senior would be unlikely to consult. Recently, however, multidisciplinary reputational rankings have been widely stocked by high school and college libraries, where they are in great demand, and they are extensively reported upon in the press.

Early academic quality rankings were based far more often upon the accomplishments of a college's graduates than of its faculty. Modern rankings are much more often based upon the accomplishments, especially the research accomplishments, of the faculty. There are a few exceptions. Some of Cattell's early rankings were based partly upon the research reputations of his institutions' science faculty, whereas today some quality rankings based upon the achievements of a school's graduates are still published. By and large, though, this generalization holds true.

It is surprising that early academic quality rankings very seldom measured the quality and quantity of faculty members' research, because during the early years of the 20th century when they were published, many universities already considered research their most important, or at least one of their most important, functions. Since even today virtually all colleges and universities, even research universities, consider teaching one of their most important missions, it is equally surprising that many recent academic quality rankings are based on faculty research reputation and publication productivity, not even partly on the faculty's teaching and advising abilities.

The reason why research is emphasized and teaching and advising are downplayed is probably because of the tremendous amount of money, especially federal money, available for academic research. Those who want to "purchase" this research wish to know departmental and institutional research capabilities, so they can spend their money wisely. Universities, for their part, almost invariably interpret to their own advantage their departmental standings in academic quality rankings based on their faculty's research reputation. The highest-ranked institutions argue that their eminence entitles them to additional support; the lower-ranked ones argue that they are not getting their fair share of research money and deserve to be more generously funded.

The publication rate of academic quality rankings has increased very sharply throughout the century, especially from the mid-1960s to the present. The history of academic quality rankings from 1925 to the present can be divided into two broad periods. The first was from 1925–1958, the era of the ascendancy of the "academic origins" studies that had been invented by Cattell. One of his followers was Samuel Fernberger, a psychologist at the University of Pennsylvania, who studied the college and university origins of academic psychologists. Another was Beverly Waugh Kunkel, a biologist at Lafayette College. In many studies, some of them co-authored with Donald B. Prentice, long-time President of the Rose-Hulman Institute of Technology, he examined the academic origins of several groups of prominent people, most frequently people listed in *Who's Who in America.*

A third was Stephen Sargent Visher, the distinguished Indiana University geographer, who published three books and more than 80 articles on the academic origins and current institutional affiliations of the "starred" (that is, most distinguished) scientists listed in Cattell's *American Men of Science.* He produced a massive work that remains the *summa* of the "academic origins" school, *Scientists Starred, 1903–1943, in "American Men of*

Science."[10] A fourth was the Wesleyan University psychologist Robert H. Knapp, who published, with Hubert B. Goodrich, *Origins of American Scientists;*[11] with Joseph J. Greenbaum, *The Younger American Scholar: His Collegiate Origins;*[12] and by himself, *The Origins of American Humanistic Scholars.*[13]

During the years 1925–1958, very few reputational rankings were published. Raymond Hughes published multidisciplinary reputational rankings in 1925 and 1934,[14] but thereafter no major, multidisciplinary academic quality ranking was published for 25 years. The era of the ascendancy of "academic origins" studies and the dormancy of reputational rankings ended in 1959, when Hayward Keniston published his reputational ranking of 25 leading universities in 24 disciplines, *Graduate Study and Research in the Arts and Sciences at the University of Pennsylvania.*[15] It ushered in the second broad period, from 1959 to the present.

In this period, reputational rankings have been ascendant. Keniston's ranking served to renew interest in reputational rankings and was followed by a spate of them, including Allan Cartter's *Assessment of Quality in Graduate Education* (1966);[16] Roose and Andersen's *Rating of Graduate Programs* (1970);[17] two rankings of professional schools by Peter Blau and Rebecca Zames Margulies in *Change* magazine, one in 1973 and the other in 1974/'75;[18] one by Everett Carll Ladd, Jr. and Seymour Martin Lipset published in the *Chronicle of Higher Education* in 1979;[19] and one published by the National Academy of Sciences in 1982.[20] Today all these reputational rankings are far better known and far more widely cited than any of the "academic origins" studies, including Cattell's seminal work and Visher's massive book.

The three books by Knapp and his collaborators during the 1950s and early 1960s, in which colleges and universities were ranked on the basis of the number of scientists and scholars they had "produced," probably hastened the demise of "academic origins" studies. They aroused widespread criticism over the years, and more than one critic pointed out that the number of scientists or scholars who had graduated from an institution revealed little about its quality unless the researcher controlled for the academic ability of the students when they entered the institution.

Today, these studies are not published nearly as often as they were before 1960. Although they are occasionally compiled for individual fields of study, especially psychology, sociology, and medicine, very few book-length "academic origins" studies, such as those by Visher and by Knapp and his collaborators, have been published in the past 25 years.

Chapter Three

EUROPEAN STUDIES OF THE
BACKGROUNDS OF EMINENT PEOPLE

An important forerunner of academic quality rankings was the studies, published mostly in Europe and especially in England, France, and Germany, about the ecological origins of eminent men and women. These works investigated such matters as where these people were born, where they grew up, where they attended school, and—of most concern here—whether and where they attended a university, since from lists of how many eminent people had attended various universities, academic quality rankings could easily have developed.[1] Most of those who wrote about the university backgrounds of eminent people took one side or another of a hot debate about whether such "geniuses," as the participants in this debate often called them, were more the "result" of their heredity or their environment.[2]

THE ENVIRONMENTALISTS

One of the first great environmentalists was the Swiss botanist Alphonse de Candolle.[3] In his *Histoire des Sciences et des Savants depuis Deux Siècles*, he listed eighteen factors he considered favorable to the advancement of science, including two directly concerning education. These two were as follows:

> Elementary, and especially middle and higher instruction, that is well-organized, independent of political or religious factions, tending to inspire research and to encourage young people and instructors devoted to science.

And also:

> Abundant and well-organized material means for various kinds of scientific work (libraries, observatories, laboratories, collections).[4]

Another early environmentalist was Alfred Odin (1864–1896), a professor at the University of Sofia in Bulgaria. In his short life he authored several works on phonology and grammar and a major work, in two volumes, on the origin of French men of letters, *Genèse des Grands Hommes: Gens de Lettres Francais Modernes.*[5] In it, he wrote:

> Everything . . . forces us to admit that education plays a role not only important but principal, decisive, in the development of the man of letters. It operates not only on average ability, but also, and with quite as much intensity, on talent and on genius.[6]

A third strict environmentalist and, along with William James, one of the few first-rate American thinkers to participate in this debate, was the early sociologist Lester Ward. An ardent believer that people could improve society and that an improved society could, in turn, serve to improve individual people in an endless cycle of progress, he wrote in *Applied Sociology* (1906):

> It is evident, then, that education is absolutely indispensable at least to a literary career, and it is practically so to any career in a civilized community. This means that all who are without it are debarred at the outset from all hope of ever joining the forces of civilization. All the achievement of the world has been done by educated persons.[7]

Later in this book he wrote, in the same vein, "genius, however brilliant, cannot succeed without education."[8]

THE HEREDITARIANS

The hereditarians were far more numerous than the environmentalists;[9] they also came much closer to producing an academic quality ranking.

The first great hereditarian was Francis Galton. He himself was a member of a distinguished family; he was related to Charles and Erasmus Darwin. In 1865 he published a two-part article in *MacMillan's Magazine* titled "Hereditary Talent and Character." In it, he examined lists of eminent people, almost all of them men, in several lines of endeavor. He found that many of them had distinguished relatives, even in fields like writing and painting in which Galton believed it was hard for parents to "pass on" their advantages to their children. So he concluded that superior intellectual ability resulted mostly from heredity.[10] In 1869 he published *Hereditary Genius*, in which he claimed to be the first person ever to use detailed statistical evidence to argue that genius was hereditary (p. vi). In 1874, in response to Candolle's *Histoire des Sciences et des Savants depuis Deux Siècles*, he published *English Men of Genius: Their Nature and Nurture*,[11] whose subtitle introduced "one of the most important and controversial distinctions in the social sciences. . . . "[12] This book, based on the replies that more than 100 scientists made to a long questionnaire Galton sent them, attempted to provide "a Natural History of the English Men of Science of the present day."[13] Of the scientists he surveyed, Galton concluded the following about their university education:

> One-third of those who sent replies have been educated at Oxford or Cambridge, one-third at Scotch, Irish or London universities, and the remaining third at no university at all. I am totally unable to decide which of the three groups occupies the highest scientific position: they seem to me very much alike in this respect.[14]

Already, then, by 1874 a "genius" study contained a calculation of the percentage of eminent men who had graduated from *particular* universities —at least, from Oxford, Cambridge, and London—not just from all universities as a group.

Another strict hereditarian was Théodule Ribot, Professor of Comparative and Experimental Psychology at the College of France, whose many works, in all their editions and translations, run to almost 200 listings in the *National Union Catalog, Pre-1956 Imprints.*[15] Ribot believed that on people of genius, as opposed to more ordinary people, education had almost no effect.

> ... the influence of education at the two ends of the series is at its *minimum.* Upon the idiot it has almost no effect: extraordinary efforts, marvels of patience and skill, often end in insignificant and ephemeral results. But as we rise toward the medium grades this influence increases. It attains its *maximum* in those average natures who, being neither good nor bad, are about what chance makes them. Then, if we rise toward the higher forms of intelligence we see it again diminish, and as the highest genius is approached, it tends toward its minimum.[16]

Sometimes the hereditarians, instead of comparing those who had graduated from universities with those who had not, compared students from a *particular* university who had been successful in school with those who had been much less successful. An example of this type of study is the anonymous 1882 article in *Cornhill Magazine* about the Cambridge University senior wranglers. (The senior wrangler was the student who, each year, achieved the highest grade in Cambridge's mathematics honors examination; since, in the late 19th century, the senior class at Cambridge averaged some 400–450 students,[17] being senior wrangler was a very great distinction.) Discussing senior wranglers going back to 1748 and how they had fared in later life, the author concluded:

...the most obvious inference...is that very little can be inferred. Universities and schools calmly speak of "producing" great men, when all that can be safely said is that they have not put an end to them.[18]

James Sully, an early British psychologist, writing about eminent men in the *English Illustrated Magazine* in 1891, named many who had had academic difficulties and had created severe disciplinary problems in school and wrote that:

> The conclusion that seems to be forced on us by the study of the lives of men of letters is that they owe a remarkably small portion of their learning to the established machinery of instruction. A good number have only imperfectly come under the influence of the educational system, while a large fraction of those who have been more fully subjected to it have been too little in harmony with its spirits and methods to derive from it any large and substantial profit.[19]

Almost 40 years after Galton had spurred the debate about whether nature or nurture "produced" eminent men and women, the hereditarian side of the debate produced an actual list of universities in order of how many eminent people had attended them. Havelock Ellis, the British editor, art and literary critic, and author of the seven-volume *Studies in the Psychology of Sex*, provided such a rank order in his *Study of British Genius* (1904) in the following passage:

> Stated somewhat more precisely, it may be said that of our 975 men, 217 were at Oxford (232 if we include those who had also been at some other university); 177 were at Cambridge (191 if we include those who had also been elsewhere); 76 came from Scotch universities (Edinburgh 28, Glasgow 21, St. Andrews 16, Aberdeen 11); from Trinity College, Dublin, have come 27 men; 23 (or 47 if we include those who had previously been at some British university) have been to one or more foreign universities (Paris 23, Leyden 9, Padua 6, Utrecht 3, Louvain 3, Gottingen 2, Bonn 2, Heidelberg 2, etc.).[20]

From this rank order of the universities attended by 975 eminent British men and women it would have been an easy step to draw conclusions about the quality of the universities themselves, but Ellis did not make any such inferences, and neither did his successors in the debate over whether nature or nurture produced geniuses. For example, Walter Bowerman, an insurance company actuary, in 1947 published *Studies in Genius*, a book which closely followed the plan and methodology of Ellis' *Study of British Genius*. In it, Bowerman examined 1000 Americans of extraordinary intellectual ability. He listed for the 642 of them who had graduated from a college or university the first college or university each had attended in order of how many had attended each. (The leading institutions, in order of how many eminent Americans began their college careers at them, were Harvard, 99; Yale, 65; West Point, 39; Princeton, 31; Columbia, 18; and Bowdoin, 14.)[21]

Maclean's Rank Order

Ironically enough, despite the decades-long debate about whether eminent people were the "product" of nature or nurture, what may possibly have been the very first work to list universities in order of how many eminent people they had produced came from the pen of a man who, although he was interested in showing the origins of Britain's "best men," expressed absolutely no opinion about whether distinguished men were the product of nature or nurture. Judging from his book, *Where We Get Our Best Men* (1900), it is clear that Alick Maclean thought distinguished people were the result of both heredity and environment, although he did not say so explicitly and did not attempt to show that one or the other provided the greater influence.[22]

Maclean selected, from a variety of sources, 3968 men who had been alive sometime during the first 60 years of Queen Victoria's reign (1837–1897), although they were not necessarily alive at the end of it. He discussed these men in terms of several characteristics, most of them background characteristics, such as their nationalities; the counties and towns in which they were born; the number that came from families which had produced three or four eminent men during this period; their fathers' occupations; the public schools (in American terminology, these would be called private schools) they had attended, if any; and the university they had attended, if any.

Based on his data, Maclean made numerous generalizations: that very high proportions of eminent men had been produced by, among "nationalities," the Jews; among towns, Aberdeen, Scotland; among rural districts, Dumfries, Scotland; among fathers' occupations, clergymen; and among public schools, Eton (pp. 48–49). Towards the end of his slim book, he provided a rank order of the universities attended by these distinguished men. Of the 3968 of them, 1230 had attended universities in England, Scotland, or Ireland, as follows:

1. Oxford (424)
2. Cambridge (381)

3. Edinburgh (132)
4. London (97)
5. Dublin (73)
6. Glasgow (52)
7. Aberdeen (42)
8. St. Andrews' (18)
9. Belfast College, University of Ireland (6)
10. Durham (3)
11. Owens College (2)[23]

Although measuring the quality of these universities by the number of eminent men they had produced was not Maclean's primary concern, nevertheless he was alert, far more so than Havelock Ellis had been, to the potential of these figures for serving as the basis for inferences about these universities as producers of eminent men. He wrote, for example, that although Edinburgh was the third largest "producer" of eminent men, "the Edinburgh figures are not high, considering the large numbers of men who have passed through that University" (p. 44). In the same vein he wrote that London University had been founded so recently "that a fairer idea of the position of 'London' will be obtained by doubling its actual figures" (p. 44). Elsewhere, in a table showing how many eminent men, by profession, Oxford, Cambridge, Edinburgh, London, and Dublin had produced, he actually *did* double London's figures. And for the three smallest "producers," he pointed out that these were "all modern institutions" (p. 44). (All of them had been founded in the 19th century and presumably had had small enrollments in the early years of the period that Maclean covered.)

Maclean's table showing universities in order of how many eminent men they had "produced" thus comes close to being an academic quality ranking. While a few other people and groups before 1900 had grouped colleges and universities into two or three *classes* based upon these schools' presumed quality, none of them seems to have produced an actual rank order—that is, one having only one university at each "position." In addition, Maclean was sensitive to the fact that his list could be used as a measure of academic quality in a way that those engaging in the nature vs. nurture debate generally were not,[24] when he commented that Edinburgh University's production of eminent men was not high, on a *per capita* basis, and that London University's contribution was actually much greater than it appeared.

Promising as these European lists of the university backgrounds of eminent people seem, they never developed into academic quality rankings. However, when academic quality rankings were invented, in the United States shortly after the turn of the 20th century, they were based upon a measure not very different from the one the European authors of these lists of the eminent people's university attendance had used. They were based on the undergraduate and doctoral origins and, especially, on the current academic affiliations of one particular type of eminent person—distinguished American scientists.

WHY EUROPEAN STUDIES OF EMINENT PEOPLE NEVER DEVELOPED INTO ACADEMIC QUALITY RANKINGS

Why did several decades of European "genius" studies and other European works on the university origins of eminent people never develop into academic quality rankings? There were several reasons, but they all stem from the fact that the center of the "genius" controversy, and also of the studies like Maclean's on the backgrounds of eminent people, was Europe, not the United States, and from the very different nature of European institutions of higher learning from those in the United States.

First, American colleges and universities at the turn of the century existed within a free-enterprise, highly competitive society, more so than did European universities of the day. In American society, there was an extraordinarily strong emphasis on being the "best," the "biggest," and so on. Administrators at American institutions of higher learning probably wanted their own school to excel other institutions more so than did their counterparts at European institutions. Universities in some European countries like France and Germany were supported by the central government and thus were assured a steady source of income whether or not they excelled relative to others.

American colleges and universities, on the other hand, the large majority of which were privately supported, needed to be considered academically good, or at least better than other colleges and universities, to attract students and financial support. American institutions of higher learning thus both wanted and needed to excel each other, more so than did European institutions; academic quality rankings, which ultimately developed in the United States, were a useful means of recording the winners and losers in such a competition.[25]

Second, in each European nation there were relatively few universities. In 1895, Alfred Odin listed 15 university cities, and therefore, since there was only one university in each, 15 universities in all France.[26] In Great Britain at the turn of the 20th century, there were about a dozen universities.[27] In Germany there were only 22.[28] In the United States, on the other hand, there were hundreds of colleges and (mostly *soi-disant*) universities around the turn of the century, some 647 by 1901.[29]

Third, in Europe there was not nearly as much range in the quality of institutions of higher learning as there was in the United States, and, therefore, less need to know what the best and worst schools were since the differences in quality, in any case, would not be very great. The degrees of all German universities, for example, were theoretically equal in prestige. A philosophy student might decide to attend Heidelberg, a Protestant university, rather than Freiburg, a Catholic one, without even considering these universities', or even their philosophy departments', comparative quality. Similarly, a psychology student might decide to study in a psychology department that specialized in experimental, rather than introspective psychology, confident that both departments would have faculties about equally well-trained and qualified to teach their courses. Although in actuality German universities did, of course, vary somewhat in quality, they certainly did not vary nearly as much as did the best and worst American colleges and universities.[30]

Fourth, not only did American colleges and universities differ enormously in quality, but the types and curricular offerings of these schools, even schools in the same field, often differed enormously. In Europe, though philosophy would be taught differently, of course, at a Catholic university than at a protestant one, and psychology differently in an experimentally-oriented department than an introspectionist one, these differences were minor compared to the disciplinary chaos that reigned in America.

To use the field of medicine as an example, when Abraham Flexner inspected 155 American and Canadian medical schools before writing his 1910 report on medical education in the United States and Canada, he found not only over 100 more or less "scientific" medical schools, but also 32 sectarian schools of various types. There were 15 homeopathic schools, eight eclectic schools, eight osteopathic schools, and one physio-medical school.[31] The situation in other fields of study was nearly as chaotic. In Europe, on the other hand, fields of study were much more sharply defined. On the continent there was no sectarian medical training, for example, and in England there was almost none.[32] Once again, since there was less diversity in European higher education, in type as well as in quality, there was less need for academic quality rankings and less likelihood, therefore, that they would be developed.

Fifth, because the European countries were all much smaller geographically than the United States, even the United States of 1900, it was much easier for Europeans to grasp the quality of the universities in their compact countries, without published academic quality rankings, than it was for Americans to grasp the quality of their far-flung colleges and universities, which even then stretched from Maine to California.

Sixth, the European universities were so much older, as a group, than were American colleges and universities, that it was easier for Europeans to ascertain the quality of their long-established universities than it was for people in the United States to judge the quality of their newly established ones. Of 21 German universities listed in the *Encyclopedia Britannica* in 1910, for example, only five had been founded after 1800, and seven of them had been established before 1500.

Seventh, in some European countries, like Germany, there were nationwide licensing examinations in nearly every discipline. Such standardized exams, which certified that those who passed them had attained a certain level of excellence, no matter what university they had attended before taking the exam, reduced the importance of attending a high-quality college or university. Passing the exam, rather than where one had studied before taking the exam, became the important measure of competence in one's field.[33]

Similarly, in the United States today, there are many academic quality rankings in some arts and science disciplines in which there is no standard licensing examination after one receives the Ph.D., and in which, therefore, the quality of the institutions the student attended serves as an important measure of his or her ability. Some of those disciplines are economics, psychology, and sociology. There are fewer rankings in fields like law, dentistry, and medicine, in which, after the student earns a degree, he or she still must pass a licensing examination.

Finally, in some European nations, like Germany, precisely because the differences among the quality of institutions were relatively small, students commonly attended several universities during their course of study. Since they could go from one to another without fearing that one would have standards far higher, or an academic program far inferior, to those at the university they had just left, they tended to migrate. Since they often attended two, three, or more universities in their academic careers, starting off at the "best" or the "right" institution was not so important as in the United States, where students more often expected to graduate from the first college or university they attended.[34] Once again, European conditions made it less necessary than in the United States to have published rankings of academic quality.

For all these reasons, then, rank orders of universities were simply not greatly needed in the European nations where the debate over the role of nature and nurture in the development of "genius" raged, so rankings did not develop out of the work in this field, or even out of studies like Maclean's on the origins of distinguished people.

Even today, when hundreds of rank orders of American colleges, universities, and individual disciplines and professional fields have been published, few studies have ever been published attempting to rank the institutions of higher learning of any European nation.

Chapter Four

THE UNITED STATES BUREAU
OF EDUCATION'S STRATIFICATIONS

A particularly long-lasting effort in the history of academic quality rankings was the United States Bureau of Education's stratifications of colleges and universities by quality. Starting with Commissioner of Education John Eaton, Jr.'s annual report for 1870, the Bureau published statistical data about American colleges. The 1871 *Report*, for example, listed 372 men's and coeducational colleges and universities and the date they were founded, their location, president, student enrollment, tuition, number of volumes in the library, religious sponsorship (if any), and some other information about them.[1]

It listed separately 136 colleges "for the superior instruction of females exclusively," providing much the same data about these.[2] As years went by, the Bureau provided more and more statistical data about each college, but it never, in its earliest years, made any effort to stratify or rank these colleges according to their quality. Indeed, it stoutly resisted the efforts by others to persuade it to do so, maintaining that " . . . fine discriminations were not its business. These can be made at need by other agencies."[3]

In 1873, the Commissioner of Education's annual report divided all men's and coeducational colleges into three categories—by type, not by quality. These categories were universities and colleges; schools of science; and professional schools. So things stood for more than a decade. In the *Report* for 1885–86, though, thirteen of the nation's better known colleges, almost all of which passed, in that era, for comprehensive institutions, were listed separately from the rest, in three small groups of from three to five schools each.[4] (They were "comprehensive" institutions in the sense that twelve of them, in addition to having an undergraduate program in arts and sciences, had at least one professional school, department, or course of study.)

But the *Report*, while singling out these 13 schools for special attention, did not go so far as to say that they were the nation's best, or even *among* the nation's best colleges and universities. The schools were Johns Hopkins (the only one without a professional school, department, or course of study), Boston University, Harvard, Dartmouth, Yale, Columbia, University of the City of New York (today called New York University), University of Pennsylvania, University of Michigan, University of Alabama, University of North Carolina, University of Virginia, and Vanderbilt.

The *Report* for 1886–87 went a little further in distinguishing a few schools from the rest. It listed separately twelve of the better privately controlled colleges and universities. These schools, too, were all comprehensive institutions, that is, schools "comprising groups of related faculties, colleges, or schools."[5] (Twenty-four state universities were also listed, in still another table headed "Statistics of State Universities for 1886–87," separately from the rest in alphabetical order by state.)[6] While the *Report* did not call the 12 comprehensive institutions the best colleges and universities in America, it did say:

> It is not pretended that the foundations [that is, the comprehensive colleges and universities] which have been selected for representation in the tables following are all universities, in the special sense of that much-abused term. It is, however, believed that the principle of selection employed is justified by the facts and tendencies as known at present. The foundations . . . illustrate every source from which the material equipments of the highest order of institutions is likely to arise, excepting State or national bounty. All of them have progressed far enough to be judged by their actual work, and nearly all of them have achieved more than national distinction.[7]

The colleges and universities listed separately from the rest in this *Report* were listed in alphabetical order by state, with no attempt to make any distinctions among them according to their excellence. The 12 comprehensive institutions listed separately were Yale, Columbian (today called George Washington) University, Johns Hopkins, Boston University, Harvard, Dartmouth, College of New Jersey (today called Princeton), Cornell, Columbia, University of the City of New York, University of Pennsylvania, and Vanderbilt.

In the *Report* for 1888–89, the University of the City of New York was dropped from the list. De Pauw (today spelled Depauw) University, which even then called itself a university despite the fact that at the time it enrolled exactly one resident graduate student, took its place. In this *Report* the U.S. Bureau of Education came very close to stating that the separately listed institutions *were* the best colleges and universities (other than state-supported institutions) in the United States. Above this *Report's* table listing twelve comprehensive colleges and universities, it called them:

> ... a group of institutions which, together with certain of the State universities ... approach more nearly to the idea of true universities than any other institutions in the country. Nearly all of them provide fellowships, two-thirds of the entire number of fellowships belonging to such foundations [that is, colleges and universities] being owned by them. They are also liberally provided with scholarships and productive funds, at least 43 per cent of the total amount of productive funds reported by colleges and universities being possessed by these institutions.[8]

The annual reports continued to list some of the best comprehensive institutions (other than state universities) separately from the rest up to and including the report for 1889–90. In its *Report* for that academic year, for example, the Bureau of Education listed separately 13 institutions — the 12 listed the previous year, plus Clark University — calling them, in the table heading, "a number of leading universities."[9] After the 1889–90 *Report*, the Bureau discontinued, without explanation, the practice of listing some of the best comprehensive institutions separately.[10] So this line of work was not destined to develop into anything resembling an academic quality ranking.

CLASSIFICATION OF WOMEN'S COLLEGES

A longer-lasting and more promising effort to stratify colleges, however, involved colleges exclusively for women. Since 1871, colleges exclusively for women had been listed separately from the other colleges and universities. In the *Report* for 1886–87, published in 1888, the Bureau of Education lamented the shoddy reporting practices of many colleges for women about whether they had the authority to grant degrees, the number of degrees they awarded each year, and the size of their college-level (as opposed to preparatory) enrollments. It complained that "many seminaries make no distinction between the elementary and the academic departments in reporting the number of their students."[11]

The Bureau therefore announced that henceforth women's colleges "organized upon the usual plan of the arts colleges" would be listed as a group in "Division A."[12] All other women's colleges would be consigned to "Division B." Seven colleges were placed in Division A that first year. Three were in Massachusetts — the Society for the Collegiate Education

of Women (today called Radcliffe), Smith, and Wellesley. Three were in
New York state—Vassar, Wells, and Ingham University.[13] The seventh
was Bryn Mawr.[14] By 1888–89 Mount Holyoke Seminary and College
(today called Mount Holyoke College) had been added to the colleges in
Division A, making eight of them.

There seems to have been some doubt at the Bureau of Education
about how useful was the separation of women's colleges into divisions A
and B. The *Report* for 1888–89, published in 1891 when the Commissioner of Education was William Torrey Harris, announced that the
separation of women's colleges into two divisions "has been found to
work quite successfully."[15] But the *Report* for 1890–91, published in 1894,
also under Harris, noted that this two-part classification "is, in a measure,
unsatisfactory, but is retained at present for want of a better."[16]

At any rate, in the *Report* for 1889–90 14 women's colleges were placed
in Division A;[17] by 1901 there were 16.[18] This stratification of women's
colleges into two groups had real promise for developing into academic
quality rankings. Colleges were stratified not "on any mechanical definition which could be applied automatically"[19]—for example, according to
enrollment, size of endowment, number of volumes in the library, and
the like—but rather on the basis of overall quality based on the judgment of the compiler of the lists. The Bureau of Education continued its
division of women's colleges into divisions A and B for more than two
decades,[20] always consigning the great majority of women's colleges to
Division B, without this practice causing any great commotion.[21]

But the Commissioner's *Report* for the year ending in June, 1911 made
what it called a "radical change" (p. 884). This *Report* stated that the
number of women's colleges in Division B that had "uncertain methods
of grading and classifying the students into college and preparatory
groups, or into college and special schools, such as music, art, etc.," was
probably larger than the number of comparable men's colleges.[22] Even
so, it continued, colleges for women would no longer be listed separately
from men's and coeducational schools, and women's colleges would no
longer be stratified into divisions A and B.

The *Report* gave the following explanation for making this change:

The basis of this classification has become uncertain and therefore
unsatisfactory. Its continuation would work to the undeserved disadvantage of some of the institutions not in Division A, which have
become approximately the equal of some of those which were classed in
that division.[23]

The report did not attempt to explain why those Division B women's colleges that had become "approximately the equal" of those in Division A could not simply be elevated to that division.

It is likely that the reason why the *Report* for the year ending in June, 1911 stopped the classification of women's colleges into divisions A and B is because at that very time the Bureau of Education's newly appointed specialist in Higher Education, Kendric Charles Babcock, was preparing a much more complex and all-embracing classification system. It was one that would classify women's colleges, along with hundreds of other colleges and universities, into one of four levels, and thus make the primitive, two-level classification scheme of women's colleges obsolete. Babcock's stratification scheme was to raise a storm of protest, and the furor it provoked ended, once and for all, the Bureau of Education's attempts to publish stratifications of colleges and universities.[24]

For years, one of the topics of conversation at meetings of the Association of American Universities had been how to evaluate the colleges from which students applied to graduate school. The evaluations would be used in order to predict how well-prepared these students, based on their undergraduate records, were likely to be; whether they should be admitted; and, if admitted, under regular or probationary status, by graduate schools.

BABCOCK'S CLASSIFICATION

At the AAU's meeting in Charlottesville, Virginia in 1910, this matter once more arose. The Bureau of Education's Dr. Babcock, former president of and professor of history at the University of Arizona, was present, and he was assigned the task of preparing a classification of colleges and universities. The main reason the graduate deans of the AAU chose an outsider to do the study was that they felt that someone who did not represent any university could be more objective in preparing the classification than could any graduate school dean or committee of deans.[25] Another consideration was the assembled deans' feeling that the Bureau of Education was "a federal office, unhampered by institutional, state, or sectional prejudices ... whose judgment would be accepted both here and abroad. ... "[26]

Babcock started his work on this classification scheme with high hopes for it, writing, at the outset of his project:

The Bureau of Education of the United States has but recently under-taken to share in the evaluation of the work and standards of institu-tions of higher education. The appointment of a specialist in higher education and the organization of the Division of Higher Education are the first steps in the fulfillment of carefully worked-out plans of the bureau for the prolonged, difficult, and delicate task of ascertaining exactly the worth of the degrees granted by the widely varying institu-tions in the United States. . . . Having no funds to give or withhold and no special propaganda to promote, and having a reasonable probabil-ity of the acceptance of its judgment both at home and abroad, the bureau already feels assured of a cordiality of cooperation in its investi-gations which has not always been granted to other investigators of like purpose.[27]

But in hoping that his classification scheme would be capable of "ascertaining exactly the worth of the degrees granted by the widely varying institutions in the United States" and in believing that it had a "reasonable probability of the acceptance of its judgment both at home and abroad" Babcock was wildly wrong on both counts. Here, in Babcock's own words, is how he made his study:

The basis for the judgment expressed in this classification and in the one proposed is not merely a study of catalogues, registers, reports, and statistical statements of the institutions concerned. Information and opinions from widely different sources have been sought and used. The Specialist in Higher Education [that is, Babcock] during the past six months made personal visits to nearly all of the large institu-tions having graduate schools; he has studied their practice in dealing with applicants holding degrees from other institutions, both before and after admission to graduate status; he has conferred with deans, presidents, and committees on graduate study; and he has inspected the credentials and records of several thousands of graduate students taking courses during the last five years, in order to ascertain how such students stood the test of transplanting.[28]

As the result of his work, he classified 344 institutions of higher learning—57 percent of the 602 American colleges and universities—into four divisions. (Actually, since Babcock divided his second level into two strata, his classification scheme actually had *five* levels of Ameri-can colleges and universities.) The basis of comparison, it is important to note, was solely the performance of each institution's graduates after they entered the nation's best-regarded graduate schools. Nothing else was considered, like these colleges' equipment and resources, the training, teaching ability, and research accomplishments of their faculties, and how well these colleges served their students who did *not* subsequently enroll in the nation's best-regarded graduate schools. Nor did Babcock consider how successfully, after these institutions' graduates completed their education, they fared in life and served their communities. Babcock's classification scheme was as follows:

Class I

"Institutions whose graduates would ordinarily be able to take the master's degree at any of the large graduate schools in one year after receiving the bachelor's degree. . . ."[29] Fifty-nine of the 344 colleges and universities (17%) were in this group, including many of today's best-regarded liberal arts colleges (Amherst, Haverford, Oberlin, Smith, Williams); most famous private universities (Harvard, Princeton, Yale); and most esteemed public universities (for example, the universities of California, Michigan, and Wisconsin). There were only a handful of colleges and universities in class I that today are not generally regarded as of the very first rank. Some of the colleges are Knox, Lafayette, and Lake Forest; some of the universities are Catholic University, the University of Kansas, and the University of Nebraska.

Class II

Class II consisted of the 161 colleges (47%) whose graduates, according to Babcock, would probably require more than one year of regular graduate work to earn the master's degree from one of the better graduate schools. Of these 161, 44 were starred, signifying that particularly able graduates of these schools might, Babcock thought, be able to receive their master's degrees, along with students from class I schools, after completing "the regular minimum amount of work."[30] These 44 starred colleges have undergone very disparate lines of development in the last 70 years. Some are generally regarded today as among the nation's very best four-year colleges (for example, Pomona, Middlebury, Swarthmore). Some are considered good universities (University of North Carolina, University of Rochester). Many, though, are seldom classified among today's most distinguished schools, including Baker University, Kansas; Drury College, Missouri; Cornell College, Iowa; and Monmouth College, Illinois. At least one from this group has even shut its doors,

Parsons College (Iowa). The 117 unstarred colleges in class II are a similarly heterogeneous group.

Class III

Class III consisted of 84 colleges and universities (12%) "whose standards of admission and graduation are so low, or so uncertain, or so loosely administered, as to make the requirement of two years for the master's degree probable."[31] This class contained several schools that have evolved, since then, into well-regarded universities—the University of Florida; Louisiana State University; Michigan Agricultural College (today called Michigan State University); and Northwestern College (today called Northwestern University). The colleges in this group that have *remained* colleges, though, and not evolved into universities, are as a group not well-known today—for example, Adrian (Michigan); Bethany (West Virginia); Eureka (Illinois); and Guilford (North Carolina).

Class IV

Class IV consisted of 40 schools (6%) whose bachelor's degrees Babcock considered "approximately two years short of equivalency with the standard bachelor's degree. . . . "[32] As with some class III schools, a few of the colleges in this group have developed into reasonably well-regarded state university campuses today. Some examples are Alabama Polytechnic Institute, today called Auburn University; Kansas State Agricultural College, today called Kansas State University; North Carolina Agricultural and Mechanical College, today called North Carolina State University; Virginia Polytechnic Institute, today Virginia Polytechnic Institute and State University; and Oregon State Agricultural College, today Oregon State University. However, as with Babcock's class III schools, scarcely a single college in Babcock's class IV that has remained a college appears to be particularly well-known or especially well-regarded today.[33]

It may be inferred from the subsequent history of the colleges that Babcock included in his classification that in the 20th century, at least, though colleges of modest reputations have sometimes evolved into well-regarded universities, they have seldom evolved into highly regarded colleges. Some colleges which were founded after Babcock's classification scheme was published are well-regarded today, like Sarah Lawrence

(New York), Bennington (Vermont), and Hampshire (Massachusetts). But few colleges listed low in Babcock's classification scheme that have remained colleges have improved their reputations greatly.

At any rate, after Babcock had finished a late draft of his classification of colleges and universities, he circulated it, seeking comments on it. In October, 1911, copies of the first tentative proofs were sent to certain deans for their criticisms. In November, 1912, a revision in galley proof form was sent to officers of the graduate and professional schools for further criticism. Before anything further could be done, the newspapers secured information about the report.[34]

Contemporary accounts differ about just how the newspapers found out about the report. Claxton, who was the United States Commissioner of Education and Babcock's superior, wrote that the Bureau did not want the report, in its unfinished form, to be publicized.

> Through an oversight the pamphlet was not marked "Proof Confidential" as it should have been, and before the error was discovered the superintendent of documents had received copies of it for distribution to the depository libraries and for sale. This explains why the pamphlet does not have any serial number on it, nor any statement that it is a document of the United States Bureau of Education. The Bureau of Education does nothing which it wishes to conceal, but its work, like any other work, can not fairly be considered as complete when it has only been begun, and even a cursory reading of this tentative statement could not fail to reveal the fact that it was not intended for general publication, and that any such use of it was not expected.[35]

When word of the report got out, there was an uproar from deans and college presidents who were enraged by their school's classification. President J.M.C. Hardy of Mississippi Agricultural and Mechanical College, which had been placed in class IV, wrote to Claxton in behalf of his own and nine other agricultural and mechanical institutions and said, in part:

> We are thoroughly in sympathy with the great work of the U.S. Department of Education, but we enter our earnest protest against publications of the kind under discussion as being only harmful and undesirable, and earnestly request that our institutions be omitted from any similar publication in the future.[36]

The chancellor of Syracuse University, James R. Day, wrote a bitter letter to the *Boston Evening Transcript* in September, 1912. In it, he complained that his university, which Babcock had placed in the second class (with a star) had, in fact, recently been ranked in the first class by the New York State Department of Education. He also pointed out that of 131 students in the city of Syracuse's central high school who had entered college in 1912, fully 119 had chosen to attend Syracuse University; that Babcock, in compiling his classification, had never set foot on Syracuse's campus; and that Syracuse (like most other institutions that Babcock classified) had not even been aware that the classification was being made.[37]

As a result of these and many other anguished protests, Commissioner of Education Claxton wrote his explanatory statement. In it, Claxton wrote that it was "unfortunate" that the designations "class I," "class 2," and so on were used "and that the word 'classification' appeared on the title page."[38] He said that the classification was "only tentative and confessedly imperfect,"[39] and that if the Bureau of Education received requests from the proper officials of any college that was displeased with its rating the Bureau would work towards having the rating corrected.[40] About a dozen colleges, he said, had already succeeded in having their original classifications changed.[41]

He continued that the classifications had been "made on the narrow basis of the rating of their bachelor's degrees as recorded at the graduate and professional schools,"[42] not on any other criterion or set of criteria. He admitted that some colleges could rightly claim that "they are less concerned about the standing of their few graduates who go elsewhere for advanced work than about meeting the obligations placed upon them by the needs of the people they serve or the educational conditions of the States or sections in which they are located."[43]

But Claxton's explanatory statement and the praise the classification received from a number of college officials, including Dean Charles Homer Haskins of Harvard University, Dean James Angell of the University of Chicago, Associate Dean William Carpenter of Columbia, Dean David Kinley of the University of Illinois, and Dean Thomas Holgate of Northwestern were not enough to quell the storm of protest. Finally, the problem reached the office of President William Howard Taft who, under tremendous political pressure not to release the report, issued an executive order banning distribution of Babcock's classification.[44]

There are two plausible reasons why Taft may have prohibited the report's circulation. First, it was towards the very end of his term. Second, incoming President Woodrow Wilson had previously served as a professor of jurisprudence and political economy and as president at Princeton. Since Wilson was, in Taft's words, "especially qualified to determine a matter of this sort,"[45] Taft said that Wilson, when he entered office, should decide the matter.

When Wilson became President, the Association of American Universities wrote to him, urging him to rescind Taft's order, but Wilson refused to do so, and the list was never officially published. After Wilson refused to approve publication of Babcock's classification, the Bureau of Education organized (1914–15) a Committee on Higher Education Statistics to consider whether a new attempt should be made to classify American colleges and universities, and, if it were decided to attempt one, to suggest how to do it. But upon considering Babcock's attempt to classify colleges on the basis of how well their students fared in leading graduate and professional schools, "the committee concluded that the continuance of the classification on this basis was at that time not desirable."[46]

As Samuel Capen, Babcock's successor as Chief of the U.S. Bureau of Education's Division of Higher Education, commented later, "the Bureau learned that there are no second and third and fourth class colleges; that it was an outrage and an infamy so to designate institutions whose sons had reflected honor on the state and nation."[47] A later observer commented equally sardonically about this episode, "obviously, the theory was rife then . . . that it is bad for business if the buyer be told exactly what he is getting for his money."[48] Thus a serious effort at stratification which might well have developed someday into an academic quality ranking of colleges and universities developed no further.

WHY BABCOCK'S CLASSIFICATION NEVER DEVELOPED INTO AN ACADEMIC QUALITY RANKING

The main reason why the United States Bureau of Education lost its opportunity to develop its early efforts to classify colleges and universities into an academic quality ranking is because of major college and university administrators' furious response to Babcock's stratification scheme. Why did Babcock's classification arouse such fury?

One reason is because the stratification had been done by a United States government agency, not by a group representing the colleges and universities themselves. When the AAU graduate school deans agreed that the Bureau of Education's judgment would "be accepted both here and abroad," they were entirely wrong about how it would be accepted in the United States. (Since the classification was never officially released, it is impossible to know with certainty how it would have been accepted in

Europe. However, because it classified only American colleges and universities, not schools in Europe, it is exceedingly unlikely that it would have raised much of a stir there, any more than publication of a stratification scheme of, for example, German universities is likely to have aroused much controversy in America). When the deans referred to its reception in Europe, they probably meant that European universities would use Babcock's classification scheme in deciding from which American schools to accept applicants for graduate school.

In hindsight, the deans should have appointed a committee from within academia, a committee which would have had legitimacy in the eyes of academicians. For a modern example of academicians' reluctance to be assessed by outsiders, in 1963 an official of the National Science Foundation told Logan Wilson, then President of the American Council on Education, and Allan Cartter that the NSF was thinking of engaging a private research firm to evaluate and rank American science departments. At that point, according to Cartter, the following happened:

> Logan Wilson and I hit the ceiling and alerted him . . . to the fact that there had been a long-standing position of the Association of Graduate Deans that *nobody* [Cartter's emphasis] ought to play around with evaluating the graduate programs who was not themselves [*sic*] responsible to the institutions themselves; either the AAU or some other group. The deans had always said that anyone who is going to accredit us or rate us has to be responsible to the institutions. We don't want any outside body doing this.[49]

Still, the United States Bureau of Education had been publishing stratifications of women's colleges for many years, without apparently drawing public expressions of rage from the administrators of women's colleges or of any other schools. Why else, then, did Babcock's stratification cause such an uproar?

First, the stratification of women's colleges had divided these schools into only two groups. Thus no college was ever rated worse than a second-class college, while Babcock's classification stratified schools into four groups—five, actually, counting the two tiers of class II— resulting in third, fourth, and fifth class institutions. Mississippi Agricultural and Mechanical College, for example, whose president wrote to Claxton requesting that his and some other agricultural and mechanical colleges be omitted from future classifications, was rated a class IV institution.

Second, the earlier, two-level stratifications of women's colleges had placed only a very few colleges in the top level. After some 25 years of separating out the best women's colleges, for example, the Bureau of Education placed only 16 in Division A and all the rest (92 colleges) in Division B. Similarly, in the 1880s, the Bureau of Education singled out only a dozen or so comprehensive or "leading" institutions for separate listing, leaving several hundred other colleges and universities in one, undifferentiated group. While it was no disgrace to be excluded from a list of the top dozen or so institutions, Babcock's class I consisted of fully 59 colleges and universities, and to be excluded from a group this large was a more serious matter.

Third, even while it singled out certain women's colleges and comprehensive institutions from the others, the Bureau of Education's early annual reports often used language so euphemistic as to minimize the possibility of hurt feelings. These reports described the schools listed separately from the rest not as the nation's best institutions but rather as those merely "organized upon the usual plan of arts colleges" or those from which, at some indefinite time in the future, "the highest order of institutions is likely to arise." Babcock, on the other hand, used much more direct language, writing, for example, that a bachelor's degree from a class IV college was the equivalent of roughly two years of work "of a standard college."[50]

Fourth, the stratification tables in the Bureau of Education's annual reports were printed in tiny type, taking up only a few pages in reports that were more than 1000 pages long and probably not very widely read by the general public or reported on by the press. Babcock's classification, on the other hand, while it is unclear exactly what form it would have taken in its final version, was unquestionably going to be distributed widely, even though it was apparently not intended for the general public. In addition, it would probably have been widely reported by the press.

Fifth, at least in the case of the two-level classification of women's colleges, most of the colleges placed in Division B were so tiny, obscure, and powerless that, even if they had wanted to, they were hardly in a position to protest very effectively. These were schools whose faculties seldom numbered above 20 and whose students, not counting those in their preparatory departments, seldom numbered as many as 100. They were schools like the Synodical Female Institute in Talladega, Alabama; Jessamine Female Institute in Nicholasville, Kentucky; and Ogontz School for Young Ladies in Ogontz, Pennsylvania. By contrast, in

Babcock's stratification scheme there were many large and powerful institutions, by the standards of the day, omitted from class I—schools like Syracuse University, Boston University, the College of the City of New York (today called City College of the City University of New York), and New York University. Institutions like these were large and influential enough to make their protests heard.

Sixth, there were real grounds for complaint about Babcock's methods. He had placed colleges and universities into classes based on only one criterion—the success of their graduates in well-regarded graduate schools. Nonetheless, he had implied that the class into which a school was placed reflected the overall standing of the institution. So colleges which excelled those in class I in most respects other than the success of their graduates in leading graduate and professional schools had legitimate grounds for complaint.

In the Bureau's early two-level classification of women's colleges, there were few Division B schools that could convincingly claim to be as good as the handful of Division A schools like Smith, Wellesley, and Bryn Mawr. Similarly, with the early separate listings of a dozen or so "comprehensive" institutions, few schools omitted from this short list could convincingly claim to be as good as Harvard, Johns Hopkins, Columbia, or Yale.

But in the case of Babcock's four-part stratification, many schools ranked below the first group could convincingly claim to excel many in that group. Such class II schools as the University of Cincinnati, the College of the City of New York, and Syracuse University could certainly claim to excel schools like Goucher, Grinnell, Knox, and Lake Forest in many ways. For example, they could claim superiority in the quality and quantity of their faculty's research, their library collections and instructional resources, and the number of courses and programs they offered students. Indeed, some class II schools could claim, with much justification, to excel certain class I schools on almost every reasonable criterion of academic quality except the one on which Babcock based his classification.

Seventh, though the United States Bureau of Education worked closely in classifying institutions with some of the nation's leading graduate and professional schools, it made little effort to gain the approval and support of most of the schools that were being rated. Many of them, indeed, knew nothing of the classification until it was circulating in draft form. Failing to involve most of the schools being classified, or even to inform them that such a classification was being made, was a strategy hardly calculated to make schools that were unhappy with their classifications quietly accept them.

For all these reasons, Babcock's 1911 classification raised a howl of protest, whereas the Bureau of Education's previous timid efforts at classification had not. Never again did the Bureau of Education attempt to stratify American colleges and universities according to their "quality."

Chapter Five

CLASSIFICATION EFFORTS BY THE COUNCIL ON MEDICAL EDUCATION AND SIMILAR GROUPS

Disciplinary associations and professional accrediting agencies also made serious, extended attempts to stratify schools according to their academic quality. These organizations often classified institutions or particular fields of study like medicine or law into two, three, four, or more strata according to their presumed academic quality. In the early years of the 20th century, several different professional organizations employed such classificatory systems, including those concerned with the fields of medicine, law, dentistry, optometry, teacher education, and forestry. Of these the earliest, most thorough, and by far the most influential classifications according to academic quality were published by the American Medical Association's Council on Medical Education, founded in 1904.[1]

RATINGS OF MEDICAL SCHOOLS

Since 1902, the *Journal of the American Medical Association* had published the results of the various states' medical licensing board examinations. In 1905, for example, it published a list of the examination results for graduates of the 42 medical schools which had produced 50 or more graduates who had taken the licensing exam in 1904. There were enormous differences in the success rates of the graduates of the various medical schools. Only 0.6% of the graduates of Harvard Medical School failed their state licensing exam, as did only 1.3% of those from Northwestern,[2] 1.7% from Johns Hopkins, and 1.9% from the University of Minnesota. However, fully 51.4% of the graduates of the University of the South (Tennessee) and 69.2% of those from Baltimore University (Maryland) failed.[3]

The *Journal of the American Medical Association* at first arranged the schools on these lists in order of the number of their graduates who had taken state licensing examinations that year, with the schools that had produced the most exam-takers being listed first, but it was obviously a simple step to arrange the list by the schools' "pass" rates. Indeed, in 1906 the Council on Medical Education divided medical schools into three classes, based on their graduates' success in passing the exams. These three strata were as follows:

1. colleges with less than a 10% failure rate
2. colleges with a failure rate of 10–20%
3. colleges with a greater than 20% failure rate[4]

In the same issue of the *Journal*, the Council on Medical Education combined the results of the 1904 and 1905 state licensing examinations and published a table grouping medical schools into five strata:

1. colleges with less than a 10% failure rate
2. colleges with a 10–20% failure rate
3. colleges with a 20–30% failure rate
4. colleges with a 30–40% failure rate
5. colleges with a failure rate higher than 40%[5]

However, the Council realized that measuring the quality of medical schools should involve more than merely calculating what percentage of their graduates passed their state licensing exams. Since 1906 it had been working on a method of classification for medical schools based on ten criteria it believed reflected academic quality. One or more officials of the Council visited all 160 medical schools in the country, rating them on a scale of ten points in each of ten areas, for a possible score of 100. The ten areas were as follows:

1. The successes of graduates of the school before state examining boards;
2. the question of requirement and enforcement of satisfactory preliminary education;
3. the general character and extent of college curriculum;
4. the medical school buildings;
5. laboratory facilities and instruction;
6. dispensary facilities and instruction;
7. hospital facilities and instruction;
8. extent to which the first two years are officered by men devoting their entire time to teaching and the evidences of original research;
9. extent to which the school is conducted as an institution for

teaching medicine, rather than as a means for the profit of the faculty, directly or indirectly;

10. the owning of a library, museum, charts, models, stereopticons, etc.[6]

Based upon its ten criteria, the Council on Medical Education then stratified all medical schools into six classes, as follows: A (scoring 90–100%); B (80–90%); C (70–80%); D and E (50–70%); and F (below 50%). Of the 160 schools rated, "81 received markings above 70, 47 markings between 50 and 70, 32 below 50."[7] All the medical schools surveyed were informed of their own score, although—partly because many medical schools objected to their scores being made public—the results were never widely published.[8]

Though a stratification system based on these ten criteria was certainly an improvement over one based merely on the percentage of each school's graduates that passed the various state licensing exams, it still did not please everyone. Henry Pritchett, President of the Carnegie Foundation for the Advancement of Teaching, an organization which since its founding in 1905 had been deeply involved in assessing the quality of colleges and universities, wrote in 1915 that the criteria being used during that year, which were nearly identical to those listed above, the only changes being in wording, "are too many, are not comparable with one another and are not in all cases capable of practical application."[9]

He said that criterion 1, the performance of graduates on state board examinations, though one that was easy to apply, "is one which will vary with each state, and with the character and strictness of the examinations."[10] Neither did he like criterion 9, about the extent of commercialism in each school, writing that schools with any degree of commercialism at all could not be very good. He disliked criterion 10, on the grounds that even if a medical school possessed a good library, that was still no guarantee that its students would use that library.

Pritchett thought that two matters were of crucial importance. These were "the basis of selection of the student body and the basis of selection of the teaching body."[11] He also considered three other criteria important— "the completeness and availability of the scientific laboratories . . . the character of the clinical facilities . . . and the income and expenditures of the school."[12]

In 1910, after a more complete inspection of American medical schools, the Council on Medical Education issued its second classification of medical schools and the first one it made public. This study was "the first complete classification of any group of higher educational institutions to be made by an accrediting organization."[13] In later years, the Council issued other classifications, modifying its criteria from time to time.

In 1912, it finished its third classification—the second one that it actually made public. In this one, it raised the number of points in each category from ten to 100, making 1000 the highest possible score; it modified the wording of some of the ten categories, while retaining their essential meaning; it reduced the number of classes from six to three; and, instead of simply assigning a letter of the alphabet to each level, it gave each alphabetical classification a descriptive heading. Class A schools were "Acceptable Medical Colleges," class B schools were "Medical Colleges Needing Certain Improvements to Make them Acceptable," and class C institutions were "Medical Colleges which would Require a Complete Reorganization to Make them Acceptable."

A score of 70% or higher was needed for a school to be listed in class A; a score of 50–70% for class B; medical schools scoring below 50% were listed in class C. There were separate classifications, also labelled A, B, and C, for "Medical Schools for the Colored Race" and for Canadian medical schools. Among American medical schools, excluding black ones, there were 62 four-year schools and ten two-year schools in class A; 29 schools in class B; and 27 in class C. Among black medical schools, there were two in class A, Howard (Washington, D.C.) and Meharry (Tennessee); one in class B; and four in class C. Among Canadian colleges of medicine, four were placed in class A, three in class B, and one in class C.[14]

In 1913, the Council issued its third published classification scheme based on essentially the same criteria, once again modifying the wording of some of them. This time, it adopted a four-strata classification system for American schools, awarding the grade of A+ to those class A schools which had as an admissions requirement a year or more of premedical science. (It did not classify Canadian medical schools this time.) Class A+, "Acceptable Medical Colleges," included 22 schools giving a four-year course and two schools giving a two-year course. Class A, "Colleges Lacking in Certain Respects but Otherwise Acceptable," included 31 four-year and six two-year medical schools; class B, "Colleges Needing General Improvements to be Made Acceptable," had 23 four-year schools and one two-year school, and class C, "Colleges Requiring a Complete Reorganization to Make them Acceptable," had 28 schools.[15]

One fault of all the classification systems, though, was that even with as many as six levels, and certainly with only three or four levels, medical schools of widely differing quality could still be placed into the same group. Commenting on a revised version of the 1913 classification that had been completed in June, 1914, Pritchett complained that to place medical schools like Vanderbilt, Tulane, and Texas in class A+, along with the very best medical schools in the country, "is good-natured prophecy, not educational justice."[16] He also lamented that to include schools "of the type of the College of Medicine at Omaha, and the Starling-Ohio School at Columbus . . . in the same class as Harvard, Johns Hopkins, and Washington University is to wipe out real distinction."[17]

Partly because many of the worst medical schools closed down and some of the others improved, the letter grades the Council assigned in its classifications rose higher and higher. In 1915, 66 of the 95 medical schools (69%) were rated class A; in 1920, 70 of 85 (82%) were in class A; and in 1927, 71 of 80 (84%) were in class A.[18]

In 1928, the Council on Medical Education formally discontinued its three-level classification system of medical schools, afterwards listing them either as "approved" (or equivalent to class A) or "unapproved" (equivalent to class B). After 1928, although it was still possible for a school to be rated "unapproved," or class B, virtually all medical schools were routinely rated class A. In 1931, for example, the Council rated all 86 medical schools in the United States and Canada as class A, giving fully 84 of them unconditional approval and only two of them conditional approval.[19] Finally, in the 1940s, the Council began to issue only a single, undifferentiated list.

RATINGS OF OTHER TYPES OF SCHOOLS

Several professional associations and organizations accrediting professional fields of study eventually developed classification schemes of their own based on those of the Council on Medical Education. In 1918, the Dental Educational Council of America (later called the Council on Dental Education) prepared its first classification of dental schools.[20] At that time there were 49 dental schools in the United States. The Council rated 16 as class A schools, 27 as class B schools, and four as class C schools; it did not rank the other two schools, considering them too poor to merit even a C ranking.

When the Council published results of dental school graduates' failure rates on the state board licensing examinations, though, it was embarrassed by the results. In 1925, for example, 21% of the graduates of class A Harvard failed the state dental board examination, as did 19% of the graduates of class A Tufts (Massachusetts). Atlanta-Southern (Georgia) and Indiana Dental School, on the other hand, both of which were not only class B schools but proprietary (that is, intended to make a profit) institutions as well, had respective failure rates of only 5% and 6%. More embarrassing still, not one graduate of either class C dental school failed any state's licensing exam in 1923 or 1924.[21]

Part of the reason for these results may have been the varying levels of difficulty of the different state licensing exams. Many Harvard and Tufts graduates, for example, probably took the board exams in Massachusetts, while many Atlanta-Southern graduates probably took the exam in Georgia, and the Massachusetts exam may simply have been harder than the Georgia exam. Even so, the fact that greater percentages of graduates of class B and even class C dental schools were passing their state licensing exams than the graduates of some class A schools could scarcely have been considered evidence of the validity of the Dental Educational Council's classification system.

In 1923, the American Bar Association's Council of the Section on Legal Education and Admission to the Bar published a classification of schools based upon whether or not they complied with prescribed standards. It then rated 38 schools that did comply with these standards as class A schools and 15 schools that did not yet comply but had promised to do so by a definite date as class B schools. Schools which had not complied and showed no intention of doing so were not listed, so this classification system was, in effect, a three-level one. In 1927, the Council discontinued this practice, and since then it has listed only a single, alphabetical list of ABA-approved schools.[22]

In 1925, the American Optometric Association appointed a joint committee that inspected 16 of the optometry schools then in existence. The others were not even considered worthy of inspections. In what was for all practical purposes a four-level system, it rated nine of them A, B, or C and declined to rate the others at all.[23]

The American Association of Teachers Colleges classified 63 four-year teachers colleges and ten junior colleges into groups A, B, and C in 1928, using standards based on those then used by the North Central Association of Colleges and Secondary Schools. The AATC stopped classifying teachers colleges in 1940.[24]

As late as 1935, the Society of American Foresters rated all institutions offering approved curricula in forestry, grading each of them A, B, or C in each of the four basic fields of forestry—silviculture, forest management, forest utilization, and forest economics and policy. It then averaged the four scores and arrived at an overall A, B, or C classification.[25]

WHY THESE RATINGS NEVER DEVELOPED INTO ACADEMIC QUALITY RANKINGS

These classification systems clearly had the potential to develop into academic quality rankings if they had added additional gradations to the point where each school had its own "position." But instead, over the years, they used fewer and fewer gradations and eventually evolved into undifferentiated lists of approved schools. One reason why they never developed into academic quality rankings is because many of these professional organizations were the accrediting agencies for their respective fields. As such, they were far more concerned with enforcing minimal standards than with distinguishing among varying degrees of excellence.[26]

Another reason, closely related to the first, was that colleges and universities themselves, once they became listed, often pressured the accrediting organizations to avoid invidious comparisons and to publish only a single, undifferentiated list of accredited schools. One of the most important purposes that accrediting agencies supposedly serve is to protect the public by warning them about low-quality schools or specific deficiencies in otherwise acceptable institutions. However, they often function more to help the schools they exist to accredit than to inform the general public; over the years they have grown to protect these institutions by publishing only a single list of "approved" schools.[27]

A third reason was many accrediting agencies' conviction that colleges and universities should be evaluated not against some absolute standard of excellence but rather in terms of their own goals. This conviction naturally tended to discourage comparisons according to quality and quality rankings. (Professional school accrediting agencies, particularly those concerned with medical education, never became as relativistic as the regional accrediting agencies. Still, many of them became, over the years, more so than when they had started.)

The following example is taken from a policy statement issued by a regional accrediting agency, although the same point could be made from the area of accrediting agencies involved with professional fields.

In 1934 the North Central Association of Colleges and Secondary Schools, the largest and historically the most influential of the six regional accrediting organizations, stated unequivocally in two places in its "Statement of Policy Relative to the Accrediting of Institutions of Higher Education" that "the facilities and activities of an institution will be judged in terms of the purposes it seeks to serve."[28] Following the North Central Association's lead, eventually all the other regional accrediting agencies came to espouse this policy, a policy which, of course, was incompatible with a strict stratification system according to academic quality. Professional accrediting organizations never went this far in the direction of relativistic assessment. However, they too generally became less insistent than they had been earlier that schools for which they were responsible meet exact quantitative criteria or else be classified lower than schools which did meet them.

For all these reasons, then, professional associations and professional accrediting organizations one by one abandoned their multilevel classification schemes and published only lists of approved schools. The Council on Medical Education, which in 1907 had classified schools into six levels, by 1912 had reduced its levels to three; since the 1940s it has published only an alphabetical list of approved schools. The ABA's Council of the Section on Legal Education and Admissions to the Bar switched from a three-level classification scheme to a single approved list in 1927. The American Association of Teachers Colleges switched to a single list by 1940.

So the multilevel stratification schemes of professional associations and agencies accrediting professional fields, which might have become more stratified and thus developed into academic quality rankings, became instead less stratified and in time evolved into undifferentiated lists of approved schools.

Chapter Six

EFFORTS BY RELIGIOUS AND STATE ORGANIZATIONS TO CLASSIFY INSTITUTIONS BY ACADEMIC QUALITY

THE METHODIST EPISCOPAL CHURCH, SOUTH'S BOARD OF EDUCATION

The Board of Education of the Methodist Episcopal Church, South was perhaps the first religious organization to stratify institutions of higher learning according to their supposed quality.[1] The Board was established in 1894. By 1907 it classified all the institutions of higher education under its jurisdiction[2] into four categories:

1. universities
2. class A colleges
3. class B colleges
4. unclassified institutions

The criteria for being listed as a college, as opposed to an unclassified institution, were based partly on an institution's income, partly on its having a minimum number of full-time faculty, and partly on its admissions requirements.

The Board's highest category was "universities," with "university" being defined, in a 1907 report by a committee of the Board, as an institution having "a productive endowment of not less than one million dollars, and organized on a basis of professional schools and of elective studies, with departments of original research" (p. 175). In the Board's *Report* for 1908, only Vanderbilt qualified for this category. Institutions were classified as universities not according to their "quality" but mostly on the basis of their structure ("organized on a basis of professional schools and of elective studies") and function ("with departments of original research").

The next two categories were for colleges, which *were* stratified on the basis of quality. The 1907 committee report said the following:

In order to be classed as a college an institution must employ not less than seven professors, or adjunct professors, giving their entire time (at least fifteen hours a week) to college instruction. It shall have, exclusive of matriculation and tuition fees, a permanent annual income of five thousand dollars, which may arise from interest on endowment fund, conference assessments, private gifts, or net earnings from board or dormitories (p. 175).

In addition, class A colleges, except women's colleges, were required to have an endowment of at least $100,000. After 1909–10, according to this committee report, in order to be placed in class A, colleges would need to require for admission at least "fourteen units (11.2 units of the Carnegie Foundation),[3] on four of which the student may be conditioned provided he offer three units of English and two and a half in mathematics" (p. 175).[4] In the Board of Education's 1908 *Report* ten colleges qualified for class A listing, including Central College (Missouri), Emory College (Georgia), and Hendrix College (Arkansas).

Colleges placed in class B did not need to have endowments as large as $100,000 and needed, after 1909–10, to require only 12 units (9.6 of them Carnegie units) for admission. Five colleges qualified for class B listing in 1908, including Emory and Henry College (Virginia), Galloway College (Arkansas), and Kentucky Wesleyan College.

Institutions that failed to meet the standards for class B colleges were placed in the fourth and lowest category. These were schools that the Board could not even bring itself to call colleges; it lumped them together under the heading "unclassified institutions," rather than "unclassified colleges." This category consisted in 1908 of 47 schools, almost three times as many as those in the other three classes combined. They were, as a group, exceptionally obscure institutions.

This effort by the Methodist Episcopal Church, South's Board of Education to stratify colleges was quite sophisticated for its time. It was multidimensional. That is, in classifying institutions it used several different criteria that the Board believed reflected academic quality. It remains one of the most sophisticated attempts ever made by a church organization to stratify the colleges under its control according to their academic quality. (Many other religious groups, such as the Presbyterian College Board, have published alphabetical lists of the colleges they sponsored or aided, without making any attempt to stratify these colleges by academic quality.)

Still, the Board stratified only Methodist institutions—in fact, only those institutions that came under the jurisdiction of the Methodist Episcopal Church, South. Other Methodist institutions of higher learning came under the auspices of the Methodist Episcopal Church, which does not seem to have published a quality stratification of the institutions under its jurisdiction, at least as early as 1908. Thus in 1908 the Board of Education of the Methodist Episcopal Church, South could classify only 63 schools, or about 10% of the American institutions of higher learning then extant. Due to the benighted condition of education in the South and Southwest at that time, it could classify only a tiny number and percentage of the best-regarded American colleges and universities of the era.

The Board of Education of the Methodist Episcopal Church, South stratified only a small number of institutions, in only one section of the country, controlled by only one religious denomination, and including only a tiny number and proportion of the best-known and best-regarded American colleges and universities of the day. For these reasons, its system never achieved the visibility it needed to be emulated by others and perhaps to have developed into an academic quality ranking.

THE IOWA BOARD OF GENERAL EXAMINERS

The Iowa Board of General Examiners had developed a sophisticated multidimensional method of classifying Iowa's colleges by 1908.[5] Its work will be considered separately from that of the state accrediting agencies because the state accrediting agencies generally accredited all the colleges and universities in a state. The Iowa Board of General Examiners, on the other hand, classified only colleges, not the University of Iowa or Iowa State University. The Iowa Board of General Examiners developed a "point" system based on eight criteria and stratified Iowa's colleges into three groups depending upon how many of them they met. The criteria were these:

1. The number of class hours for the heads of departments and students shall not exceed twenty a week.
2. A faculty properly qualified shall consist of graduates of colleges who have pursued graduate work equivalent at least to that required for a master's degree.
3. The library shall consist of at least five thousand volumes. . . .
4. The laboratory equipment shall be worth not less than $5000. . . .

5. The means of support is defined as requiring a permanent endowment of not less than $200,000. . . .

6. The average salary of heads of departments, exclusive of the salary of the president, shall be at least $1000.

7. The college must maintain at least seven separate departments or chairs. . . .

8. The graduates must show the completion of a four-year secondary course and a four-year college course above the usual eight grades of common schools. . . . [6]

These standards were very low, even for 1908 in rural Iowa, where most of these colleges were located. Even in rural Iowa in 1908 there was nothing very impressive about a college library of 5000 volumes and a college whose department heads averaged salaries of at least $1000/year. In 1910, for example, Illinois' rural Mt. Morris College (Mt. Morris) had 30,000 volumes in its library, St. Ignatius College (Chicago) had almost 31,000, and even Chicago's University High School had 12,000.[7] In 1909 the Carnegie Foundation paid its stenographer slightly more ($1080/year) and its filing clerk only slightly less ($900/year) than the $1000/year that heads of departments at Iowa colleges had to be paid if their colleges were to be rated class A.[8] But although the Board's standards were not impressive, its eight-point rating system was; a good, multidimensional academic quality ranking system could well have developed out of it.

Based upon how many of the eight criteria they met, Iowa's colleges were classified as follows:

1. Those meeting all eight criteria were placed in group A. This group consisted of ten colleges, including Coe, Cornell, Parsons, and Drake University (which, its name notwithstanding, was essentially a college).

2. Colleges meeting from five to seven of the eight criteria were placed in group B. This group had seven colleges, including Central University (it, too, was essentially a college), Luther College, and Tabor College.

3. Colleges meeting three or four of the criteria were placed in group C. This category had three colleges—Buena Vista, Charles City, and St. Joseph's.

The eight criteria were unusually wide-ranging, covering, as they did, faculty teaching loads and student course loads; the faculty's educational attainment; the size of the library collection; the value of the laboratory equipment; the size of these colleges' endowments; the salary of their department heads; their number of departments; their admission standards; and their graduates' eligibility for graduate work.

But promising as this multidimensional rating system was, like some other systems it was doomed to oblivion, largely because of its setting's obscurity. Because it was used to classify only a handful of colleges (20 of them in 1908) in one sparsely populated state, it did not have the visibility it needed to be adapted by those organizations assessing the quality of colleges and universities throughout the United States.

CLASSIFICATION EFFORTS BY
STATE ACCREDITING AGENCIES

Another early effort in the history of multilevel classification systems was efforts by organizations empowered by the individual states to accredit colleges and universities in their own states and, in some cases, institutions in other states and even foreign countries.[9] New York state had had such an institution since its legislature established the Board of Regents of the University of the State of New York in 1784. Iowa and Utah had state accreditation agencies by 1900; Washington, Virginia, and Maryland had them by 1914.[10]

Several different kinds of agencies have been empowered by one state or another to accredit institutions. These agencies have varied from state to state but include state departments of education, state boards of education, state universities, and various other state associations, commissions, and similar agencies.[11] Some states have historically restricted their accrediting activities mostly or entirely to teacher education.[12]

These accreditation efforts usually resulted in undifferentiated lists of approved colleges. However, in a few cases state agencies *did* produce stratified lists of accredited schools, using criteria that they thought reflected academic quality. One of the most ambitious attempts by any state accrediting organization to classify institutions by academic quality took place in Illinois. In 1916, after two years of study, the Illinois Committee on Admissions to Higher Institutions finished preparing criteria for classifying institutions in Illinois and other states. Its rating system was multidimensional, based on these ten criteria:

1. graduation requirements
2. entrance requirements
3. number of departments
4. faculty preparation

5. number of students in recitation and laboratory sections
6. value of buildings
7. income from endowment
8. library and laboratories
9. lighting, heating, etc.
10. general standards and spirit of administration and faculty[13]

According to how well they met these criteria, institutions were rated A+, A, B, or C, a ranking scheme that was changed shortly thereafter to A, B, C, or D. This was one of the few times in the history of early multilevel classification schemes that the range of available grades became lower, rather than higher, as time passed.

Though it seems that no other state accrediting agency ever employed a four-level classification scheme, some other states did develop two-level or three-level classification systems. Writing in 1940, Fred J. Kelley and his collaborators reported that California had, at that time, three levels in its classification scheme—A, B, and C. States which employed two-level classification systems in 1940 were Kansas, Wisconsin, and Illinois, which had scaled down its classification scheme since 1920 from four levels to two.[14]

In 1940, at least two states, Iowa and Minnesota, maintained a separate classification category for institutions that were provisionally accredited. That is, the academic credits allowed the students of such institutions were determined "according to the scholastic records made by them after transferring to the university."[15] This was a rudimentary two-level stratification scheme.

In addition, several states included on their list institutions that were on probationary status and had been given a certain number of years to comply with the standards in which they were deficient, after which they were either placed on the list without probationary status or dropped from it entirely.[16] These, too, were rudimentary two-level classification schemes. So Illinois' short-lived four-tier system and California's three-tier system seem to have been two of the few instances in which state accreditation agencies developed classification systems having more than two levels.

None of the various multilevel classification efforts made by several states ever developed into academic quality rankings. Indeed, over time they usually became less, not more, differentiated, as was the case with the stratification schemes of many other groups, and they usually wound up simply as undifferentiated lists of approved institutions. The primary reason why they did not develop into academic quality rankings was that most of these state accrediting agencies were concerned entirely, or at least mostly, with institutions inside their own states and did not classify schools located elsewhere.

Therefore, like the Board of Governors of the Methodist Episcopal Church, South and the Iowa Board of General Examiners, they simply did not have enough schools to work with to produce a comprehensive quality ranking. Even within their own states, they were often instructed to accredit only those schools that had teacher training programs. Such classification efforts, covering only some colleges and universities within a single state, were unlikely to develop into academic quality rankings.

Of course, some states, notably New York, did accredit—or, to use New York's terminology, "register"—schools throughout the United States and in foreign countries. New York's Board of Regents inspected any United States school so long as the school paid for the inspection.[17] It also registered schools in foreign countries based on a number of sources of information. These included "their catalog statements and other publications, government reports, correspondence concerning particular phases of the institution's work and . . . information obtained in various other ways, including inspection, where possible."[18]

But even states like New York that kept information about colleges and universities in other states and foreign countries did so for the purpose of deciding whether to employ as teachers and confer professional licenses on people who had been educated outside New York state. These states had no particular interest in distinguishing among levels of excellence, but rather in establishing minimum levels for schools whose graduates would be considered qualified for teaching appointments and professional licenses. By 1940, despite its inspection programs, catalog examinations, and the like, New York's own lists very closely resembled those of the national and regional accrediting agencies,[19] suggesting that its independent efforts to ascertain the quality of those schools were probably not very great by then.

So accreditation efforts by the various accrediting organizations of the states never developed into academic quality rankings. This was true even of states like Illinois and California that employed multilevel classification systems, and even of states like New York that collected information on the quality of institutions in other states and countries.

Chapter Seven

INSTITUTIONS WITH
PHI BETA KAPPA CHAPTERS

Phi Beta Kappa was one organization whose list of campuses where it had formed chapters possibly could have been used as a measure of academic quality. However, institutions with Phi Beta Kappa chapters, as a group, have seldom been considered a roster of the nation's best colleges and universities.

In its early decades, Phi Beta Kappa was a unique organization, without any close parallel.[1] At the turn of the 19th century, Phi Beta Kappa chapters at Harvard, Yale, and Dartmouth regularly admitted to membership about a third of all those students receiving A.B. degrees,[2] and Phi Beta Kappa chapters admitted about a third of their college's A.B. degree recipients for many years after that.[3] The organization also contained elements of a social fraternity, a secret society, and a literary and debating society. On the one hand, at its meetings "chief attention was given to literary exercises, especially to composition and debating."[4] On the other, Phi Beta Kappa "had all the characteristics of the present-day fraternity: the charm and mystery of secrecy, a ritual, oaths of fidelity, a grip, a motto, a badge for external display. . . ."[5]

Though its existing members considered, in an informal way, an institution's academic quality in deciding whether or not to start a chapter at it, other factors unrelated to academic quality were important, too. First, Phi Beta Kappa considered granting charters only to colleges and universities with undergraduate programs in the liberal arts and sciences. Thus Clark University, which in the early years of this century had one of the nation's strongest graduate schools but a much weaker undergraduate program with its own separate administration and faculty, was turned down for membership. Clark was not granted a charter until 1953, when its undergraduate school had greatly improved. The Massachusetts Institute of Technology, which in the early years of the century was almost entirely a technical institution, did not receive a charter until

1971, when it had moved in the direction of being a comprehensive university and had strong programs in the humanities and social sciences.

Second, for about 100 years Phi Beta Kappa membership was very heavily concentrated in the Northeast. Though it had been founded at William and Mary (Virginia) in 1776, 20 of the next 24 schools admitted to membership, 1780–1882, were located in the six New England states and New York. The only exceptions were the University of Alabama (which, having been admitted in 1851, in 1861 went inactive for more than 50 years) and three colleges in Ohio—Western Reserve, Kenyon, and Marietta.

Third, in order for a school to establish a chapter, it needed to have at least three faculty members or administrators who were graduate members of other Phi Beta Kappa chapters request a charter for their current institution.[6] Some schools, especially small colleges outside the Northeast, might be academically respectable but still not have three such people on campus.

Fourth, Phi Beta Kappa did not actively solicit new chapters. The only schools considered for charters were those from which groups applied for one. If people at well-regarded colleges and universities did not, for one reason or another, apply for charters, those schools did not receive any. Thus the only school from the South which was granted a Phi Beta Kappa chapter in the 19th century was the University of Alabama, though others—for example, Vanderbilt and Tulane—would probably have been granted a charter if they had applied for one.

The third school from Ohio to receive a chapter was Marietta College (in 1860), which received one long before better-regarded Ohio State University (1904) and Miami University (1911) did. Similarly, Phi Beta Kappa chapters were established at Western Reserve College in 1847, the University of Vermont in 1849, and Hobart College (New York) in 1871, none of which was particularly well-regarded, long before they were established at the more highly regarded University of California (1898), Princeton (1899), University of Michigan (1907), and University of Virginia (1908).

Nevertheless, by 1905 or 1910, the roll of institutions with Phi Beta Kappa chapters was probably a fairly good list of the best-regarded colleges and universities in the United States with undergraduate programs in the liberal arts and sciences. It included both colleges and universities, both public and private institutions, and men's, coeducational, and women's colleges. Around 1905–10, the list of schools at which it had established chapters probably came closer to being a list of the best American colleges and universities offering undergraduate liberal arts and science programs than either before or after.

It certainly came nearer to being such a list than it had in the 19th century when, until about 1890, Phi Beta Kappa had largely neglected schools outside the Northeast. Even so, when in the early years of the 20th century the Association of Collegiate Alumnae and the Association of American Universities used the list of schools the Carnegie Foundation for the Advancement of Teaching had approved for their professors to receive its pensions as a basis for selecting their own members, they did not use the roster of schools with Phi Beta Kappa chapters.

Perhaps one reason was because some well-regarded technological schools like MIT and Stevens Institute of Technology could not be granted charters. Perhaps another was that no institutions could be members of Phi Beta Kappa, the way institutions could be members of, for example, the Association of American Universities. Rather, a group of individuals on a campus was granted permission to establish a chapter there. Perhaps it was partly because Phi Beta Kappa was perceived as a social organization, not an organization, like the Carnegie Foundation, generally considered as established for the public welfare.

Today, institutions with Phi Beta Kappa chapters are seldom considered a roster of first-rate colleges and universities, or even of first-rate schools offering undergraduate liberal arts and science programs, although individual institutions may boast, in their catalogs and other literature, that they have Phi Beta Kappa chapters. The main reason is because Phi Beta Kappa's list of chartered institutions is so inclusive—the organization had 234 active chapters in 1984—that membership today is often considered more a sign of academic respectability than of excellence. Today, as opposed to in its early years, Phi Beta Kappa has a very careful selection process. It has a standing Committee on Qualifications which, "after thorough examination of nonmember institutions, invites those considered qualified for charters to submit applications."[7] The standards of this committee, according to one source, are "stricter than those of any accrediting agency. . . . "[8] In Phi Beta Kappa's triennial application period, 1979–1982, 90 schools applied for a chapter, and only six were granted one.

Even so, Phi Beta Kappa has established chapters at many colleges and universities not generally considered to be among the nation's best, including Centre College (Kentucky), Hope College (Michigan), Trinity

College (Washington, D.C.), Hofstra University (New York), Hamline University (Minnesota), San Diego State University (California), Trinity University (Texas), University of Redlands (California), and the University of Santa Clara (California).

Today, with well over 200 schools having charters, including dozens that are seldom found upon any list of America's most distinguished colleges and universities, the roster of Phi Beta Kappa campuses is, with good reason, very seldom used as a roster of the best American colleges and universities.

Chapter Eight

THE AMERICAN ASSOCIATION OF UNIVERSITY WOMEN'S MEMBER SCHOOLS

An early effort to form lists of the best colleges and universities was the work of the American Association of University Women (before 1921 called the Association of Collegiate Alumnae) in deciding which colleges and universities, among those that offered baccalaureate degrees to women, to admit as members.[1] Some organizations did work that resulted in lists of what could be called the "best" institutions of the day, although the organizations themselves had little intention of producing such lists. The Association of Collegiate Alumnae (hereafter called the ACA), on the other hand, in its early years deliberately attempted to admit only the best colleges and universities granting baccalaureate degrees to women and to formulate rational standards for determining what the best schools were.

The ACA was founded in Boston in 1882 by 65 women. The eight colleges and universities from which they had graduated, not all of which would necessarily have been considered among the best schools of the day, were automatically admitted to membership.[2] The debates, over the next few years, about which other schools to admit and why were apparently long and acrimonious enough to make the ACA wish to establish guidelines concerning what types of schools to admit. One of the procedures the organization used in its early years in deciding which institutions to admit was to inspect their campuses. The ACA was thus one of the first groups to use campus visitations, of the type later used by the Association of American Universities, the Carnegie Foundation for the Advancement of Teaching, and other organizations to form lists of approved, accredited, or acceptable institutions.[3]

In 1895, the ACA's president and secretary were instructed to appoint a committee to decide what standards colleges applying for membership should be required to meet. A year later this committee made its report, recommending that the ACA pursue three "lines of inquiry."[4] These were "the educational qualifications of the corps of instruction," the institution's financial status, particularly its endowment and "average available income," and its physical plant—buildings, libraries, laboratories, and so on.[5] In addition, the ACA was called upon to make sure that the school's faculty taught only college-level students and was not required to teach precollege students in any preparatory school or classes that might be connected with the institution.

This short list of factors to be considered was striking for what it omitted. In the first place, it said nothing about a school's students, their academic ability, or the amount and quality of their academic preparation for college. Second, it said nothing about the school's curriculum— about what programs and courses of study it offered. Third, like many academic quality rankings, past and present, it did not seek to evaluate a school's administrators—for example, their number, their ratio to students, their background, and their effectiveness. Fourth, though it recommended evaluating the faculty's "educational qualifications," it did not suggest inquiring about their number, teaching ability, and research accomplishments, or about the school's student-teacher ratio.

Apparently, the ACA did not feel obliged to follow its own list of lines of inquiry very closely, for in 1897, upon admitting four new schools, it described the criteria it had used in admitting them, showing that more and somewhat different criteria had been used. These were as follows:

1. The "standard of entrance requirements; the care with which this standard is guarded. . . . "

2. Graduation requirements: "the grade of work and the amount of work demanded; the breadth of the curriculum. . . . "

3. The faculty: "their training, experience, and pedagogical force; their number in proportion to the number of students and of courses; their organization and unity; the executive force of their president."

4. Resources, including the college's endowment, its total income, and its physical plant and equipment.[6]

Two of these criteria covered the preparation and quality of work of the students. In addition, the curriculum, the faculty-student ratio, and even the ability of the president were included. All in all, this was a longer and more comprehensive list of criteria than the one the ACA had produced a year earlier.

In 1904, the ACA's Committee on Corporate Membership, which decided which colleges to admit, issued its most thorough set of requirements for admission yet. It contained stipulations about each institution's Board of Trustees; its material resources, including both endowment and physical plant; its faculty, including its size, salary, educational background, and the faculty-student ratio; and its admissions and degree standards.[7]

In some cases, these recommendations were quite specific, as when they stipulated that "there shall be no preparatory department under the government or instruction of the college faculty."[8] In most cases, though, they were quite vague, as when they called for "at least four years of serious secondary school work" prior to admission[9] or when they asked for "class sections restricted to such numbers as ensure proper individual instruction"[10] without hinting at what size those might be.

Still, this list of criteria stands as a forerunner of later multidimensional academic quality rankings. In making recommendations, however vague the language was, concerning campus "resources," the faculty's educational background and compensation, and admissions and graduation requirements, the ACA had included many of the criteria that those who attempted to make academic quality rankings in later years would measure.

In its early years the ACA was quite cautious about admitting new members, and it grew very slowly. By 1907, its 25th anniversary, there were only 24 institutional members, the eight charter members plus Barnard, Bryn Mawr, Columbia Teachers College, MIT, Radcliffe, Stanford, the universities of California, Chicago, Illinois, Minnesota, and some others. This group of schools was probably not very different from what a list of the 24 best-regarded American colleges and universities of the day would have looked like. But the careful investigations required of each school that applied for membership were proving very difficult and time-consuming. Talbot and Rosenberry wrote that:

> . . . the investigation . . . had proved to be a most arduous and burdensome task. Not only was the gathering of data difficult, but the correlation and arrangement was growing increasingly hard of accomplishment. The day of the trained statistician was not yet here and yet the task of estimating institutions, especially on the material side, was fast becoming one of specialization (p. 80).

To make their work easier, beginning in 1910 the ACA began to use the lists of approved or acceptable institutions that had been established by other groups. Its use of such lists provided by other organizations is summarized well by Fred J. Kelly and his collaborators in *Collegiate Accreditation by Agencies Within States:*

For many years [the ACA] made its own investigations of the academic and financial status of institutions applying for membership, but in 1910 it voted to accept the judgment of the Carnegie Foundation for the Advancement of Teaching in these matters, leaving for its committee on standards special consideration of the provision made by the institutions of suitable conditions for women.[11]

Afterwards it was:

... the practice of the association to continue to recognize the work of some other accrediting agency in setting up academic standards, while continuing to apply its own additional tests. In 1912, it voted to consider for membership the institutions in Class I of the classification made by the United States Bureau of Education. Finding the criterion in this classification too difficult to apply, it changed its requirements of academic standards to include the institutions on the list of the Association of American Universities. To this list it voted, in 1919, to supplement the lists of the regional accrediting associations, a practice which it continued until 1929, when as the American Association of University Women it returned to its former practice of recognizing only the institutions accredited by the Association of American Universities.[12]

Not until 1963 did the American Association of University Women stop maintaining lists of the best colleges and universities granting baccalaureate degrees to women. Many of the groups which established lists of the best colleges and universities formulated these lists quite independently of each other. The AAUW, though, is an example of an organization that used the lists of other organizations as a basis for making its own.

For many years, the institutional membership of the ACA had increased only slowly; from 1882 to 1907, it had grown at the rate of less than one new institution per year. Around World War I, possibly because its new procedure of relying heavily on the lists of others in selecting its own members greatly speeded up the selection process, it began to admit schools at a more rapid pace, and it continued this pace after the war. In 1929 alone it recommended 27 schools for membership, more than it had admitted during its first 25 years. By 1931 it had 194 member schools, a number certainly too large to serve as a list of excellent colleges and universities giving bachelor's degrees to women.

Still, the ACA's early work is an important forerunner of modern academic quality rankings. The 24 members as of 1907 were probably a reasonably good list of the best-regarded colleges and universities that conferred baccalaureate degrees on women at that time, and had the membership stayed reasonably small, its membership roster might have continued to be such a list. Furthermore, the ACA was one of the first organizations ever to conduct campus visitations for the purpose of evaluating colleges and to establish a multidimensional method for evaluating college quality. Its lists of criteria for evaluating colleges show what one well-educated, turn-of-the-century group of people who investigated the matter very thoroughly considered the most important criteria concerning the academic quality of colleges and universities.

Chapter Nine

COLLEGES AND UNIVERSITIES RECEIVING GRANTS FROM THE GENERAL EDUCATION BOARD

A nother list that had the potential to develop into a roster of leading institutions was the list of colleges and universities to which the General Education Board (hereafter called the Board), early in its history, gave endowment grants.[1] The Board had been founded by John D. Rockefeller, Sr. in 1902 as a philanthropic organization benefiting, as its name implies, many different types and levels of education. Its purpose, as stated in its Congressional Charter, was "the promotion of education within the United States of America, without distinction of race, sex, or creed."

By 1964, when the Board exhausted its funds and brought its active program to a close, it had given away a total of $324.6 million to a great number and variety of educational institutions and groups.[2] These included American colleges and universities, medical schools, public elementary and secondary schools, libraries, and agricultural projects.

At first, it concentrated on improving public school education in the South. Though in its first few years the Board had given two or three small grants to higher education, it really got into higher education philanthropy in a big way in 1905 when Rockefeller gave it $10 million "to promote a comprehensive system of higher education in the United States."[3] By 1914 it had given endowment grants to slightly more than 100 colleges and universities.

THE BOARD'S FUNDING CRITERIA

The Board was guided, in its choice of which colleges to fund, by three criteria. First, it considered how good a college was academically and how promising its future seemed. Its officers believed that America had far too many colleges and that many of these would inevitably languish or die; early in its history it wanted to fund only institutions that had promising futures.

71

Second, the Board wanted to aid mostly schools that were sponsored by religious denominations, organizations which had "founded and maintained most of our really substantial private foundations."[4] From 1902–1914, it gave a grant to only one state university—the University of Virginia.[5]

Third, the Board considered the economy and population of the geographical area the college was located in and how promising its area's future seemed. As Abraham Flexner said in his history of the Board's early years:

> Our college planning, in so far as it endeavors to develop institutions that have not yet attained full power, must give great weight to the consideration that the modern university thrives and is most useful in close association with population, industry, and wealth.[6]

In arguing that a modern university thrives "in close association with population, industry, and wealth," Flexner was challenging a strong current of American thought which held that institutions of higher learning should be situated in rural settings. Many state universities established in the 19th century were deliberately located far from population centers, such as the University of Massachusetts (founded in 1863), situated in the rural western part of the state, 90 miles from Boston; the University of Illinois (1867), situated not in Chicago, but 130 miles south of it in Urbana; and the University of Connecticut (1881), located not in the populous southwest or central parts of the state, but in Storrs in the rural northeast. Similarly, New York state established most of its teachers colleges in rural, sometimes even remote areas of the state, placing them in such communities as Potsdam, Brockport, Fredonia, Cortland, Oneonta, and Plattsburgh.

Even around the turn of the century, there was still a very strong strain of thinking that colleges and universities should be situated in rural areas. As Daniel Coit Gilman, the president of urban Johns Hopkins University, said at the inauguration of a new president of Washington and Lee University, located in rural Virginia:

> It was a little country college in eastern France where Pasteur's life was begun. It was a little country college at Metz where Tocqueville received that classical discipline which preceded his studies of American democracy. . . . It was Dartmouth which drew from Daniel Webster before the Supreme Court in Washington that familiar and pathetic passage: "It is, sir, as I have said, a small college, and yet there are those who love it."[7]

John Corbin, in an early 20th century guidebook to six universities, stated:

> [A university's] character is determined by its location, as is always the case with an institute of learning, at least in many fundamentals. In order to maintain any distinctive atmosphere and spirit, the University of Pennsylvania has a life-and-death struggle to resist the devouring force of Philadelphia, while Columbia fled for its life out of the heart of New York to Morningside Heights.[8]

The same author wrote about the University of Chicago that "its location, a mere quarter of an hour from the heart of the metropolis, is likely to prove unfavorable to the atmosphere of liberal culture."[9]

In recent years, state universities whose original campuses were situated in sparsely populated areas have often opened new campuses in their state's major population area. The University of Wisconsin, for example, whose original campus was in Madison, opened a campus in Milwaukee (1956), and the University of Massachusetts opened one in Boston (1965). Some colleges have moved from urban to suburban settings, as Goucher moved from Baltimore to suburban Towson, Maryland in 1950, and the State University of New York at Buffalo moved most of its programs from Buffalo to suburban Amherst shortly after 1970. Others, like the University of Chicago, have strongly considered moving from an urban to a suburban location, yet virtually no colleges and universities in recent years have moved from urban to rural settings. Even so, a disproportionately large number of America's best colleges (as opposed to universities), like Amherst, Williams, Oberlin, Middlebury, Dartmouth, Hamilton, Bowdoin, and Carleton, remain in small towns.

At any rate, in its early years, wanting to learn how much support colleges and universities received from their own area, particularly how many students they attracted from nearby, the Board drew maps showing what percentages of a college's students resided within 50 and 100 miles of it. In all sections of the country, even sparsely settled ones, the Board found that most colleges drew the majority of their students from within a 100-mile radius. Swarthmore (Pennsylvania), for example, drew 64% from within 50 miles and 79% from within 100 miles; Rochester (New York) drew 87% from within 50 miles, 93% from within 100 miles; Furman (South Carolina) drew 60% from within 50 miles, 72% from within 100 miles; Millsaps (Mississippi) drew 49% and 80%; Beloit (Wisconsin) 48% and 73%; and Pomona (California) 80% and 86%.

Only a few colleges were exceptions to this rule, most of them institutions that were both located in sparsely populated areas and nationally known, a combination of circumstances conducive to attracting many students from far away. Williams, for example, located in rural Massachusetts, drew only 14% of its students from within 50 miles and 23% from within 100 miles; nearby Smith drew 14% and 35%. Vassar, in Poughkeepsie (New York) drew 9% and 42%. All things being equal, the Board preferred to aid colleges that had a large pool of potential students nearby from which to draw.

All these criteria for conferring endowment grants were freely acknowledged by Flexner in his history of the General Education Board, published in 1915. In addition, Raymond Fosdick, writing much later, mentioned two more criteria. The first was that the Board wanted to develop some strong colleges in every area of the country to be part of what it envisioned as a "comprehensive system of higher education."

Therefore, in geographical areas that had no first-rate, and perhaps not even any reasonably good or promising schools, the Board sometimes granted funds to the best schools available, "to bring the more needy sections up to a level with the less needy."[10] The Board's desire to distribute its money more or less evenly around the country, and not to concentrate it in the East, where a disproportionately large number of the best private institutions were located, is reflected in the fact that it gave roughly equal amounts of its funds to colleges in the "southern" states, the "western" states (which included states in the Midwest), and the eastern states.[11]

The second was that, in order to appear impartial, the Board, in distributing its wealth among schools of various religious denominations, occasionally had "to consider assistance for a college simply because the sponsoring sect complained of being neglected."[12]

Finally, it appears that the Board was not particularly eager to fund technological schools. Though it gave one of its largest grants to Stevens Institute of Technology, it had given nothing at all, as of 1914, to MIT, Rensselaer Polytechnic Institute, Throop Polytechnic Institute (today called Caltech), Case School of Applied Science (today Case Western Reserve University), Georgia School of Technology (today known as the Georgia Institute of Technology, or Georgia Tech), or any other technological school.

The Board thus had many criteria for dispensing its money, only one of which was the school's current academic quality, and even that one was vitiated by the fact that the college had not only to be considered good academically in the present but also to appear to have a promising future. Therefore, it might seem unlikely that a list of the colleges to which the Board had made grants from 1902–1914 would resemble a list of the best-regarded colleges and universities in the United States.

Actually, though, if one excludes state, municipal, and technological institutions—admittedly, that is excluding quite a lot—the list is probably a reasonably good approximation of the more esteemed private colleges and universities in each state and region. There were some obvious omissions, though. For example, neither Dartmouth nor Vassar received grants in this period, possibly because the Board considered their geographical locations unpromising. Clark, which was then considered one of the nation's best institutions for graduate study, received no money. Neither did the University of Chicago, perhaps because it had recently been established by John D. Rockefeller, Sr., and was in excellent financial condition. Or perhaps Rockefeller, having founded it, had a special interest in that university and preferred to make grants to it directly, without going through the Board.

Such a list was not likely to develop into an academic quality ranking because no distinctions were made among institutions. It might have developed into a list of 100 or so of the better private colleges and universities, with some allowances made for the fact that standards were lower for institutions from regions which had few highly-regarded colleges, the kind of list that could be used by other foundations in deciding which schools to fund. However, the Board continued to make grants prolifically; by 1925 it had given money to 291 colleges and universities, not counting medical schools,[13] and such a number was simply too large and inclusive to serve as a list of America's most highly regarded private colleges and universities.

Chapter Ten

INSTITUTIONS RECEIVING PENSION FUNDS FROM THE CARNEGIE FOUNDATION FOR THE ADVANCEMENT OF TEACHING

The Carnegie Foundation for the Advancement of Teaching (here-after called the Foundation or the CFAT) was another philanthropic organization whose list of the schools it benefited could plausibly have been considered a roster of America's best regarded colleges and universities.[1] At least, the roster of institutions whose faculties were eligible to receive its pensions could, with some qualifications, have been used as such a list early in its history.

In 1905, Andrew Carnegie established the Foundation for the purpose of distributing pensions to retired college and university professors and their widows from selected institutions. His goals were to provide pensions for a group of people he considered seriously underpaid—he called college teaching "the least rewarded of all the professions"[2]—and also to improve educational efficiency in two ways. The first was by inducing older professors to retire by giving them the financial security to do so, in order that they could be replaced by younger, presumably more productive ones. The second was, by virtue of establishing a good pension program for retired professors, to attract able people into the profession.[3]

He endowed the fund with $10 million and selected 25 men to serve on its Board of Trustees. Twenty-three of them were the presidents of colleges and universities; only a few of these schools were sectarian institutions, and none were state universities. Most of them were major, private, nonsectarian universities. Their presidents included many of the most eminent figures in American higher education of the time, including Nicholas Murray Butler of Columbia, Charles William Eliot of Harvard, William Rainey Harper of Chicago, and Woodrow Wilson of Princeton. The trustees elected Henry Pritchett, then President of MIT, to be President of the CFAT.

In setting up the CFAT, Carnegie had stipulated that the pension funds were to be for professors in "Universities, Colleges, and Technical Schools in our country, Canada and Newfoundland."[4] He excluded both publicly-controlled and denominational institutions on the grounds that their respective states and Canadian provinces, on the one hand, and the religious denominations that controlled and partly supported them, on the other hand, were the appropriate groups to fund the pensions of professors at these schools.[5] Still, he left the CFAT Board of Trustees wide latitude in defining what constituted a denominational institution.

CHOOSING ELIGIBLE INSTITUTIONS

The first task of the CFAT's officers and trustees, faced with the responsibility of deciding upon which professors to confer pensions, was to define what, precisely, was a college, for hundreds of schools of that era called themselves colleges or even universities although they were, for all practical purposes, secondary schools. After much deliberation, the CFAT finally decided to employ the definition of "college" then used by the state of New York. It was as follows:

> An institution to be ranked as a college, must have at least six (6) professors giving their entire time to college and university work, a course of four full years in liberal arts and sciences, and should require for admission, not less than the usual four years of academic or high school preparation, or its equivalent, in addition to the pre-academic or grammar school studies.[6]

To this definition, the CFAT added the following:

> A technical school, to be eligible, must have entrance and graduation requirements equivalent to those of the college, and must offer courses in pure and applied science of equivalent grade.
> To be ranked as a college an institution must have a productive endowment of not less than two hundred thousand dollars.[7]

These were minimal requirements; those the CFAT actually applied in admitting institutions were often more stringent. Still, the minimal requirements were multidimensional, based as they were on all the following: size of faculty, in the form of a minimum of six full-time professors; curriculum, in the form of a four-year course of study in liberal arts and sciences; and financial resources, in the form of a productive endowment of at least $200,000. A great many colleges and universities, including many that were not particularly well-regarded academically, would have been eligible under these criteria. It was exactly these small and less than flourishing schools that Carnegie had traditionally been eager to help.

Theron Schlabach wrote, concerning Carnegie's gifts to colleges before he established the CFAT, that Carnegie "thought that smaller schools, not being so distracted by sports and other nonacademic concerns, gave better education than the larger ones. Despite the protests of leading educators he stepped up his giving to the less wealthy colleges."[8] Schlabach, referring to the decision of the CFAT trustees to impose strict educational standards on schools wishing to participate in the pension fund, wrote that the "decisions of the trustees created a system of benefactions that effectively shut out many small colleges in which Carnegie had a long-standing interest. . . ."[9]

But once Carnegie appointed the CFAT Board of Trustees he scrupulously avoided interfering with its decisions, and this Board, composed as it was mostly of presidents of prestigious universities, was not inclined to accept struggling institutions into the pension program. The most important figure in the decision to accept only schools that were academically well-respected was CFAT President Henry Pritchett. He wanted to create a stratified, German-style educational system in the United States and therefore to support the institutions that were already the strongest, rather than to use CFAT funds to help develop marginal institutions.[10]

The trustees, in determining which institutions to approve for pensions, collected a large amount of information about American and Canadian universities, concentrating on three factors:

The educational standards of the institutions;
The relations of each institution to the State, both in the matter of control and support;
The relation of each institution to religious denominations.[11]

Though Carnegie had intended to include Newfoundland's institutions of higher learning in his pension program, the CFAT's Board of Trustees eventually excluded the five Newfoundland institutions that called themselves colleges because all of them were both subsidized by the government and under the supervision of a "superintendent appointed on denominational grounds."[12]

In evaluating schools' applications for membership the CFAT did not use, beyond its minimal standards, any absolutely rigid requirements. Rather, it decided which schools to accept on a case by case basis. In addition to the minimal criteria, it paid close attention to a college's entrance standards, especially the kind and amount of high school work it required for admission. In addition, it disapproved of schools that had preparatory departments, especially where those departments were not rigidly segregated from the rest of the institution. It also disapproved of colleges and universities that maintained any connection with proprietary law and medical schools. Before any school could be accepted, it had to be inspected in person by an official of the CFAT.

Finally, in 1906, after a great deal of work, the CFAT selected 46 colleges, universities, and technical schools in the United States and two universities in Canada as acceptable. The CFAT considered none of them to be under the control of any denomination or any level of government and all of them to meet its financial and educational standards.[13] Four of these schools—Cornell University, the University of Vermont, MIT, and the University of Pennsylvania—received some support from their respective states. Still, in none of these cases did the CFAT consider this support as amounting to the "controlling factor" in the school's financial support.[14]

The schools were not evenly distributed geographically. As Schlabach pointed out:

> Of the forty-eight schools, exactly half were in the New England states and New York, and about two-thirds east of the Ohio-Pennsylvania border . . . .only one institution, Tulane University, was farther south than Maryland.[15]

Though it was scarcely intended as a list of the most or even the more highly esteemed American privately controlled colleges and universities, in fact it served reasonably well as such a list. It excluded all denominational colleges, but not many of these, judging from other contemporary lists of the "best" colleges and universities, would have been included on any organization's roster of America's best-regarded colleges and universities, anyway.[16]

Very few of the nation's handful of municipal universities would likely have been considered eligible on the grounds of academic quality—the City College of New York and the University of Cincinnati, perhaps, but probably no others. The list of 46 American institutions did include many small, little-known schools, such as Colorado College, Hobart, and Ripon; some women's colleges, like Smith, Vassar, Wellesley, and Wells; and some technological schools, like Case School of Applied Science, Clarkson School of Technology, and Stevens Institute of Technology.

With the obvious exception of the best-regarded state universities the CFAT list was right from the start a fairly good list of some of the most esteemed colleges, universities, and technological schools in the United States. Each year, for several years after it admitted its first 48 schools, the CFAT admitted some new institutions. In its 1907 *Annual Report*, for example, it reported the admission of three new colleges—Dickinson, Randolph-Macon Woman's College, and Bates. In its 1908 *Annual Report* it noted the admission of seven new schools, including its first municipal institution, the University of Cincinnati.

Ever since the CFAT had been established in 1905, state universities had been clamoring to be declared eligible for Carnegie pensions, against the opposition of many members of the CFAT Board of Trustees. Several trustees thought that state universities should be supported by their states and that if the CFAT assumed the responsibility for conferring pensions on faculty members at state universities, their states would be reluctant ever to fund pensions. Some trustees may have also considered the improving state universities of the Midwest and California as threats to their own schools. At any rate, after three years of intense lobbying by the state universities, in 1908 Andrew Carnegie committed $5 million more to fund pensions for professors and their widows at state universities. In 1909, the CFAT accepted seven more schools, including its first four state universities—Michigan, Minnesota, Missouri, and Wisconsin—and its first Canadian provincial university, the University of Toronto.[17]

Also in 1909, the CFAT dropped two institutions from its accepted list. One was Randolph-Macon Woman's College which, after being accepted, had adopted a resolution that all candidates for its Board of Trustees must be approved by the Methodist Episcopal Church, South. It therefore had reverted, by the standards of the CFAT, to being a "denominational" institution. The other was George Washington University, one of the original group of 48 accepted institutions, which the CFAT dropped for two reasons. First, it had let its endowment fund drop below the required amount of $200,000. Second, and far more serious in the eyes of the Foundation, it had retired two of its professors, against their wishes and while they were in the prime of life. It had done so on the grounds that the CFAT would provide pensions for them and so that the university, which was in a period of financial stringency, could hire younger, less expensive professors to replace them.[18]

In its 1911 *Annual Report* the CFAT reported the admission of another state institution, the University of Virginia. This made nine state universities and provincially-controlled schools, in all, that it had accepted—eight American state universities and the University of Toronto. After that the Foundation closed its doors to state institutions for more than a decade, accepting no more until it reported the admission of the University of Alabama in its 1922 *Annual Report.*[19]

By 1913, the CFAT had accepted 73 institutions.[20] Perhaps the missing school with the best academic reputation was the University of Chicago, which was ineligible because of its close ties to the Baptist Church. Vanderbilt was missing, too, probably due to its close ties with the Methodist Episcopal Church, South. It, too, was probably more highly regarded academically than some universities on the CFAT's accepted list. Similarly, Bryn Mawr, which was probably considered better academically than some of the women's colleges on the Carnegie list, had not yet been accepted.

CHANGING SELECTION CRITERIA

In its earliest years, the CFAT selected members, within the limits of its guidelines, mostly according to what it felt to be the academic quality of the individual schools that applied. Around 1908 or 1909, though, the Foundation's criteria for deciding which schools to accept seem to have changed sharply. From 1905 until about 1908, the Foundation apparently wanted to select, from among those schools that were nondenominational and not controlled by any state, the schools with the highest academic standards, and it sometimes held out the promise of acceptance to induce schools to raise their standards. But by 1909, the CFAT began to use membership in its pension program as a carrot to try to improve not just individual schools but the structure of American higher education as a whole. (In doing so, it was acting similarly to the General Education Board, which in its early years attempted not only to strengthen individual institutions but also to improve, through judicious distribution of its grants, the entire "system" of American higher education as well.)

Instances of the CFAT's rejecting colleges and universities based on criteria having to do with matters extraneous to those schools' academic quality are numerous. In 1909, Pritchett wrote to the Governor of Ohio, stating that because Ohio had three state-supported universities—Ohio State University in Columbus, Ohio University in Athens, and Miami University in Oxford—instead of only one, as Pritchett would have preferred, none of the three would be accepted as members, even though

Pritchett regarded Ohio State, at least, as a "real" university.[21] The CFAT refused to accept another university, which the *Fourth Annual Report* did not name, even though it was, according to the report, a "strong institution," because of "the articulation of the university . . . with three-year high schools."[22] (The Foundation would have preferred that the institution accept only the graduates of four-year high schools.)

The CFAT's *Annual Report* for 1910 adopted a position very similar to that of the General Education Board at about the same time, stating criteria for acceptance concerning not only an institution's intrinsic quality but its geographical region and its local "competition" from other colleges and universities, as follows:

> Geographically, what is the need for a college in its locality? What other colleges or universities, if any, contribute to the need which the college seeks to fulfil? (*sic*)
> In view of its geographical location, what is the probable future of the college?
> What proportion of the income of the Foundation is now being paid to colleges and universities in the same state?[23]

Applying these criteria to specific situations, the CFAT's *Fifth Annual Report* noted that Ohio had 51 chartered colleges and universities, "more than are possessed by the British Islands with a population nine times as great." Since the CFAT had already accepted five of these 51, it doubted whether it could accept any privately endowed college from Ohio in the near future, no matter how excellent it might be.[24]

Even though Knox College was the only institution from Illinois on the accepted list, the CFAT refused to consider accepting Lombard College, because it was located in the same small city (Galesburg, with a population of 18,000) as Knox. The CFAT reasoned that it was "obviously not in the best interest of education that two colleges should compete with each other in a community of this size."[25]

In short, by 1909 the CFAT was considering, in deciding what colleges to accept, not only whether they were free of denominational control and had adequate educational standards and financial resources, but also the promise of their region and the number of nearby colleges against which they had to compete. Such a policy for admitting schools was scarcely one that would seem likely to result in a list of the better-regarded American colleges and universities. Yet, in large measure because the CFAT had admitted its first 48 American institutions before it began to apply such criteria, as of 1913 the 70 American colleges and universities on its accepted list were probably a reasonably good group of the best-regarded colleges and universities in the United States.

This turn of events was an ironical one. No one had ever intended that the CFAT's list of member institutions be one of America's most highly-regarded colleges and universities. Yet by 1913, although state universities were still probably underrepresented, a list of the CFAT's members came reasonably close to resembling such a list.

Chapter Eleven

THE ASSOCIATION OF AMERICAN UNIVERSITIES' ACCREDITATION OF UNDERGRADUATE PROGRAMS

A nother list of leading institutions resulted from the early practice by the Association of American Universities (hereafter called the AAU) of accrediting the undergraduate programs of colleges and universities. Actually, in 1914 the AAU approved in principle a three-level stratification scheme for the colleges and universities it accredited, based on how well their students fared in graduate and professional school.

Still, the AAU's work is being considered among that of organizations which published lists of supposedly academically superior institutions, not among those that published multilevel classification schemes, because it apparently never used the three-level stratification scheme it developed. At least, it never published a stratification of colleges and universities in any issue of its annual *Journal of Proceedings and Addresses.*

THE AAU AND EUROPEAN UNIVERSITIES

The AAU was founded in 1900, partly in response to a call by five leading American universities that wished "to secure in foreign universities, where it is not already given, such credit as is legitimately due to the advanced work done in our own universities of high standing.... "[1] Its original members were fourteen of America's best-regarded universities of that era.[2]

Shortly afterwards, in 1904, the University of Berlin notified the AAU that it would accept graduate work at American universities towards its doctor of philosophy degree only if such work were taken at schools that were AAU members. Other universities in Germany and Holland followed suit. In 1908, an AAU committee chaired by Charles William Eliot, President of Harvard, issued a report containing the following statement:

Foreign governments . . . now recognize the universities which are members of this Association and refuse recognition of those which are not. It is the duty of this Association either to standardize American universities, and thus justify the confidence which foreign governments repose in them, or to notify those governments that there are American universities outside this Association whose work and standing are not inferior to universities now members of the Association.[3]

In 1912 the University of Berlin's faculty of philosophy reiterated its 1904 policy.[4] The AAU therefore decided to adopt the second course of action the committee charged by President Eliot had recommended in 1908 and notify foreign governments that America had other colleges and universities "whose degrees are regarded by the Association as of equal value"[5] with its own members' degrees. But the AAU did not wish to draw up such a list itself. Its Executive Committee, in a "Special Report . . . ," wrote as follows:

> . . . it would plainly be impossible with any machinery that is now at hand for the Association to make such a list, which would involve not only an immense amount of correspondence, but also a great deal of personal scrutiny as to actual conditions. The Association, too, should not be called upon to bear the onus of a classification that would almost inevitably awaken opposition. . . . [6]

Its Executive Committee therefore decided to draw up a roster that would combine all the institutions on three other, already existing lists:

> . . . the members, present and future, of the Association of American Universities.
> . . . those other institutions on the accepted list of the Carnegie Foundation for the Advancement of Teaching. . . .
> . . . those institutions which are not included in the accepted list of the Carnegie Foundation because they are in some sense sectarian as defined in the terms of the gift of the fund, but otherwise conform to its standards of acceptability. Such a list has readily been furnished by the Carnegie Foundation with the understanding that it is to be used for the present purpose.[7]

In 1913, the AAU sent the German ministries of education a list of all these colleges and universities, 119 in all.[8] In doing so, the AAU was, to say the least, disingenuous in claiming that these 119 institutions, a number more than five times as large as its membership list of 22, all had degrees equal in value to those of the AAU schools. Virtually all of the AAU's members were among the best-regarded universities of the day, like Columbia, Cornell, Harvard, Johns Hopkins, and the universities of

California, Chicago, and Wisconsin. Its list of 119 institutions, by contrast, included such unsung colleges as Cornell (Iowa), Drury (Missouri), Franklin (Indiana), and William Jewell (Missouri).

The AAU could always claim that these schools, because they were colleges, not universities, were therefore ineligible for AAU membership, their outstanding quality notwithstanding. But the AAU would have been hard put to say why the many universities among the 97 additional schools, if *their* undergraduate degrees were fully equal in quality to those of the AAU members, had not been admitted as members of that organization. The AAU was, in effect, telling the continental universities that the 97 colleges and universities on the list that were not AAU members were good enough for the continental universities to take their graduates on equal terms with those of graduates of AAU institutions, but not so good that the AAU itself would accept them as members.

BABCOCK'S COMMITTEE
ON THE CLASSIFICATION OF COLLEGES

Having established a list of schools whose degrees were allegedly equal in quality to those of the AAU schools to give to the continental universities, in 1914 the AAU appointed a Committee on the Classification of Colleges to review and update this list. To chair this committee it selected none other than Kendric Babcock, now Dean of the College of Literature, Arts, and Science at the University of Illinois, who while at the United States Bureau of Education had produced that organization's never officially released five-level classification of colleges and universities. It is not surprising that the AAU appointed Babcock to chair such a committee. It had long wanted his 1911 report that President Taft had suppressed to be released. In 1913 it had gone so far as to send a letter to President Wilson asking him to allow publication of Babcock's list, saying that by doing so Wilson would "assist the cause of higher education throughout the country...and confer a boon not only upon the members of this Association, but upon all the Colleges concerned."[9]

Wilson did not do so, but Babcock's Committee on the Classification of Colleges drew up a three-strata classification system very similar to the one he had done earlier for the U.S. Bureau of Education. Its three divisions were as follows:

Group A. Institutions whose graduates should ordinarily be admitted to the graduate schools of this Association for work in lines for which they have had adequate undergraduate preparation, with a reasonable presumption that advanced degrees may be taken with the minimum amount of prescribed work and in the minimum time prescribed. . . .

Group B. Institutions from which only those graduates of high standing in their classes who are individually recommended by the department of undergraduate instruction corresponding to that in which they purpose to do their graduate work may be admitted on the same basis as graduates from the institutions in Group A.

Group C. Other institutions whose graduates should be admitted to graduate schools, but with the presumption that more than the minimum time and minimum amount of work will be ordinarily required for an advanced degree.[10]

Babcock's two classificatory schemes—the first one for the United States Bureau of Education in 1911 and the second one by his Committee on the Classification of Colleges for the Association of American Universities in 1914—were generally similar. There were some important differences, however, all in the direction of making the second classification system less inflammatory.

In the first place, whereas the first scheme had four levels, the second had only three; now there would be no fourth-class colleges. Second, the provocative word "class" was changed to the milder word "group." Now no college would be even a third-class college, but rather a college in group C.

Third, the 1914 report to the AAU was less precise about how long it would supposedly take graduates of particular groups of colleges to earn degrees from major graduate schools. In 1911, Babcock had said that graduates of a class I college or university would commonly be able to earn the master's degree in "one year" after receiving the bachelor's degree,[11] and that for those graduates of class III schools "the requirement of two years for the master's degree [is] probable."[12] In 1914, however, Babcock's Committee on the Classification of Colleges said about the schools in group A merely that their graduates could take advanced degrees "in the minimum time prescribed,"[13] without specifying how long this period of time would be. For graduates of schools in group C the Committee said that "more than the minimum time . . . will be ordinarily required,"[14] again without specifying it.

Finally, Babcock's Committee on the Classification of Colleges used softer language than did Babcock in his 1911 report. In 1911, for example, Babcock had said that even from a strong (that is, starred) class II school only "a brilliant student with a brilliant record" could possibly earn a degree from a good graduate school as fast as could those who graduated from class I institutions.[15]

However, in 1914 his Committee on the Classification of Colleges said that to earn degrees from major graduate schools in minimal time such students did not necessarily have to be brilliant or have outstanding records. They only had to be "graduates of high standing in their classes who are individually recommended by the department of undergraduate instruction corresponding to that in which they purpose to do their graduate work,"[16] Similarly, in 1911 Babcock had written of class III schools whose "standards of admission and graduation are so low, or so uncertain, or so loosely administered. . . . "[17] No such provocative language appears in the description of groups A, B, and C in 1914.

Despite these concessions to the sensitivities of college and university administrators, Babcock and the AAU, thwarted by Taft and Wilson, had finally triumphed in publishing a classification system quite similar to Babcock's original one. This system, based as it was only upon graduates' presumed preparation for graduate work, would obviously be useful to the continental universities. These institutions' primary interest, after all, was whether they should accept graduates of a particular American college or university and how well-prepared they could expect its graduates to be, rather than what amount of endowment income a college had or how well equipped was its chemistry laboratory.

But this triumph seems to have been a hollow one, for although in 1914 the AAU accepted in principle Babcock's three-strata scheme based on the readiness of an institution's alumni for graduate and professional school, it never published a stratification of colleges and universities based on this scheme in its *Journal*. The 1915 and 1916 volumes of the *Journal* contained no listings of approved schools. The 1917 *Journal* did print a list of approved colleges, consisting of the CFAT's accepted list plus several additional schools. It pointed out that all these schools fall into one of Babcock's three groups, but the list grouped all the schools together, not stratifying them in any way.[18]

LATER DEVELOPMENTS

In 1923, the Committee on the Classification of Colleges was author-ized to accredit schools based upon still another method—institutional self-reports, followed by campus inspections and, in some cases, rein-spections. At first these visitations were performed by David Robertson of the American Council on Education, with the visitations financed both by inspection fees of $100 levied against the colleges visited and a grant of $3000 from the CFAT.[19] Its selection criteria this time, in contrast to the AAU's early methods of evaluating institutions, were definitely multidimensional.

In the AAU's *Journal of Proceedings* of its 26th annual conference, held in 1924, it published its minimal standards for inclusion on its approved list. The list included requirements in these areas: admissions standards; graduation requirements; size of faculty; training of faculty; teaching load of faculty; minimum operating income; quality of equipment and library; any preparatory schools associated with the college being kept entirely distinct from the college; the "tone of the institution"; and its success in preparing students to do satisfactory graduate or professional work.[20]

The AAU's Committee on the Classification of Universities and Colleges, as it was now called, went on to request the right to inspect some institutions already on the approved list, at no cost to the institutions, on the grounds that some of them might have declined in quality since being approved. Its explanation for doing so was as follows:

> A preliminary examination of nine institutions now on the accepted list has convinced the Committee that three of these should be inspected at an early date. It has reasons to believe that some others have deterio-rated since they were placed on the approved list.[21]

So, within eleven years, the AAU had devised three entirely different methods of determining America's better colleges and universities:

1. In 1913—based on whether they were members of the AAU, on the accepted list of the CFAT, or would have been on the CFAT's accepted list if they had been nonsectarian.

2. 1914—based on how prepared their graduates were considered to be to enter leading graduate schools.

3. 1923—based on a multidimensional list of criteria as revealed by college self-reports and campus inspections.

Whereas how well a college's graduates performed in graduate and professional schools was still considered "fundamental in determining whether the institution should be included on the approved list,"[22] many other factors were included as well. The AAU continued its approved list for many years. But by the end of World War II, many of its members were increasingly unhappy with its continued involvement in accreditation, for a variety of reasons.

> Many of the presidents and deans were unhappy, to say the least, with the amount of time and emphasis devoted at their meetings to matters related to accrediting at the expense of other important educational issues. . . . they could not consistently support a program whose validity was being questioned by different studies[23] and on which graduate schools were placing decreasing reliance as far as admission of students was concerned. . . . For these and other reasons it was quite logical that the AAU would decide to end its accrediting activity. . . . [24]

It did so in 1948.[25]

The AAU's list of approved institutions, which lasted for more than three decades, and the three-level stratification scheme it adopted in principle, even though it published the list of schools selected on this basis in one, undifferentiated list in the *Journal,* failed to develop into an academic quality ranking. They failed to do so because the AAU, throughout its accrediting years, 1913–1948, never saw itself as primarily an accrediting organization. Under the pressure of a policy adopted by some continental universities that could be taken as an insult to American higher education and that would have greatly limited most American college graduates' access to some of the leading universities of the day, it established a list of approved schools and frequently revised it. Still, accrediting colleges and universities was never the AAU's primary interest or function, only a time-consuming sideline. As other accrediting agencies flourished; as conditions in American higher education, due partly to the efforts of these agencies, became less chaotic and more standardized; and, finally, as its members objected to the time and effort that this sideline was requiring, the AAU ended its accrediting activities.

Chapter Twelve

THE WORK OF THE SIX REGIONAL
ACCREDITING AGENCIES

The United States' six regional accrediting agencies issued lists each year of those colleges and universities that met their minimal standards.[1] Though these lists can scarcely be taken as those of outstanding institutions, they can be regarded as those of schools which at least met certain minimal standards of quality. The regional accrediting organizations were established from 1885 to 1924, but they generally did not begin actual accreditation of colleges and universities until long after they were founded. For example, the North Central Association of Colleges and Secondary Schools, the first of the six to issue a list of accredited institutions, was founded in 1895 but did not publish its first list of accredited colleges and universities until 1913.[2]

The work of the various regional accrediting organizations was never very likely to develop into academic quality rankings, because they usually issued only lists of approved colleges, not multilevel stratifications. The Southern Association of Colleges and Secondary Schools was an exception to this rule, though. Established in 1895, the Association adopted its first list of accredited colleges and universities in 1920. It issued, along with its list of approved institutions, "a so-called four-year non-member list . . . composed of colleges which do not quite meet the standards, but which approximate them to a sufficient degree as to permit of their graduates being accepted as teachers in accredited secondary schools."[3] This was, in essence, a two-level stratification system.

In general, though, accreditation by regional accrediting organizations, as opposed to those organizations accrediting professional fields, was binary from the beginning. Why did accrediting organizations in several professional fields originally develop multilevel quality classifications, even though those eventually devolved into undifferentiated lists of approved schools, while the regional accrediting organizations, with

93

isolated exceptions such as the work of the Southern Association, did not develop them at all?

The main reason is because the accrediting agencies for professional fields were responsible for evaluating and approving schools in only one academic area, such as medicine, pharmacy, law, or forestry. The regional associations, on the other hand, were faced with the task of evaluating *whole* institutions—colleges, universities, technological schools, and so on. American professional schools in any field at the turn of the 20th century differed widely in goals and quality. Still, there existed far more agreement about what should be their goals, mission, and curriculum, and about what constituted an acceptable level of academic "quality" for them than there did about the goals, curriculum, and academic standards for all the institutions of higher education in a multistate region.

The fact that regional accrediting agencies were confronted with the task of somehow evaluating schools that differed enormously in size, goals, and academic programs made it very hard for them to stratify schools into classes according to their putative academic quality. This resulted in their simply publishing undifferentiated lists of schools that met the accrediting agencies' minimal standards.

Chapter Thirteen

ABRAHAM FLEXNER'S *MEDICAL EDUCATION IN THE UNITED STATES AND CANADA* AND SIMILAR STUDIES

There was still another type of work from which academic quality rankings might have developed. It was the book filled with facts and statistics about American colleges, universities, or individual departments. Abraham Flexner's *Medical Education in the United States and Canada* (1910), hereafter called the *Flexner Report* or the *Report*, was the most famous and influential of this type.[1]

In his *Report*, Flexner described each of the 155 medical schools which then existed in the United States and Canada. He never ranked them, nor did he even stratify them into classes according to their academic quality. Still, more than 75 years after its publication, the *Flexner Report* remains one of the best known and influential studies of academic quality ever written in America. It has been influential in at least two ways. First, it inspired several successor reports that followed it very closely in format and method. Second, and more important, scholars almost universally agree that the *Flexner Report* dramatically changed the nature of medical education in the United States, although they disagree about how it changed it and how beneficial these changes were.

For many years Flexner was portrayed as a giant whose 1910 *Report*, all by itself, had caused the closing of many medical schools and brought about sweeping reforms in American medical education.[2] More recently, his influence, although still regarded as considerable, is thought to have been not quite that great. The reform of American medical education, it has been pointed out by many, had been occurring on many fronts since at least the last third of the 19th century.[3] Flexner himself, in his *Report*, acknowledged that in recent years American medical education had improved.[4]

Not only had medical education as a whole been improving, but medical schools had been closing at a rapid rate even before Flexner published his *Report.* One writer has said the following about Flexner's influence:

> Flexner's report thus aided a process already underway. The rate of consolidation and elimination of medical schools was as rapid before the report as after. Between 1904 and 1915 some ninety-two schools closed their doors or merged, forty-four of them in the first six years to 1909 and forty-eight in the second six years to 1915.[5]

In recent years, it has even been argued that the *Flexner Report*, far from being a document that resulted in progressive reform, was primarily one that worked to protect the interests of America's capitalist class:

> ... [the *Report*] succeeded in limiting the class composition of medical practice by restricting entry to the medical field to only those individuals who could afford four years of medical school (i.e. essentially upper middle class white men).[6]

Although the *Flexner Report* is not generally seen today as responsible, all by itself, for the closing of dozens of American medical schools, and though the reform of medical education was occurring before it was written, it has still been one of the most influential reports ever published on the quality of professional schools, or, for that matter, any type of education. The economist Reuben Kessel wrote, "if impact on public policy is the criterion of importance, the Flexner report must be regarded as one of the most important reports ever written."[7]

The story of how Flexner was asked by the Carnegie Foundation for the Advancement of Teaching to write his study of American medical schools has been told many times and will not be repeated here.[8] At the time, he was virtually unknown. Although he had published a book, *The American College: A Criticism*, it had been "a commercial failure, and a critical failure as well."[9] Flexner was not even a physician, and he initially thought that the CFAT was confusing him with his brother, Simon Flexner, who was a medical doctor. But the CFAT wanted someone who was not a physician and could therefore not be accused of serving his own self-interest or trying to advance the interest of any medical sect. In engaging Flexner, its reasoning was similar to that of the United States Bureau of Education, a few years later, which chose Kendric Babcock, who was not then associated with any college or university, to classify American colleges and universities.

The famous *Report* actually had four parts. The first was a long introduction by Henry Pritchett, President of the CFAT. In it, he summarized Flexner's major findings, defended Flexner's whirlwind visits as an appropriate method for judging the quality of medical schools,[10] and called, as did Flexner, for a sharp reduction in the number of physicians and medical schools. He also voiced the hope that "this report will make plain once for all that the day of the commercial medical school has passed" (p. xvi).

Flexner's own material was divided into three sections. First came a long essay sketching the history of medical education in the United States. It described the conditions in medical schools during the first two years of study, which were largely devoted to lectures and laboratory work, and during the next two years, which were largely devoted to clinical study. It also discussed the income and expenditures of medical schools.[11] This essay included, in addition, brief sections on the medical sects of the era and their medical schools; the state boards; and the medical education of women and blacks. The *Report* ended with an appendix showing, for all the medical schools in the United States and Canada, their number of faculty members, student enrollment, annual income from fees, and annual operating budget.

But the part that caused most of the furor and did the most to change the course of American medical education was the one in which Flexner listed all the medical schools in the United States and Canada, state by state (or province by province), city by city, and school by school. For each one, he briefly described its entrance requirements, teaching staff, income, and laboratory and clinical facilities. For most states, after his description of each of its medical schools, he ended with a section titled "general considerations," in which he described, often caustically, medical education in general in those states and suggested what should be done to improve it. In these "general considerations," Flexner pulled no punches, any more than he did in his descriptions of individual schools, as the following passages illustrate:

About Arkansas:

Both the Arkansas schools are local institutions in a state that has at this date three times as many doctors as it needs; neither has a single redeeming feature. It is incredible that the state university should permit its name to shelter one of them (p. 188).

About Oregon:

Neither of these schools has either resources or ideals; there is no justification for their existence. The entire coast is oversupplied with doctors by immigration; unless something better can be made than can be thus readily obtained, the state will do well to let the field lie fallow (p. 292).

About Illinois:

The city of Chicago is in respect to medical education the plague spot of the country.... Of the fourteen undergraduate medical schools ... described, the majority exist and prepare candidates for the Illinois state board examination in unmistakable contravention of the law and the state board rules (p. 216).

THE *FLEXNER REPORT* AS A FORERUNNER OF ACADEMIC QUALITY RANKINGS

The following are some important features of the *Flexner Report* as a precursor of academic quality rankings. First, Flexner obtained most of his information by inspecting the medical schools personally. Visiting the schools one was judging was a common practice of early individuals and groups that wished to ascertain the quality of these schools. The Council on Medical Education, shortly after it was organized in 1904, visited all the medical schools in the United States for the purpose of classifying them by quality; officials of the CFAT personally inspected each school before accepting it into the Foundation's pension program; and the Association of Collegiate Alumnae visited institutions before admitting them to membership. As early as 1902, a representative of the American Osteopathic Association's committee on education had inspected all osteopathic colleges before reporting on them.[12] These practices contrast sharply with the methods of those who have done modern quality rankings. Recent researchers have generally used already existing information (the faculty's number of publications, the number of volumes in the library, the number and/or percentage of eminent graduates, for example) or have relied on groups of experts to rank these schools according to their reputation, but have seldom attempted to visit all, or even some, of the schools they ranked.

Second, Flexner "covered" every medical school in the United States and Canada, including very marginal ones and those sponsored by medical sects. This practice was in sharp contrast to the method of those who have done recent quality rankings. They usually attempt to rank only the top few dozen schools in a discipline, or in some cases only the top ten or fifteen.[13]

Third, Flexner visited his schools at a whirlwind pace. His inspections of schools, many of them in the company of N.P. Colwell, Secretary of the Council on Medical Education, generally lasted only a few hours. In his autobiography, he quoted with approval the remark of Frederick Gates, long-time Chairman of the General Education Board, that "you don't need to eat a whole sheep to know it's tainted."[14]

Flexner was very forthright about the speed with which he conducted these visits:

> In half an hour or less I could sample the credentials of students filed in the dean's office. . . . A few inquiries made clear whether the faculty was composed of local doctors. . . . [15] A stroll through the laboratories disclosed the presence or absence of apparatus. . . . Finally, the situation as respects clinical facilities was readily clarified by a few questions. . . . In the course of a few hours a reliable estimate could be made respecting the possibilities of teaching modern medicine in almost any one of the 155 schools I visited in the United States and Canada.[16]

Throughout his life Flexner, an inveterate visitor of college and university campuses in the United States and Europe, greatly preferred personal inspections to information elicited by survey research or from already-existing records. In his autobiography, he described as follows the habits of two of his colleagues on the General Education Board, where Flexner worked for many years, on a trip to black colleges and state departments of education in the South:

> Dr. Buttrick and Dr. Sage had been in the habit of pursuing the same method that I had pursued in the study of medical schools. They came to few conclusions on the basis of correspondence and reports. They went and saw for themselves, precisely as I had done. They never made use of a questionnaire, because they knew instinctively that no two persons interpret a questionnaire in the same way and that no questionnaire, however elaborately or carefully drawn, could elicit the information that a keen eye could discern. I readily fell in love with their way of doing things.[17]

Relying, as he did, mostly on the data at hand and on what he could see in his whirlwind inspections, Flexner probably overemphasized some aspects of the schools he visited and underemphasized others. He paid a great deal of attention to these schools' physical facilities, their bricks and mortar and the equipment they owned, since these were easily observed. He also placed much emphasis on their entrance requirements, both their stated requirements and their actual ones, as evidenced by the records of the students they had enrolled.[18]

Here, in his own words, is what Flexner looked for. Although nowhere in his *Report* did he describe these things explicitly, he did enumerate them in his later autobiographies, as follows:

> First, the entrance requirements. What were they? Were they enforced?
> Second, the size and training of the faculty.
> Third, the sum available from endowment and fees for the support of the institution, and what became of it.
> Fourth, the quality and adequacy of the laboratories provided for the instruction of the first two years and the qualifications and training of the teachers of the so-called pre-clinical branches.
> Fifth and finally, the relations between medical school and hospitals, including particularly freedom of access to beds and freedom in the appointment by the school of the hospital physicians and surgeons who automatically should become clinical teachers.[19]

Focusing as he did on medical education, Flexner paid almost no attention to the quality and quantity of the faculty's research at the schools he visited. The faculty at the majority of the institutions he visited, of course, had little or no research to report. Still, in the case of those schools where faculty members did perform research—Johns Hopkins, Harvard, and Western Reserve, for example—he said almost nothing about it.[20]

Flexner paid very little attention to the actual quality of the teaching at these schools, contenting himself with inspecting and reporting on the classrooms, the laboratory and clinical facilities, the faculty members' credentials, and whether or not they were employed full-time by their school. If, in the midst of the wretched physical conditions he found at many schools, competent teaching somehow took place, if many of these schools' graduates somehow turned out to be caring, skillful physicians, Flexner would have been nearly oblivious to these facts.[21]

Flexner's Frankness

Fourth, Flexner was perhaps more blunt, even brutal, than anyone has been, before or since, about the deficiencies of individual schools, at least in a report intended for the general public. Some of his opinions were as follows:

About the St. Louis College of Physicians and Surgeons:

> The school occupies a badly kept building, the inner walls covered with huge advertisements....there is a make-believe laboratory for experimental physiology....Anatomy was "over"—only empty tables were found in the dissecting-room, the sole access to which is by way of

a fire-escape. . . . A small, poorly lighted, badly ventilated, and over-crowded hospital is part of the school building. . . . The school is one of the worst in the country.[22]

The St. Louis College of Physicians and Surgeons sued Flexner, as a result of these and other comments, for $150,000 on the grounds of libel, but the case "was dismissed for want of prosecution."[23]

About the Still College of Osteopathy, Des Moines, Iowa:

[The laboratory facilities] are mainly limited to signs. "Anatomy" is painted prominently on a door which, on being opened, reveals an amphitheater; "Physiology" on a door which, on being opened, reveals a class-room with an almost empty bookcase, but no laboratory equipment; the key to "Histology" could not be found; "Chemistry" proved to be a disorderly elementary laboratory with some slight outfit for bacteriology besides. . . . Everything about the school indicates that it is a business. One is therefore not surprised to find the following advertisement in the local newspaper: "Have your case diagnosed at Still College of Osteopathy, 1442 Locust Street."[24]

About the California Medical College at Oakland:

The school occupies a few neglected rooms on the second floor of a fifty-foot frame building. Its so-called equipment is dirty and disorderly beyond description. Its outfit in anatomy consists of a small box of bones and the dried-up filthy fragments of a single cadaver. A few bottles of reagents constitute the chemical laboratory. A cold and rusty incubator, a single microscope, and a few unlabeled wet specimens, etc., form the so-called "equipment" for pathology and bacteriology. . . . The school is a disgrace to the state whose laws permit its existence.[25]

Although the head of Harvard Medical School's pathology department had predicted that Flexner would not, because of hometown loyalty, be able to bring himself to criticize the medical schools in Louisville—Flexner had taught high school and later run his own preparatory school in that city—Flexner wrote the following about the hospital facilities available to the medical school of University of Louisville:

The obstetrical ward is not open to students; there is no pavilion for contagious diseases. The hospital facilities are therefore poor in respect to both quality and extent: unequal to the fair teaching of an even smaller body of students, they are made to suffice for the largest school in the country.[26]

About Louisville's Southwestern Homeopathic Medical College he wrote, "there is no outfit worth speaking of in any department; the building is wretchedly dirty. . . . There is nothing to indicate recent dissecting."[27]

Nor was Flexner afraid to take on the nation's leading medical schools. About Harvard, among some favorable remarks, he wrote that "there is a noticeable lack of sympathy between the laboratory and the clinical men."[28] About Columbia's College of Physicians and Surgeons he wrote, "nowhere has the school rights; at Bellevue (municipal hospital), custom establishes a qualified security, liable, however, to be disregarded; elsewhere the basis is purely personal."[29]

Flexner did not save his caustic comments about schools until he wrote his *Report* but occasionally offered them verbally during his inspections. This behavior, not surprisingly, sometimes got him into trouble. Shortly after he started his tour of medical schools, several reports reached the CFAT that he was unstable, causing Pritchett some concern. Pritchett wrote on one occasion to the Harvard pathologist who had predicted that Flexner would not be able to bring himself to criticize Louisville's medical schools:

> Before asking Mr. Abraham Flexner to begin work here in connection with the study of professional education, I consulted with a number of persons concerning his ability and character. Since he has begun work, however, a number of criticisms have come to me about him, generally in the way of casting some doubt upon his judgement and indicating somewhat erratic tendencies. There also seems to have been something at Harvard which caused friction.[30]

In the same vein, Pritchett also wrote about Flexner as follows:

> . . . on the testimony of his friends I have had no question that he was a man of high character. Within the past few days, however, a good many criticisms have come to me concerning him, something to the effect that he is erratic and hard to get along with and somewhat uncertain in judgement.[31]

With all the features of medical schools that Flexner did not like, the question arises, what did he like? Flexner knew exactly what he liked, so far as medical education was concerned—a school as much as possible like Johns Hopkins.[32] His devotion to Hopkins, from which he had received a bachelor's degree after two years of attendance, was total. As late as 1930, in his *Universities: American, English, German,*[33] he held up Hopkins as an ideal, although the school by then had seen its best days. Flexner, in that book, probably gave Hopkins too much credit for excellence and failed to give schools like Harvard and the leading state universities enough.[34] As clearly as he saw many of the problems of medical schools of his time, he was not always prescient about the future course of higher education. Writing in 1930, he asserted, "the political upheavals which occur in American universities are beyond imagining in Germany."[35]

BOOKS INFLUENCED BY THE *FLEXNER REPORT*

Although after his *Report* Flexner himself never published another book that contained detailed, school by school descriptions, several others did, in books sponsored by the CFAT and other organizations. The reports discussed below all follow the *Flexner Report* in three ways:

1. They were based upon personal inspections of all the schools of a particular type, inspections made either by the author of the report or by a team of inspectors.

2. They began with a long essay discussing the history and general present conditions of the type of school under consideration.

3. After the essay on general conditions, they contained descriptions, organized state by state (and, for reports that included Canada, province by province) of each school. These were not "essayistic" descriptions but rather presentations in textual form, instead of in charts and tables, of essentially the same factual information about each school.

Gies's *Dental Education in the United States and Canada*

At least two studies put out by the CFAT, despite the fact that both of them were published more than 15 years after the *Flexner Report,* follow the format of that study very closely. The first was William Gies's *Dental Education in the United States and Canada* (1926).[36] Even its title obviously imitated that of the *Flexner Report,* and Pritchett described it as "an effort to do for dental education . . . the same service that the Foundation undertook to perform for medical education."[37]

After a detailed treatment of the history of dentistry, the history of dental education in the United States, and the organization and structure of contemporary dental education in the United States and Canada, Gies printed school by school descriptions of almost 50 dental schools in the United States and five in Canada, all of which he had personally visited at least twice. His descriptions were generally far longer than Flexner's, possibly because Gies was describing only about one-third as many schools; they also contained much more detailed statistical data, especially about these schools' finances and their students' backgrounds and characteristics. Gies also reported, for each school, whether it had earned an A, B, or C classification from the Dental Educational Council.

Gies's descriptions, even of the worst dental schools, were generally matter-of-fact, without the brutality of Flexner's comments. For instance, the Atlanta-Southern (Georgia) Dental College was a class B school that required no college work for admission, possessed a library of only 404 bound volumes, and had no unbound volumes or pamphlets at all for the use of a student body of about 300, resulting in a ratio of about 1.3 books per student.[38] Furthermore, it was a proprietary school, owned by a stock company. Such a school would have driven Flexner to fury, but Gies, though he left no doubt, in his "summary" of this school, that he held it in low regard, described it dispassionately and without Flexner's vitriol.

Reed's *Present-Day Law Schools in the United States and Canada*

Another CFAT report that closely followed Flexner's *Medical Education in the United States and Canada* was Alfred Reed's *Present-Day Law Schools in the United States and Canada* (1928).[39] It, too, began with a detailed essay which discussed the political and historical events that had shaped contemporary legal education in the U.S. and Canada, the present organization of legal education in these two countries, and the length of time required to earn a law degree. It then provided school by school descriptions of law schools in the United States and Canada, some 200 in all. All these descriptions were based upon Reed's personal inspections. About 15 years earlier, in connection with another CFAT study then in progress, Reed had visited all the U.S. law schools, and in 1924, in preparation for *Present-Day Law Schools...*, he visited the ten Canadian law schools.[40]

Although Reed's book contained more material than did the *Flexner Report* and Gies's book on the history, organization, and present general condition of the institutions it discussed, it contained much the shortest sections on individual law schools. Whereas Gies's descriptions of dental schools, counting both his textual and tabular material, generally ran to a few densely packed pages and more than 1500 words, Reed went to the opposite extreme.

His sections about each school provided only the most basic facts about it—its annual fees, the year it had opened, its income, admission requirements, the size of faculty, and so on. They contained very little information, other than what could be inferred from these bare facts, about these schools' "quality." Unlike Flexner and Gies, who generally discussed, after the description of each school in a state, the medical and dental education of that state as a whole, Reed provided no such discussion. While none of the three reports ranked schools or even stratified them into levels according to "quality," Gies probably went the farthest in that direction, publishing the letter classifications of the Dental Educational Council and furnishing very detailed information about each school. Flexner went next farthest. Reed, although he wrote an especially long essay on the general condition of legal education at the front of his book, offered by far the least information on individual schools and the least data from which one could judge their respective "quality."

The U.S. Bureau of Education's *Negro Education*

Perhaps the most remarkable successor to the *Flexner Report* of 1910 was not sponsored by the Carnegie Foundation at all. It was the massive two-volume work, published by the United States Bureau of Education and financed partly by the Phelps-Stokes Fund, a New York state philanthropic organization, titled *Negro Education: A Study of the Private and Higher Schools for Colored People in the United States* (1917).[41] This work was produced over three years by a large staff of researchers, headed by Thomas Jesse Jones, a white man who held a Ph.D. in sociology from Columbia University and who had worked for eight years in the research department of Hampton Institute, a college-level school for blacks in Virginia.

Volume I of this study described the general condition of education for blacks in the South—its history, organization, financing, control, physical facilities, the help provided, over the years, by various philanthropic organizations, and so on. Volume II contained descriptions, arranged state by state and school by school, of "all private schools for colored people, whether elementary or higher . . . [and] all schools above the elementary grades, whether public or private."[42] The report described, in all, 747 schools, "of which 625 [were] private schools, 28 state institutions, 67 public high schools, and 27 county training schools."[43] Remarkably, "every school reported upon was visited by one or more [of the U.S. Bureau of Education's] agents, and the larger schools were studied by specialists in different types of education."[44]

This massive second volume, more than 700 pages long, contained a brief description of each black college, high school, and private elementary school. Descriptions of each elementary and secondary school were generally short, from 100–300 words long, covering such subjects as its number of teachers and students, its curriculum, physical plant, income, and expenses, followed, at the end, by recommendations for improving the school. In their length, content, and matter-of-fact tone, these descriptions were not very different from Reed's descriptions of law schools.

The vignettes of college-level institutions, though, were generally much longer than those of lower schools. These descriptions provided the same information as those for the lower level schools, but in more detail, especially concerning the institutions' curriculum and courses of study.

This work, covering, as it did, 747 schools and running to more than 1100 pages, was perhaps the most massive study ever done that employed the general format of the *Flexner Report*. Like that *Report* and the other studies considered in this chapter, it did not rank or attempt to stratify by quality the schools it covered. Still, like the other reports, it is worth discussing because of the large amount of information it provided from which inferences about the academic quality of these institutions might be drawn.

Chapter Fourteen

JAMES MC KEEN CATTELL AND THE INVENTION OF ACADEMIC QUALITY RANKINGS

The man who actually "invented" academic quality rankings 15 years before Raymond Hughes published his reputational ranking in 1925 was the eminent early psychologist, James McKeen Cattell. Cattell had a long and distinguished career, living until the age of 83 and publishing his last article only the year before he died. An incomplete bibliography of his publications runs to 167 items. He did important research, over the years, on a great many psychological topics, and he won great fame as a psychologist during his lifetime, being named president of the ninth International Congress of Psychology in 1929. In 1903, a panel of distinguished psychologists he selected to rank the nation's leading research psychologists rated him the second most distinguished research psychologist in the United States, behind William James and ahead of G. Stanley Hall, Edward B. Titchener, Josiah Royce, and John Dewey.[1] During his lifetime, he served as editor of a number of important journals, including the *Psychological Review, Science, Popular Science Monthly* (later called *Scientific Monthly*), and *School and Society*. But despite Cattell's lifetime of impressive achievement as a scientist and as "a powerful force in the development of the scientific and intellectual community,"[2] not much solid work is available about him.[3]

He was the son of the president of Lafayette College, from which he graduated in 1880 at the age of 20, first in his class. Later he studied at Leipzig with Wilhelm Wundt, earning his Ph.D. in 1886. He then worked with Francis Galton at Galton's anthropometric laboratory in London. Galton's statistical methods and his interest in individual differences, unusual for the period, that was evident at least as early as his *Hereditary Genius* (1865), both influenced Cattell. In 1887, Cattell returned to the United States, teaching that year at Bryn Mawr College and the University of Pennsylvania; in 1889, the University of Pennsylvania appointed him to what Cattell later claimed was "the first American professorship

107

wholly in psychology."[4] In 1891 he was appointed professor of psychology at Columbia. During more than a quarter century there he produced much important research in many areas of psychology, but he was a contentious and irascible person, and he was constantly embroiled in controversies. One scholar, in an article generally sympathetic to Cattell, nonetheless admitted that he was "a difficult man to get along with," one who was "combative, blunt, and altogether lacking in tact," who disturbed his colleagues with his "incessant agitation" and who "advocated the deliberate use of ridicule."[5]

He quarreled frequently and bitterly with the administration of President Nicholas Murray Butler, with other members of the Columbia faculty, and with psychologists from all over. Finally, in 1917 he was dismissed from Columbia for "having petitioned several Congressmen to send conscripts to Europe only with their consent, and for having written his petition on stationery bearing his Columbia address."[6] His dismissal became one of the most celebrated academic freedom cases of World War I.[7] Thereafter, Cattell spent most of his time at his home, on top of the aptly named Fort Defiance Hill, 40 miles north of New York City. He had edited his journals from his home even while he was at Columbia, and he continued an active intellectual life at home. He devoted most of his time to editing his various journals and reference works and continued to publish, from time to time, studies of the backgrounds of eminent American scientists.

THREE STRAINS OF WORK

Cattell's analysis of the educational backgrounds and the current academic affiliations of eminent scientists ultimately resulted in the first academic quality ranking. This line of research stemmed from at least three strains of work he had been engaged in since early in his career.

First, like Francis Galton, he had long been interested in eminent people as a subject for research. As early as 1895 he had published, in the *Psychological Review,* a brief abstract of a study "demonstrating the distribution in time and race" of 1000 eminent people.[8] Later he greatly expanded this abstract and published the results of his study as an article.[9] In it, he described the procedure he had used to select the 1000 most eminent people in history, in order of their eminence, by examining six biographical dictionaries and encyclopedias from four nations and selecting those people whose biographical listings were the longest. Since these people dated back in time to the ancient Greeks, for many of them there was little or no information in the reference works he examined about their education. At any rate, many of them had lived long before the rise of universities in the late 12th century and obviously could not have attended one. Therefore, Cattell wrote nothing in this article about these people's education. He did, though, discuss how many of them had lived in various centuries, their nationalities, the fields of endeavor in which they had excelled, and other topics for which information was available for most of them.

A second strain of Cattell's work that eventually led to his research on the academic backgrounds of eminent scientists was his long-standing interest in individual differences among people, especially the differences in their mental abilities. The study of individual differences and variations among human beings goes back at least as far as Lambert Quetelet's *Treatise on Man and the Development of his Faculties,*[10] first published in 1835. Nonetheless, when Cattell began to publish psychological research in the mid-1880s most investigators, with the prominent exception of Galton, were much more interested in measures of central tendency—what people had in common and the mean scores of their experimental subjects—than in the differences among them. As one of Cattell's most famous students later wrote about psychological research *c.* 1890, just after Cattell began his own psychological research:

> Neither the English psychological tradition . . . nor the new experimental work . . . showed any clear promise of enriching mental science by studies of the variations of individual men in response to the same external situation. Except for certain stock references to temperament, imagery, or the like, diversities were hidden in averages, or even discarded as erroneous.
> Against this narrowness Professor Cattell was perhaps the first rebel from within the ranks of psychologists. . . . [11]

Cattell, at the beginning of his career, did much work on individual differences among people. His early psychological papers were filled with tables showing not only the mean scores his subjects attained but their differences from each other as well,[12] and his work on different degrees of eminence achieved by scientists is an extension of this work on individual differences.

Interestingly, Cattell, in an autobiographical fragment, traced his interest in individual differences back to his love of sports. He wrote:

Stress is laid here on sports and games because interest in these apparently led to my early work on individual differences and the order of merit method. It seemed as natural to measure the rate at which people read as the rate at which they ran; to place them in order of merit for psychological traits as for eligibility to the college football team on which I played or the baseball team of which I was manager.[13]

The third strain of work that led to his invention of academic quality rankings was Cattell's penchant, reflecting his desire to quantify difficult-to-measure things, for assigning inanimate objects and even people to their "correct" position in a series. In 1892 he had published, in collaboration with the well-known philosopher George Stuart Fullerton, a monograph titled, *On the Perception of Small Differences*, about the smallest differences his subjects could perceive in movement, weight, and the intensity of light.[14] By 1895 he had made plans to list what he called the 1000 most eminent people in world history in order of their relative importance.[15]

In 1902, he combined his interests in observing the smallest degrees of difference that people could detect and in forming rank orders of people and things. He conducted an experiment in which he created 211 virtually imperceptible shades between black and white, placed each one on a card, and asked subjects to arrange these cards in order from the darkest to the lightest.[16] From measuring how well his subjects could discriminate among the different shades of grey, Cattell moved to measuring the eminence of scientists according to the place to which knowledgeable scientists in their field assigned them. There was the important difference, however, that in arranging the cards containing shades of grey, his subjects were trying to reproduce a rank order that existed in the objective world, while in ranking scientists according to their order of scientific merit, Cattell's scientific judges were *creating* the objective reality, since no "objective" ordering of their merit existed outside the judgments of those who rank-ordered them.

These three strains of Cattell's early work, then—his interest in eminent people, in measuring individual differences, and in assigning things and people to the place that they "belonged," according to the amount they possessed of some quality—all coalesced. They led to Cattell's work, over three decades, in arranging scientists in order of their relative merit according to how leading scientists ranked them relative to other scientists in their field.

CATTELL'S *AMERICAN MEN OF SCIENCE*

Cattell's reference work, *American Men of Science: A Biographical Dictionary*, played a crucial role in the development of academic quality rankings. He published the first edition of *American Men of Science* in 1906, writing in its preface that "the chief service it should render is to make men of science acquainted with one another and with one another's work."[17] To obtain the names of people from whom to select those worthy of biographical sketches, he sent forms requesting autobiographical information to about 10,000 people he thought might be engaged in scientific research. They were members of scientific organizations, people listed in the "catalogues of institutions of learning,"[18] contributors to scientific journals, and those listed in various reference works, especially *Who's Who in America*. From these 10,000 he selected more than 4000, a number he thought included most of those "in North America who have carried on research work in natural and exact sciences."[19] For all of them he published brief biographies, naming the scientific fields in which they did research and listing details about their education, the degrees they had earned, the scientific honors and awards they had received, and their employment history.

From the more than 4000 scientists Cattell singled out about 1000 of the most eminent and placed an asterisk, or "star," in their biographies. His reason for singling out these was as follows:

> . . . to secure a group for scientific study. . . . My original interest in this work of reference was to secure data for a statistical study of the conditions, performance, traits, etc., of a large group of men of science. . . . [20]

In choosing the approximately 1000 people who were to be starred, he first selected what he considered the twelve most important natural and exact sciences. For each of these branches of science he asked ten leading scientists to serve as raters. He then gave all ten raters in each field "slips made with the names and addresses of all those known to have carried on research work of any consequence,"[21] winding up with the names of 2481 scientists, counting those scientists who worked in more than one branch of science once for each of their fields. Each rater then arranged the scientists in his or her field according to what the rater considered their scientific merit.

Cattell then took the ten lists, averaged the ratings, and called these averaged ratings rosters of the leading scientists in each field, in order of their scientific merit. For each field, he "starred" a number approximately proportionate to the number of scientists working in that field. The scientific disciplines from which he "starred" scientists and the number of scientists he starred were as follows: "chemistry, 175; physics, 150; zoology, 150; botany, 100; geology, 100; mathematics, 80; pathology, 60; astronomy, 50; psychology, 50; physiology, 40; anatomy, 25; anthropology, 20."[22] Cattell did not include any applied or practical branches of science, such as engineering, among his twelve scientific fields. The fact that he selected the twelve branches of science he did and not others may have influenced the development of scientific disciplines for a long time. Years later, the eminent geographer Stephen Visher, who himself published a great deal of work analyzing the backgrounds of the scientists starred in various editions of *American Men Of Science*, was to make the following claim for Cattell's influence:

> A suggestive bit of evidence of [Cattell's] influence is seen in the comparatively much lesser development, 1903–1943, in America of those sciences which Cattell did not recognize by starring their leaders. Indeed, the great stimulation which public recognition by starring afforded to the workers in the 12 sciences which he recognized tended to attract ambitious young scientists away from sciences in which public recognition is not so available.[23]

After his first edition in 1906, Cattell edited or coedited five other editions of *American Men of Science*, which appeared in 1910, 1921, 1928, 1933, and 1938. In each, he substantially increased the number of scientists he listed, including 34,000 by the 1938 edition. He also increased the number of scientists who were "starred," although at a much less rapid pace than the rate of increase of the number of scientists merely listed, so that it became harder and harder to be "starred." The number of scientists working in some scientific disciplines expanded much faster than the number in others, but Cattell continued to allocate "stars" among the disciplines in approximately the same proportion as in the original 1906 edition. Consequently, in fields in which the number of scientists expanded especially rapidly it became very difficult to be "starred," much more so than in the original edition, when about one-fourth of all the scientists included in the book were "starred." The descendant of *American Men of Science* is still published regularly. It is now called *American Men & Women of Science*. Its 15th edition was published in 1982,[24] although the practice of "starring" was discontinued with the eighth edition, published in 1949.

At the end of the biographical listings in four of the six editions of *American Men of Science* which Cattell edited or coedited, he included an essay analyzing the backgrounds and present-day characteristics of the scientists starred in that edition. These essays generally included information on their birthplace, the city and state of their current residence, their age when they were first "starred," and so on. The subject that Cattell analyzed in by far the most detail, though, in these essays was the scientists' college and university attendance and their present university or other institutional affiliation. In work published from 1903–1933, he presented detailed tables showing the college or university from which they had received their baccalaureate degree, where they had done graduate work (short of receiving the Ph.D.), from which institutions they had received their Ph.D., and by what college, university, or other institution they were currently employed. "Other institutions" by which many starred scientists were employed included the Geological Survey, the Department of Agriculture, and the Smithsonian Institution.

TOWARDS AN ACADEMIC QUALITY RANKING

It is fascinating to observe how Cattell, over a period of about seven years, completely changed his mind about what his data on the academic backgrounds and present academic affiliations of his "starred" scientists meant. In 1903, he published an article that discussed the 200 psychologists listed in the first edition of *American Men of Science*.[25] In it appeared a table (p. 371) showing the number of American psychologists who had received the B.A., had done graduate study short of receiving the Ph.D., and had received their Ph.D. at various American and European universities, in order of how many of the psychologists had studied or received a degree at each. If a future psychologist had received both an B.A. and a Ph.D., or had received a B.A. and also done graduate work at the same university, that university got "credit" twice. If the student had done graduate work at two or more universities, both or all of them got "credit" for the student's attendance. Of the American universities, Columbia and Harvard were tied for first, with 42, and Clark was third (31).

In publishing this table, though, Cattell was careful to disavow that it was a measure of these institutions' academic quality in psychology:

> After the men have graduated from college, and when their work has been chosen, they are gathered for their special studies into a few universities. It does not seem, however, that they are turned into

~~psychologists at these universities. They simply select for study the~~
universities that have reputation and facilities, being often attracted
by fellowships or the hope that the university will assist them in
securing positions. The direction of the work is sometimes determined
or influenced by the university, the merit of the work but slightly, if
at all.[26]

In stating that he thought that these universities influenced the quality
of their graduates' work "slightly, if at all," Cattell was, for all practical
purposes, saying that his list should not be taken as a list of the "best"
departments of psychology.

In 1906, he moved a step closer towards treating his data on the
academic origins and present institutional affiliations of scientists as
actually reflecting the quality of these institutions. Discussing eminent
American scientists and where they lived, he wrote:

Other states have improved their positions. Thus, thanks to its great
university, Michigan has 22 men in the first group as compared with
five in the second. [That is, Michigan had 22 men among the 500
highest ranked of the 1000 "starred" scientists and five men among the
second 500.] Thanks again to its universities, Illinois has increased its
number of scientific men from 42 to 63, of whom 36 are in the first
class.[27]

In the same article he referred to the universities that had had more of
these future starred scientists study at them than did other universities
not just as institutions that these scientists had happened to pass through,
as he had in 1903. Rather, he referred to them as institutions that
excelled in these disciplines in which many future "starred" scientists
had studied. He wrote:

The Johns Hopkins University has excelled relatively in chemistry,
physics, zoology, and physiology; Harvard in zoology and botany;
Columbia in zoology, botany, and mathematics; Cornell in physics and
botany; Clark in psychology, and Michigan in botany and pathology.
Of the foreign universities, Berlin has excelled in physics, Leipzig in
psychology and Gottingen in chemistry and mathematics.[28]

Though Cattell had thus taken a step closer to regarding his tables
showing the academic origins of eminent scientists as measuring departmental strength in these disciplines, he had not quite done so. Although
he displayed a table showing, for the 1000 starred scientists, how many
had received their bachelor's degree, done graduate work short of receiving a Ph.D., and received their Ph.D. at various American and foreign
universities, Cattell stopped short of calling this table a list of the best

institutions at which to study science. He titled it merely, "Attendance of the Thousand Men of Science at Different Institutions."[29]

THE FIRST ACADEMIC QUALITY RANKING

Finally, in 1910 Cattell published an academic quality ranking. First, he decided that his list of starred scientists needed to be updated, since data for the first one had been collected back in 1903. He asked the ten scientists who had been ranked at the top of each of the twelve branches of science, a total of 120, to make new lists of the leading ten people in their discipline, in order of their scientific eminence. Sixty-eight of them did so, and he averaged their rankings, forming, as he had earlier, a rank order of the leading scientists in order of their scientific merit for the same twelve scientific fields.

After these calculations and some other adjustments had been made, there were substantial differences between the 1903 and the 1910 lists; 238 scientists had been placed, for the first time, among the leading 1000, and 201 had lost their places. Cattell displayed three tables which showed, respectively, those institutions which had added and lost the most scientists who had been newly added to or dropped from the list of starred scientists (table II, p. 440); the institutions that had conferred a B.A. or Ph.D. on the most people newly added to or dropped from the starred scientists (table III, p. 441); and the institutions that currently employed the most starred scientists, with the starred scientists' ratio to all instructors and to the students at each institution (table X, p. 465). Although, in his earlier articles, Cattell had devoted most of his attention to the institutions at which his scientists had been educated, in this article he presented extensive data on the institutions that currently employed them.

Discussing a table showing universities and some other institutions which employed many scientists in order of how many of these scientists they had gained and lost between 1903 and 1910 Cattell, moving closer to considering these data as measuring the quality of university science departments, wrote:

> It seems almost incredible that it should be possible to measure the efficiency with which an institution is conducted by such simple means, yet the differences can not be attributed to chance.[30]

Elsewhere in the same article he discussed the ratio of faculty members at a number of universities who were "starred" scientists to the total faculty, and he wrote that these ratios showed the "relative strengths" of these departments (p. 465). Again implying that he now equated a school's proportion of starred scientists with its "quality," he added, "students should certainly use every effort to attend institutions having large proportions of men of distinction among their instructors" (pp. 465–466).

Finally, Cattell devised a complex weighting system to derive from the number of starred scientists at leading universities and other organizations employing large numbers of starred scientists the first academic quality ranking. Here, in his own words, is how he did it.

> In order . . . to sum up in one figure the strength of a university or department, weights have been assigned to the men [that is, the 1000 starred scientists] on this basis—a man in the lower four hundred being the unit, those in the other hundreds were assigned ratings as follows: VII and VI = 1.2; V = 1.4; IV = 1.6; III = 1.9; II = 2.2; and I = 3. The first hundred were subdivided, the lower fifty being assigned 2.5, and the upper twenty-fives, respectively 3 and 4 (p. 468).

This, then, was the first academic quality ranking ever published. It was a rank order, not just a classification of schools into a few groups. In addition, it was based on a criterion—how many eminent scientists were connected with each institution, with the more eminent scientists weighted more heavily than the less eminent—that Cattell by this time certainly thought reflected academic quality. That Cattell by this time definitely considered the list a roster of institutions in order of their academic quality is certain, because he wrote that in it he intended "to sum up in one figure the strength of a university or department" (p. 468). In addition, he titled the table, "the Scientific Strength of the Leading Institutions."[31] It is shown in table I.

It is ironic that with all the organizations that had been trying hard for years to devise ways to stratify colleges, universities, and individual departments according to their quality, the man who actually "invented" academic quality rankings more or less backed into this invention. It is especially ironic that the method he used—calculating the number of eminent scientists employed by universities and other institutions—was one which at first he himself had thought showed little promise for measuring academic quality.

Cattell continued to write articles analyzing the academic origins and present distribution of eminent scientists for many years, usually publishing them in *Science*. In them, he showed the leading institutions of

Table I

THE SCIENTIFIC STRENGTH OF THE TWENTY LEADING INSTITUTIONS IN 1910
ACCORDING TO CATTELL

	Weighted Number	*Gain or Loss*
Harvard	146.0	+16.3
Chicago	94.6	+18.0
Columbia	79.3	−13.3
Johns Hopkins	63.4	+ 4.2
Yale	61.7	+12.2
Cornell	57.6	+ 4.6
Wisconsin	49.0	+22.3
Geological Survey	43.8	−12.2
Department of Agriculture	40.9	− 4.9
Massachusetts Institute of Technology	37.7	+ 9.5
Michigan	37.1	− 3.5
California	32.4	− 5.0
Carnegie Institution	30.9	+19.4
Stanford	30.0	+ 4.8
Princeton	28.6	+ 7.5
Smithsonian Institution	26.0	− 7.3
Illinois	25.0	+16.7
Pennsylvania	24.4	− 4.5
Bureau of Standards	18.9	+ 0.1
Clark	16.0	+ 2.0

Reprinted from *James McKeen Cattell: Man of Science, 1860-1944*, ed. by A.T. Poffenberger, vol. 1 (Lancaster, Pa.: Science Press), copyright © 1947, p. 468, with permission of R. R. Bowker.

the time according to how many eminent scientists they each had "produced" and currently employed. Throughout these years—he published his last study of eminent scientists in 1933, in the fifth edition of *American Men of Science*—he never fundamentally changed his system of ranking institutions.

CATTELL'S LASTING INFLUENCE

Cattell's influence on later academic quality rankings was quite substantial. For decades after his 1910 ranking, dozens of other studies were done ranking colleges and universities according to how many important and accomplished people of all kinds—not just scientists— had studied at them. Whereas Cattell had produced the first rank order of colleges and universities by examining his 1000 starred scientists' current affiliations, most of the researchers who followed him went back to the method he had used earlier of showing the number of eminent people in various fields who had attended these colleges and universities as students.

Ranking colleges and universities by the number and percentage of their students who became eminent in later life in various fields of endeavor, as opposed to ranking them by the research accomplishments of the faculty members currently employed there, had one decided advantage. It was that all colleges and universities could be rated by the graduates they "produced," while only a few could be ranked by the research achievements of their faculty members, since only a small percentage of colleges and universities had, or aspired to have, a research faculty. These studies had the decided disadvantage, though, of always and inevitably being 20 or 30 years behind the times, since it takes at least this long for a college's graduates to be listed in *Who's Who* or *American Men of Science* or to accomplish the other achievements that these studies commonly use as their measure of eminence.

The method that Cattell invented and had applied to eminent psychologists as early as 1903 and which, he concluded by 1910, could be used in revised form to measure the "strengths" of science departments and of university science programs as a whole, became by far the most frequently used method of ranking colleges and universities from the 1920s until about the mid-1960s. By the mid-1960s, though, the method of ranking colleges and universities by the number and proportion of eminent alumni they "produced" had declined, for at least three reasons.

First, the research of Alexander Astin and others had shown that the number and percentage of eminent alumni a college or university produced were largely dependent on the intellectual ability of the students it admitted.[32] Ironically, Cattell's original view that future scientists more or less "passed through" colleges and universities on their way to scientific eminence, rather than achieved scientific eminence mostly because of the scientific "quality" of the colleges and universities they attended, was the one which most modern researchers have come to accept.

Second, Allan Cartter's *Assessment of Quality in Graduate Education* (1966)[33] when it appeared was the most authoritative reputational academic quality ranking ever done. It stimulated a number of reputational rankings, at the expense of most other kinds of academic quality rankings, including "academic origins" and "current employment" studies.

Third, new kinds of reference works had been published, especially the *Science Citation Index* (first published in 1961) and the *Social Sciences Citation Index* (first published in 1966). These came to be used often as a basis for academic quality rankings, displacing, to some extent, "academic origins" and other types of studies. Still and all, "academic origins" studies were very numerous and very influential for many years. For a massive, surprisingly little-known collection of more than 100 "academic origins" studies, see George Pierson's *Education of American Leaders: Comparative Contributions of U.S. Colleges and Universities.*[34]

Even today, when reputational rankings are, generally speaking, the best known and the most influential kinds of academic quality rankings, some studies still calculate the number and/or percentage of famous alumni institutions have produced. These are mostly studies of particular fields, not multidisciplinary rankings. In them, the influence of James McKeen Cattell's work lives on.

Chapter Fifteen

THE NATIONAL ACADEMY OF SCIENCES' RANKING OF 1982 AND AMERICA'S BEST GRADUATE SCHOOLS, 1925-1982

For a dozen years after it appeared in 1970, Roose and Andersen's *Rating of Graduate Programs* remained the most authoritative quality ranking of American arts, sciences, and engineering doctorate-granting departments ever published.[1] In 1982, though, it was supplanted by the five-volume *Assessment of Research-Doctorate Programs in the United States* (hereafter called the *Assessment*), produced by the Committee on an Assessment of Quality-Related Characteristics of Research-Doctorate Programs in the United States (hereafter called the committee).[2]

This study, the Rolls-Royce of academic quality rankings, is by far the biggest, best, most expensive, most thoughtfully conceived and carefully carried-out academic quality ranking yet done. Whereas the Roose/Andersen study covered departments at 130 universities, this one included programs at 228; whereas the Roose/Andersen study had thirty-four pages analyzing its departmental rank orders, this one had several hundred pages of analysis. Whereas all the previous multidisciplinary reputational rankings of graduate departments were based on one or two criteria—either the quality of the faculty, the effectiveness of the program, or both—this study included not only these but two more reputational measures and then, depending on the particular discipline being assessed, eight to twelve other criteria as well. These included three measures concerning a program's size, four on the characteristics of its recent graduates, one on the size of its university's library, and, for all fields but the humanities, two on research support and two more on the recent journal articles attributed to its program or faculty.

In its extensive analysis of the results for each discipline, the committee showed the intercorrelations among all the measures used to assess it and compared, for all disciplines included in each volume, the scores they received on the various measures of "quality." In addition, in an effort to answer questions that have long been asked about reputational rankings, the committee performed several useful analyses on what effect various attributes of the raters have on the way they rate programs. These attributes included their disciplinary subspecialties, their geographical proximity to programs, whether they were alumni of a program, whether they were provided some basic factual information on the programs they rated, and so on.

TWO FAULTS

As carefully as it was conceived and as painstakingly as it was done, the *Assessment* suffered from two serious faults. First, although it presented data about many factors that ostensibly reflect "quality," the relation of many of these factors to academic quality was tenuous. Two of them, concerning students' postgraduation employment plans, appeared so farfetched as measures of academic quality to three members of the committee that they issued a strongly worded minority statement protesting their inclusion.

Other measures used in this study—for example, the size of programs, as indicated by their number of faculty, recent graduates, and currently enrolled doctoral students—though they often correlated highly with programs' reputational rankings for faculty quality and program effectiveness, seem conceptually distinct from these measures. It is by no means evident that size causes excellence, or smallness mediocrity. Indeed, Johns Hopkins' English department, which tied for last in faculty size among the 106 English departments rated, nevertheless tied for 7th in reputation for faculty quality.

A few criteria, such as the number of recent published articles attributed to the program and the "overall influence" of these articles, seem more nearly related to academic quality, but even these measures are of only limited usefulness, for many reasons. Two such reasons are that they fail to consider any form of faculty scholarly productivity other than journal articles and that, since they are based upon the total number of articles published, they are strongly biased in favor of large programs.

A second serious fault is that the committee listed the schools in each discipline not in descending order from highest to lowest ranked according to one, some, or all of its "quality" measures, but rather in alphabetical order, from Adelphi to Yeshiva, or whatever. It is easy to see the dilemma the committee faced in deciding how to present its data. It could scarcely have averaged the twelve to sixteen measures it used for each discipline and listed schools by their rank on these, because for many or most of these measures their relation, if any, to academic quality is far from clear. If the committee had chosen the five or six of its measures that seemed most nearly to reflect academic quality, then it would implicitly have denigrated all those measures it had *not* used in its composite scores.

The committee ultimately decided not to rank its schools by quality in any way whatsoever and presented its data in a way that made it exceedingly difficult to find out an institution's standing in any discipline or to compare institutions' programs with each other. It listed the names of every university it covered in each discipline in alphabetical order. Next to each school's name, spread over two broad pages, appeared up to sixteen columns of figures—double columns, actually, for almost every column displayed a raw score and a standard score. Then came four more columns listing the standard errors for the scores on the reputational survey. The net effect was that for clarity, convenience, and ease of use, the five volumes, taken together, can be compared to the Manhattan telephone directory if it listed everyone not by name but by blood type.

By publishing endless columns of figures for institutions in each discipline it covered, without summarizing, combining, or averaging these figures, or ranking the institutions in any way, this most reluctant of all academic quality rankings is like the Bible for some religious sects, of which anyone is welcome to make any interpretation he or she wishes.

What should the committee have done? At the very least, in addition to displaying its endless columns of figures, it should have taken one of its reputational measures, either for the faculty's "scholarly quality" or the program's "effectiveness," and ranked all programs in each discipline according to this measure. Doing so would have allowed useful comparisons of programs with each other and of how programs rate today with how they ranked earlier.

LEADING DOCTORATE-GRANTING INSTITUTIONS

The *Assessment* covered 2,699 programs in thirty-two disciplines. Raw scores for almost all the twelve to sixteen measures used for each discipline were converted into standard scores with a mean of 50 and a standard deviation of 10, so that for each measure, about 95 percent of all departments had a standard score between 70 and 30.

In this chapter, we will focus on the measure of the faculty's reputation for scholarly quality. Doing so is necessary in order to permit comparisons with earlier studies. Eight programs received ratings on their faculty's reputation for scholarly quality that were at least 2.5 standard deviations above the mean for their discipline. They are shown in table II. Five of these programs were in engineering; the others were in science. In these "hard" fields, for some reason, the top-ranked programs received higher standard scores than did those in the "softer" humanities and social sciences. All eight of these programs were in disciplines that had at least fifty-eight programs evaluated by the *Assessment*—that is, larger disciplines.

Table II
THE HIGHEST-SCORING PROGRAMS IN FACULTY'S REPUTATION FOR SCHOLARLY QUALITY

Rank	Institution	Program	Standard Score
1.	MIT	Microbiology	77
2.	MIT	Electrical Engineering	76
2.	MIT	Mechanical Engineering	76
4.	UC (Berkeley)	Civil Engineering	75
4.	UC (Berkeley)	Electrical Engineering	75
4.	Rockefeller U.	Microbiology	75
4.	Stanford U.	Computer Science	75
4.	Stanford U.	Electrical Engineering	75

Reprinted by permission from David S. Webster, "America's Highest Ranked Graduate Schools, 1925–1982," *Change*, vol. 15, no. 4, May/June, 1983, p. 16.

Seven programs scored 2.5 standard deviations or more below the mean on their faculty's reputation. They are shown in table III. Six of these, including the three lowest ranked, are in the biological sciences. While these programs may be the lowest scoring among those reported by the *Assessment*, it should be noted that not all programs in the country were included in the study. Institutions were allowed to choose those programs they wished to include in the survey and were less likely to include information on smaller, less well-known programs within their institutions than on larger, better known ones.

We calculated institution-wide scores for the leading universities but decided not to average the scores on different measures because of all the problems in doing so. Instead, we employed the single criterion of the faculty's reputation for "scholarly quality," because it has been used in more multidisciplinary reputational rankings, over the years, than has

Table III
THE LOWEST-SCORING PROGRAMS IN FACULTY'S REPUTATION FOR SCHOLARLY QUALITY

Rank	Institution	Program	Standard Score
1.	U. of North Dakota	Botany	20
2.	U. of Southern Mississippi	Cellular and Molecular Biology	21
3.	Loma Linda U.	Cellular and Molecular Biology	23
4.	Indiana State U.	Physiology	24
4.	U. of Mississippi	Microbiology	24
4.	Northern Illinois U.	Linguistics	24
7.	Catholic U.	Microbiology	25

Reprinted by permission from David S. Webster, "America's Highest Ranked Graduate Schools, 1925–1982," *Change*, vol. 15, no. 4, May/June, 1983, p. 16.

reputation for program "effectiveness." Thus, of all the committee's measures, it provided the best basis of comparison with past rankings.

We considered counting all those programs that earned standard scores of 70 and above for their faculty's scholarly reputation, but since only about twenty universities had even óne program rated this high, this method would not work. And we considered counting all programs rated 60 or above, but doing so gave no more credit to an extremely highly regarded program than to a reasonably well regarded one.

Finally, we credited an institution with two points for each program rated 70 or over and one point for each rated 60–69. (Note that the *Assessment*, in contrast to earlier rankings, rated *programs*, not departments. In some cases, particularly in the biological sciences, it rated two or even three programs in the same discipline. For example, it might have rated three biochemistry programs at a single university—one in its biology department, another in its chemistry department, and a third in its medical school. When a university was rated in two or more programs in the same discipline, we counted only the program with the highest score.)

In measuring institutions' overall strength in doctoral education, even this technique is by no means without faults, for several reasons. First, if a program's faculty failed to achieve a standard score of 60 or higher, it received no "credit," although this can mean several different things: that it scored 59 and is thus regarded as well above average; that it scored 32 and is thus regarded as far below average; that the school offered no doctorate-granting program at all in that discipline; that it offered one that had conferred so few doctorates in recent years that it was not included in the *Assessment;* or that, as happened occasionally, the school simply failed to provide its data on time.

Second, the programs ranked in this study, with a few exceptions, were located in graduate schools of arts and sciences and engineering schools, not in professional schools other than schools of engineering. The institutional scores thus fail to consider the large majority of professional school programs at these universities.

So schools like Princeton and MIT, neither of which has, as distinguished universities go, a wide range of professional schools, were likely to have been rated higher than they would be if professional schools had been counted, too. Other institutions with many well-regarded professional schools, as evidenced by the two Blau/Margulies studies of the mid-1970s,[3] were likely to rank lower than they otherwise would have; these included Columbia and Ohio State University.

Third, the *Assessment* included only thirty-two of the largest disciplines —largest in terms of how many Ph.D.s had been conferred in recent years—and omitted many of the smaller ones. Those it omitted, to mention only ones covered by the Roose/Andersen study, included Russian, astronomy, developmental biology, population biology, entomology, and pharmacology. The *Assessment* also omitted many interdisciplinary departments, committees, and programs. These included some exceptionally strong programs, such as the University of Pennsylvania's department of history and sociology of science, Columbia's department of East Asian languages and cultures, and the University of Chicago's committee on social thought.

So the aggregate figures should not be taken to reflect the universities' strength, across the board, in graduate education, but rather their strength in Ph.D.-granting programs in the arts, sciences, and engineering in those disciplines that had recently granted substantial numbers of research doctorates. The *Assessment*'s thirty highest-ranking institutions, plus ties, according to their reputation for their faculty's scholarly quality, are shown in table IV.

The remarkable strength of the University of California at Berkeley is immediately apparent. It achieved a standard score of 60 or higher in thirty disciplines, compared to twenty-five for Yale, the runner-up in this respect. Only in microbiology and physiology did Berkeley fall below 60, scoring 58 in the former and 55 in the latter. It had more programs in the humanities scoring 60 or more than any other school and was tied for first in all the other fields except the biological sciences. It had fifteen programs with standard scores of 70 or over, three more than Harvard and MIT, the runners-up. In fact, Berkeley had more

Table IV
LEADING PH.D.-GRANTING INSTITUTIONS IN THE ARTS, SCIENCES, AND ENGINEERING,
ACCORDING TO DATA IN THE
ASSESSMENT OF RESEARCH-DOCTORATE PROGRAMS IN THE UNITED STATES

NUMBER OF PROGRAMS IN EACH FIELD WITH STANDARD SCORES
OF 60 OR HIGHER IN REPUTATION FOR "FACULTY QUALITY"

Rank Order	Institution	Phys. Sci., Math	Hum.	Eng.	Biol.	Soc. Sci.	Programs Rated 60 or Higher	Programs Rated 70 or Higher	Total Score
1	U. of California (Berkeley)	6	9	4	4	7	30	15	45
2	Stanford U.	6	4	4	4	6	24	10	34
3	Harvard U.	5	5	—	4	6	20	12	32 ⎤
3	Yale U.	6	7	—	6	6	25	7	32 ⎦
5	MIT	5	2	4	3	3	17	12	29
6	Princeton U.	5	7	4	—	5	21	7	28
7	U. of Chicago	5	4	—	4	7	20	7	27
8	UCLA	5	5	2	6	6	24	—	24 ⎤
8	U. of Michigan	2	6	3	4	6	21	3	24 ⎬
8	U. of Wisconsin (Madison)	5	3	2	5	6	21	3	24 ⎦
11	Columbia U.	5	6	—	4	6	21	2	23 ⎤
11	Cornell U.	6	6	3	4	3	22	1	23 ⎦
13	U. of Illinois (Urbana)	4	2	4	4	3	17	2	19
14	U. of Pennsylvania	2	5	1	3	5	16	1	17
15	Caltech	4	—	4	1	—	9	6	15
16	U. of Minnesota	3	—	2	2	4	11	2	13 ⎤
16	U. of Texas (Austin)	3	3	3	2	2	13	—	13 ⎦
18	U. of North Carolina	2	3	—	2	4	11	—	11 ⎤
18	Northwestern U.	1	1	3	1	5	11	—	11 ⎦
20	U. of Washington (Seattle)	2	—	1	5	2	10	—	10
21	U. of California (San Diego)	2	2	—	3	1	8	—	8 ⎤
21	Indiana U. (Bloomington)	1	4	—	—	3	8	—	8 ⎬
21	New York U.	1	4	—	1	1	7	1	8 ⎥
21	Rockefeller U.	1	—	—	4	—	5	3	8 ⎦
25	Brown U.	1	3	1	—	2	7	—	7 ⎤
25	Duke U.	—	—	—	5	2	7	—	7 ⎬
25	Purdue U.	2	—	4	1	—	7	—	7 ⎦
28	CUNY Graduate School	—	3	—	—	3	6	—	6 ⎤
28	U. of Virginia	—	3	—	1	1	5	1	6 ⎦
30	Carnegie-Mellon U.	1	—	2	—	1	4	1	5 ⎤
30	Johns Hopkins U.	—	1	1	1	2	5	—	5 ⎦

Reprinted by permission from David S. Webster, "America's Highest Ranked Graduate Schools, 1925–1982," *Change*, vol. 15, no. 4, May/June, 1983, p. 18.

programs rated 70 or higher than all but thirteen universities had rated 60 or higher.

The institution-wide scores listed in the far right column conceal some great differences in strength among the five broad fields of study covered by the *Assessment.* Some institutions, like Stanford, UCLA, Wisconsin,

Michigan, and even MIT, had programs with standard scores of 60 or over in all five fields. Other institutions, though, had some gaps.

Columbia and Yale, both of which offer doctorate-granting programs in at least three of the four engineering areas surveyed, had none rated 60 or over. Princeton, which had at least four programs rated 60 or higher in four of the five fields, offers the doctorate in only two of the six biological sciences covered and was not rated as high as 60 in either of them. The University of Minnesota, while having at least two programs rated 60 or above in the other four fields, had none in the humanities. Some institutions had their strength concentrated in one area. Omitting from consideration such specialized institutions as Caltech and Rockefeller University, which could be expected to have their strength concentrated in a few fields, at Duke five of seven programs rated 60 or above were in the biological sciences, as were five of ten at the University of Washington (Seattle). At Northwestern, five of the eleven programs rated 60 or above were in the social sciences; at Indiana University (Bloomington), four of the eight rated this high were in the humanities, as were four of seven at New York University and three of five at the University of Virginia.

We determined the leading institutions for each of the five broad fields of study covered by the *Assessment*, using as our basis the number of disciplines in each field in which it had at least one program that scored 60 or higher. For example, in the mathematical and physical sciences, for which the *Assessment* covered six disciplines, four schools listed in table III had at least one program scoring as high as 60 or higher in all six, and so on. The top fifteen institutions (plus ties, if any) for each of the five broad fields are shown in tables V through IX.

IMPROVEMENTS IN PROGRAMS' REPUTATIONS

The *Assessment* included a third reputational measure for which it reported data as "improvement in program quality" from 1976 to 1981. "Improvement" was, to put it mildly, a euphemism, since it is highly unlikely that, in the half-decade of financial austerity and widespread cutbacks preceding the *Assessment*, all 2,699 programs covered would have "improved." The committee itself consistently referred to "change" in program quality, not "improvement," on its survey forms.

In general, most evaluators thought there had been little or no change overall in programs. Few of the schools that are frequently ranked as top

Table V

THE TOP 15 INSTITUTIONS IN THE MATHEMATICAL AND PHYSICAL SCIENCES

Rank	Institution	Number of Disciplines Scoring 60 or Over
1	U. of California (Berkeley)	6
1	Cornell U.	6
1	Stanford U.	6
1	Yale U.	6
5	UCLA	5
5	U. of Chicago	5
5	Columbia U.	5
5	Harvard U.	5
5	MIT	5
5	Princeton U.	5
5	U. of Wisconsin (Madison)	5
12	Caltech	4
12	U. of Illinois (Urbana)	4
14	U. of Minnesota	3
14	U. of Texas (Austin)	3

Reprinted by permission from David S. Webster, "America's Highest Ranked Graduate Schools, 1925–1982," *Change*, vol. 15, no. 4, May/June, 1983, p. 19.

Table VI

THE TOP 15 INSTITUTIONS (PLUS TIES) IN THE HUMANITIES

Rank	Institution	Number of Disciplines Scoring 60 or Over
1	U. of California (Berkeley)	9
2	Princeton U.	7
2	Yale U.	7
4	Columbia U.	6
4	Cornell U.	6
4	U. of Michigan	6
7	UCLA	5
7	Harvard U.	5
7	U. of Pennsylvania	5
10	U. of Chicago	4
10	Indiana U. (Bloomington)	4
10	New York U.	4
10	Stanford U.	4
14	Brown U.	3
14	CUNY Graduate School	3
14	U. of North Carolina (Chapel Hill)	3
14	U. of Texas (Austin)	3
14	U. of Virginia	3
14	U. of Wisconsin (Madison)	3

Reprinted by permission from David S. Webster, "America's Highest Ranked Graduate Schools, 1925–1982," *Change*, vol. 15, no. 4, May/June, 1983, p. 20.

Table VII
THE TOP 15 INSTITUTIONS IN ENGINEERING

Rank	Institution	Number of Disciplines Scoring 60 or Over
1	U. of California (Berkeley)	4
1	Caltech	4
1	U. of Illinois (Urbana)	4
1	MIT	4
1	Princeton U.	4
1	Purdue U.	4
1	Stanford U.	4
8	Cornell U.	3
8	U. of Michigan	3
8	Northwestern U.	3
8	U. of Texas (Austin)	3
12	UCLA	2
12	Carnegie-Mellon U.	2
12	U. of Minnesota	2
12	U. of Wisconsin (Madison)	2

Reprinted by permission from David S. Webster, "America's Highest Ranked Graduate Schools, 1925–1982," *Change*, vol. 15, no. 4, May/June, 1983, p. 20.

Table VIII
THE TOP 15 INSTITUTIONS IN THE BIOLOGICAL SCIENCES

Rank	Institution	Number of Disciplines Scoring 60 or Over
1	UCLA	6
1	Yale U.	6
3	Duke U.	5
3	U. of Washington (Seattle)	5
3	U. of Wisconsin (Madison)	5
6	U. of California (Berkeley)	4
6	U. of California (Davis)	4
6	U. of Chicago	4
6	Columbia U.	4
6	Cornell U.	4
6	Harvard U.	4
6	U. of Illinois (Urbana)	4
6	U. of Michigan	4
6	Rockefeller U.	4
6	Stanford U.	4

Reprinted by permission from David S. Webster, "America's Highest Ranked Graduate Schools, 1925–1982," *Change*, vol. 15, no. 4, May/June, 1983, p. 21.

twenty schools are listed in table X, for instance. At any rate, nine programs were rated three or more standard deviations above the mean in improvement. They are listed in table X. Seven of these programs, all except music at Rochester and anthropology at Florida, are located west

Table IX

THE TOP 15 INSTITUTIONS (PLUS TIES) IN THE SOCIAL AND BEHAVIORAL SCIENCES

Rank	Institution	Number of Disciplines Scoring 60 or Over
1	U. of California (Berkeley)	7
1	U. of Chicago	7
3	UCLA	6
3	Columbia U.	6
3	Harvard U.	6
3	U. of Michigan	6
3	Stanford U.	6
3	U. of Wisconsin (Madison)	6
3	Yale U.	6
10	Northwestern U.	5
10	U. of Pennsylvania	5
10	Princeton U.	5
13	U. of Minnesota	4
13	U. of North Carolina	4
15	CUNY Graduate School	3
15	Cornell U.	3
15	U. of Illinois (Urbana)	3
15	Indiana U. (Bloomington)	3
15	MIT	3
15	U. of Rochester	3

Reprinted by permission from David S. Webster, "America's Highest Ranked Graduate Schools, 1925–1982," *Change*, vol. 15, no. 4, May/June, 1983, p. 21.

Table X

PROGRAMS RATED EXTREMELY HIGH IN REPUTATION FOR "IMPROVEMENT," 1976–1981

Rank	Institution	Program	Standard Score
1.	U. of California (San Diego)	Political Science	86
2.	U. of Texas (Austin)	Physics	83
3.	U. of Arizona	History	81
4.	U. of California (Santa Barbara)	Electrical Engineering	80
4.	Colorado State U.	Chemistry	80
4.	U. of Florida	Anthropology	80
4.	U. of Rochester	Music	80
4.	U. of Texas (Austin)	Civil Engineering	80
4.	U. of Utah	Mathematics	80

Reprinted by permission from David S. Webster, "America's Highest Ranked Graduate Schools, 1925–1982," *Change*, vol. 15, no. 4, May/June, 1983, p. 22.

of the Mississippi River. Six, all except those at Rochester, Colorado State, and Utah, are in the Sunbelt.

Some institutions showed great improvement in one or more of the five broad fields of study. The following list is the result of an unsystematic sampling of about twenty schools we thought might show such improvements and is far from complete. Some fields that were reputed to have improved greatly are as follows: social sciences at the University of Arizona, 67.5; engineering at the University of Texas at Austin, 67.5; mathematical and physical sciences at the University of Texas at Austin, 67.2; social sciences at the University of Florida, 65.7; engineering at the University of Houston, 64.5; social sciences at the University of Virginia, 64.5; humanities at the University of Virginia, 64; humanities at the University of Arizona, 63.2; math and physical sciences at the University of Arizona, 62.4

While again we sampled only about twenty universities, some showed especially impressive institution-wide gains. The University of Houston's standard score on reputation for improvement in the last five years was 64.8 (Houston was rated, however, in only eight disciplines, half of them in engineering); Arizona State University scored 62.1, based on ten disciplines; the University of Virginia 60.5, on twenty-six disciplines; and the University of Arizona 60.4, based on twenty-five disciplines.

Looking at the "improvement" scores another way, of the thirty-two disciplines covered, a total of thirty-five institutions were rated first (in three disciplines, two schools tied for first). Institutions listed as the most improved or tied for the most improved in more than one discipline were as follows: University of Arizona (four disciplines); University of Texas (Austin) and University of Virginia (three each); and University of Florida, University of Houston, and University of Utah (two each). Four of these six schools, all but Virginia and Florida, are west of the Mississippi River, and four of them, all but Virginia and Utah, are in the Sunbelt.

One institution that fared very well between the Cartter (1966) and Roose/Andersen (1970) studies was SUNY/Buffalo. In many disciplines, a large proportion of raters surveyed by Roose/Andersen thought that it had improved in the past five years. For example, 66 of 71 judges who expressed an opinion thought its classics department had improved, 58 of 61 thought it had improved in English, 45 of 55 in economics, 41 of 49 in history, and 46 of 53 in psychology. These were perhaps the most impressive "improvement" ratings achieved by any of the 130 schools Roose/Andersen covered. Lately it has fallen upon leaner times. In the *Assessment*, it received an improvement rating of only 46.0, below the mean.

DECLINES IN PROGRAMS' REPUTATIONS

There were also some sharp declines recorded in the *Assessment,* although again, there was little overall change attributed to the majority of the programs evaluated. Eight programs were rated three or more standard deviations below the mean for reputed "improvement" in program quality, 1976–1981. They are listed in table XI. While seven of the nine programs with the highest standard scores for improvement were located west of the Mississippi, all eight of the programs with the lowest scores for "improvement" are east of it.

Table XI
PROGRAMS RATED EXTREMELY LOW IN REPUTATION FOR "IMPROVEMENT," 1976–1981

Rank	Institution	Program	Standard Score
1.	SUNY (Buffalo)	Statistics	15
2.	Johns Hopkins U.	French	16
3.	Johns Hopkins U.	Classics	18
3.	Johns Hopkins U.	Spanish	18
5.	Emory U.	Mathematics	19
6.	Case Western Reserve U.	Geosciences	20
6.	New School for Social Research	Political Science	20
6.	Penn State U., Graduate School	Microbiology	20

Reprinted by permission from David S. Webster, "America's Highest Ranked Graduate Schools, 1925–1982," *Change,* vol. 15, no. 4, May/June, 1983, p. 22.

An unsystematic sampling of some institutions turned up several that scored well below the average for improvement in one or more of the *Assessment*'s five broad fields. The social sciences at Columbia had a combined "improvement" score of 38.4; engineering at the University of Michigan and mathematical and physical sciences at SUNY/Buffalo, both 37.8; math and physical sciences at Johns Hopkins (37.4); engineering at Columbia (37); humanities at Johns Hopkins (36.1); humanities at Case Western Reserve (34.8); social sciences at the New School for Social Research (34.4); math and physical sciences at Case Western Reserve (31.8); biological sciences at Case Western Reserve (31); and social sciences at Case Western Reserve (29.5).

Three institutions, of the 20 or so we checked in detail, showed institution-wide scores, in reputation for "improvement," of more than one standard deviation below the mean. One was Johns Hopkins which, despite having the art history program rated as the most improved in the United States (73), still received exceptionally low "improvement" ratings in classics (18), Spanish (18), and French (16). It received "improvement" scores below the mean in 22 of the 26 disciplines in which it was rated, for a campus-wide score of 37.7.

Case Western Reserve got below-average "improvement" scores in all 21 disciplines in which it was rated. Indeed, except for engineering (42.7), it averaged nearly two standard deviations below the mean in the other four fields, taken as a group. It had a school-wide score of 33.3. The lowest "improvement" score of the institutions we checked was for New York City's New School for Social Research, which received below average "improvement" scores in all six disciplines in which it was rated and had an institution-wide total of 32.3.

One institution that seems to have turned itself around from a sharp decline in reputational rankings is Columbia. Of the 31 disciplines in which it was rated in both the Cartter and Roose/Andersen studies, in the latter study it improved its position in two, stayed the same in five, and declined in 24. Many of these declines were very steep, especially considering that the rankings employed virtually identical methodologies, thus increasing the likelihood that Columbia's decline in ratings was "real" and not an artifact of changes in methodology. In the four years between the two reports, Columbia's reputation for quality of graduate faculty declined in classics from tied for 6th to tied for 12th, in German from tied for 9th to 16th, in music from 3rd to 9th, in political science from 5th to 11th, in psychology from 14th to tied for 27th, in biochemistry from 11th to tied for 26th, in physiology from tied for 10th to tied for 27th, and in geology from 4th to 9th.

So it is heartening to see that Columbia, despite its low "improvement" scores in the social sciences and engineering, attenuated, if it did not completely reverse, its decline in reputation. The *Assessment* gave several of its programs good "improvement" scores, including computer sciences (67), microbiology (61), chemistry (60), economics (59), and cellular and molecular biology (59), and its institution-wide "improvement" score of 45.1 was not very far below the mean.

In fact, its "improvement" score was very close to SUNY/Buffalo's score of 46.0. Ironically, the two institutions that, according to the Roose/Andersen study, may have respectively risen most and slipped worst during the late 1960s recently seem, so far as their rate of reputed "improvement" is concerned, to have converged.

TRENDS, 1925–1982

Now we will look at the results of the seven multidisciplinary reputational rankings of graduate departments that have appeared since 1925. Since only one of them totaled its departmental ratings to get institution-wide ones, it is necessary to aggregate the departmental scores for all the others, and since these rankings, even though they were all "reputational," varied widely in methodology, their institution-wide totals must be calculated in different ways.

Six of them, all except the 1982 *Assessment*, are listed below, along with a description of how we calculated institution-wide totals for each.

1. Hughes (1925) asked his judges to rate departments from 1 to 5, according to their quality of graduate work.[4] He then ranked schools by multiplying their 1 ratings by four, their 2 ratings by three, their 3 ratings by two, and their 4 and 5 ratings by one. We added his scores for each department to get an institution-wide total.

2. Hughes (1934) did not rank order departments but rather, based on his raters' responses, listed in alphabetical order the highest-scoring departments in each discipline, starring as "distinguished" those that more than half his judges considered in about the top 20 percent and calling the rest "adequately staffed and equipped" to confer the doctorate.[5] We gave an institution 2 points for each starred department and 1 for each that was listed.

3. Keniston (1959) aggregated his departmental scores into institution-wide ones.[6] We have used his totals.

4. Cartter (1966) ranked the highest-rated departments in each discipline and then grouped together several schools, without distinguishing among them, as having "good" graduate faculties and several more as having faculties that were "adequate plus."[7] Raymond Ewell devised the following system to rank institutions covered in this study.[8] He gave a department 5 points each time its graduate faculty was rated as "adequate plus" and 10 points each time it was rated as "good." To those departments that received a numerical rank, he gave as many points as their inverse rank, plus 14. For example, a school that was listed as first of the fifteen that were ranked in a given discipline would get 15 points plus the automatic 14, or 29; one listed 7th of 15 would get 9 points plus the automatic 14, or 23, and so on. We have used Ewell's institution-wide totals.

5. Roose/Andersen (1970).[9] Since this study was a virtual replication of Cartter's, we have applied Ewell's method to it.

6. Ladd/Lipset (1977.)[10] George Callcott calculated institution-wide scores from this study by giving an institution 10 points for being ranked first in any discipline, 9 for being ranked second, and so on down to 1 for being ranked 10th.[11] We have used Callcott's totals.

The results of the seven rankings, 1925–1982, cannot be considered precise indications of the rise and fall of these universities' research doctorate programs for several reasons, of which these two are the most important. First, though they were all "reputational" rankings, they asked different groups of judges about different mixes of departments and universities. Hughes' 1934 study included far more agricultural disciplines, in which Iowa State College, of which he was president at the time, excelled, than did any other study, including departments of animal nutrition, plant pathology, plant physiology, and soil science. Keniston limited his raters to the departments at only twenty-five leading comprehensive universities. Ladd and Lipset's ranking included several professional schools, such as business, law, and medicine, that are not ranked by any other study.

Second, because of the very different ways in which they rank departments, we had to use very different methods of combining their departmental rank orders into institution-wide scores. Nevertheless, table XII provides some fascinating information about the rise and fall of graduate schools throughout much of this century.

It shows the positions of the top twenty-five departments, plus ties, in each of the seven studies, 1925–1982, except for the Keniston study, in which Keniston ranked only twenty of the twenty-five schools he included in his survey. The column at the far right shows the change in position between an institution's 1925 and 1982 ranks.

Considering only those institutions that appeared among the top twenty-five schools in six rankings (and the top twenty in Keniston's), three made especially impressive gains. MIT, reflecting its evolution from a technical school to a more nearly comprehensive university, improved fourteen places, from 19th (1925) to 5th (1982), with its biggest leap coming since 1970. Stanford, perhaps the brightest success story among major universities of the twentieth century, steadily advanced from 14th (1925) to 2nd (1982). UC/Berkeley climbed from 9th (1925) to first (1982), but it had actually jumped to first by Hughes' 1934 ranking and has been ranked either first or second in every study since then.

Among schools that were not ranked among the top twenty-five in the earliest studies, or were not ranked at all, UCLA has done exceptionally

Table XII

INSTITUTIONS' RANKING IN THE SEVEN MAJOR REPUTATIONAL RANKINGS
OF GRADUATE SCHOOLS, 1925-1982

Institution	Hughes (1925)	Hughes (1934)	Keniston (1959)	Cartter (1966)	Roose/ Andersen (1970)	Ladd/ Lipset (1979)	Assess- ment (1982)	Change, 1925- 1982
U. of Chicago	1	5	6	9	7	6	7	− 6
Harvard U.	2	1*	1	2	2	1	3*	− 1
Columbia U.	3	3	3	7	12	11	11*	− 8
Yale U.	4	7	4	6	5	4	3*	1
U. of Wisconsin (Madison)	5	4	8	3	6	7	8*	− 3
Princeton U.	6	11*	7	10	8	8	6	T
Johns Hopkins U.	7	9	16	13	19	17	(30)*	−23
U. of Michigan	8	8	5	4	4	5	8*	T
U. of California (Berkeley)	9	1*	2	1	1	2	1	8
Cornell U.	10	6	9	11	11	12	11*	− 1
U. of Illinois (Urbana)	11	11*	10	8	9	10	13	− 2
U. of Pennsylvania	12	14*	11	15	14	15*	14	− 2
U. of Minnesota	13	10	12	12	16		16*	− 3
Stanford U.	14	13	13	5	3	3	2	12
Ohio State U.	15	14*	18	22		19*		−
U. of Iowa	16	17*				23*		−
Bryn Mawr College	17	24*						−
Caltech	18	17*		18	20	13*	15	3
MIT	19	16		21	15	9	5	14
Northwestern U.	20	21	17	17		23*	18	2
U. of Missouri (Columbia)	21	19*						−
Clark U.	22							−
U. of Pittsburgh	23							−
Indiana U. (Bloomington)	24		15	19	18	13*	21*	3
U. of Nebraska	25							−
New York U.		22	19	23			21*	
U. of North Carolina		24*			24*	23*	20	
U. of Texas (Austin)		23		20	17	19*	16*	
Iowa State U.		19*						
Washington U. (St. Louis)		24*						
UCLA			14	14	10	15*	8*	
U. of Washington (Seattle)			20	16	13		19	
Purdue U.				24	21	18	25*	
Brown U.				25	23		25*	
Duke U.					22		25*	
Michigan State U.					24*			
U. of Rochester						19*		
Juilliard School						19*		
U. of California (San Diego)							21*	
Rockefeller U.							21*	
	n = 25	n = 25	n = 20	n = 25	n = 25	n = 25	n = 25	

Reprinted by permission from David S. Webster, "America's Highest Ranked Graduate Schools, 1925-1982," *Change*, vol. 15, no. 4, May/June, 1983, p. 23.

* = 2 or more institutions tied at a position

T = 1925 and 1982 ranks were identical

− = Institution ranked in top 25 in 1925 but lower than 25th (plus ties) in 1982

well. Established in 1919, it first appeared among the top twenty-five in the Keniston study of 1959, in which it ranked 14th. In the *Assessment* it ranked 8th, by far the best showing of universities founded in this century and perhaps the best showing ever of a predominantly "commuter" institution. The University of Texas at Austin has also done well. It did not make the top twenty-five in Hughes' 1925 study, but since then it has steadily improved its position from 23rd (1934) to 16th (1982).

Among those universities that have declined in overall reputation for graduate training in the arts, sciences, and engineering, Johns Hopkins stands out. Though we normally did not calculate the standing of universities that fell below the top twenty-five and ties in any ranking, we did follow Johns Hopkins in the 1982 *Assessment.* It tied for 30th, a drop of twenty-three places since 1925. Among schools which ranked among the top twenty-five in all seven studies, Columbia dropped from 3rd to 11th (actually, from 1959 to 1970 it dropped from 3rd to 12th, and in the two most recent studies it held steady at 11th). The University of Chicago, too, has lost much ground since 1925. Ranked first that year, it declined steadily until 1966, when it ranked 9th, and since then has improved a couple of notches to 7th in 1982.

Some other schools, not ranked among the top twenty-five in every study, have obviously declined in reputation. One is Ohio State University, which ranked 18th or higher in each of the first three studies but by 1982 had disappeared from the top twenty-five. The University of Iowa dropped, too. It ranked 16th and 17th in Hughes' two studies but made the top twenty-five studies only once since then. The University of Missouri at Columbia was ranked 21st and 19th in the two Hughes studies but has not ranked in the top twenty-five since then.

Only twelve universities were ranked in the top twenty-five (top twenty in the Keniston study) in all seven academic quality rankings, and by averaging their ordinal positions in each one, a school's "average" rank, 1925–1982, has been calculated and is shown in table XIII.

THE FUTURE

Whatever faults the 1982 *Assessment* had, with its publication the art of ranking graduate school arts, sciences, and engineering programs took a big step forward. Actually, for reasons worthy of study in themselves, reputational rankings of graduate school arts and sciences programs are far superior methodologically to any multidisciplinary ranking that has

Table XIII
THE LEADING AMERICAN UNIVERSITIES IN REPUTATIONAL RANKINGS
OF GRADUATE SCHOOLS, 1925–1982

Rank	Institution	Average Rank
1.	Harvard U.	1.7
2.	U. of California (Berkeley)	2.4
3.	Yale U.	4.7
{ 4.	U. of Chicago	5.9 }
{ 4.	U. of Wisconsin (Madison)	5.9 }
6.	U. of Michigan	6
7.	Columbia U.	7.1
8.	Stanford U.	7.6
9.	Princeton U.	8
10.	Cornell U.	10
11.	U. of Illinois (Urbana)	10.3
12.	U. of Pennsylvania	13.6

Reprinted by permission from David S. Webster, "America's Highest Ranked Graduate Schools, 1925–1982," *Change*, vol. 15, no. 4, May/June, 1983, p. 24.

ever been published of graduate professional schools. Two types of quality rankings are especially needed now.

First, we need good, multidisciplinary rankings of graduate professional (other than engineering) schools. Although good rankings have occasionally been published for individual professional school fields, the best multidisciplinary reputational rankings of professional schools that have ever been published, those by Blau and Margulies in *Change* during the mid-1970s, have many faults and are, at any rate, outdated.

Second, it is time to attempt the difficult task of ranking undergraduate colleges, or at least the undergraduate programs of colleges and universities. Doing so will certainly be difficult, for most doctorate-granting programs of, say, history and physics have reasonably similar goals, but how can a ranking be devised that will compare, either along one dimension or several, schools with such different, sometimes contradictory goals as Antioch and the United States Military Academy, Berea and Washington and Lee, the California College of Arts and Crafts and the City College of New York? Still, such ratings have occasionally been attempted, the most successful of them being two rankings put out by a firm called College-Rater that are now virtually unknown, of "the nation's leading undergraduate colleges and universities."[12]

Almost any reasonably good ranking would be better than what is available now: college catalogs, often filled with self-serving rhetoric, and the many college guidebooks, perceptively analyzed by Jon Nicholson of Carleton College in *Change* magazine,[13] which generally avoid presenting much information directly concerning academic quality.

Far more students at any time are looking for an undergraduate college than a graduate or professional school. And prospective undergraduates have many more institutions to choose among. Yet, paradoxically, far more academic quality rankings rate graduate programs of arts and sciences and graduate professional schools than undergraduate colleges. It is time to tackle the unquestionably serious problems involved and produce some academic quality rankings of undergraduate programs.

Chapter Sixteen

CONTEMPORARY METHODS OF ASSESSING COLLEGE AND UNIVERSITY QUALITY

In 1977, two Indiana University faculty members published a long article in the *American Psychologist* ranking the psychology departments at American colleges and universities.[1] The ranking was based on the number of articles each institution's faculty members had published, from 1970–75, in thirteen journals sponsored by the American Psychological Association. Harvard's psychology department, which during these six years included such eminent figures as Robert F. Bales, Roger Brown, Jerome Bruner, Richard Herrnstein, Jerome Kagan, David McClelland, and B. F. Skinner, was ranked 28th in the country, behind the psychology departments at the University of Missouri at Columbia, Temple, Michigan State University, and the University of Oregon.

In 1979, John Robey of New Mexico State University published an article in *PS* presenting two rank orders of the one hundred leading American political science departments, one of which was based on faculty's *per capita* article publication in six political science journals from 1968 to 1977.[2] At the very top of this rank order was the political science department of Florida Atlantic University, a school founded only eighteen years earlier. Harvard was ranked 30th, behind the political science departments at Emory, Cincinnati, Georgia, Purdue, and Houston, while the University of California at Berkeley was ranked 39th, Yale 40th, Chicago 42nd, Princeton 74th, and MIT 81st. Columbia's renowned political science department failed to crack the top one hundred. (Incredibly, Columbia's large department even failed to crack the top one hundred based on its faculty's *aggregate* article publication in the six journals.)

In 1980, two professors at the University of Virginia's McIntire School of Commerce published an article containing a list of the twelve "top-ranked undergraduate business programs" in the United States according to, among others, senior personnel executives of America's largest industrial firms, banks, and public utilities.[3] These senior personnel executives named Harvard, Stanford, Columbia, the University of Chicago, and Northwestern as having undergraduate business schools among the nation's twelve best, unfortunately overlooking the fact that none of these institutions even *has* an undergraduate school of business.

Clearly, the art and science of ranking American colleges, universities, and individual departments according to their academic "quality" has a long way to go before the results of such studies are generally accepted. Hundreds of quality rankings of American institutions of higher learning and their various academic departments and professional schools have been published since James McKeen Cattell published the first one in 1910.[4] These rankings have employed dozens of methodologies, many of them used only once. But in the last twenty-five years, six types of methodology have been used more than any others. Three of them are based on the accomplishments of colleges' and universities' faculty members, two of them on the accomplishments of their students, and one on the amount and quality of their "resources"—their educational expenditures, physical plant, and so on.

RANKINGS BASED ON FACULTY ACCOMPLISHMENTS

Reputational Rankings

"Reputational" rankings are based on the opinions of experts—deans, department chairpersons, and senior scholars in an academic discipline or professional field—who rank departments in order of their faculties' reputation for scholarship. Though only a small proportion of the quality rankings published since 1910 have employed this methodology, most of the best-known, multidisciplinary rankings have used it. These include Allan Cartter's *Assessment of Quality in Graduate Education* (1966), Roose and Andersen's *Rating of Graduate Programs* (1970), the two rankings of professional schools by Blau and Margulies published in *Change* magazine in the mid-1970s, and the ranking by Ladd and Lipset published in the *Chronicle of Higher Education* in 1979. They also include the ranking published by the National Academy of Sciences in 1982, which used reputational rankings along with many other kinds.

One advantage of reputational rankings is that those who supposedly know most about academic quality in a discipline can be and often are employed as raters. Another possible advantage of reputational rankings is that, of all the major types of quality rankings, they produce results with the most face validity, results that most nearly match what the educated general public considers the hierarchy of colleges and universities to be. It is hard to imagine any reputational ranking of political science departments that could possibly be devised which would rank Florida Atlantic University first in the United States and fail to include Columbia in the top one hundred, and such rankings, therefore, have a certain intuitive appeal and gain easy public acceptance.

A major disadvantage of reputational rankings, however, is that they can effectively rate only departments whose members have substantial research reputations. Such rankings are useful for differentiating, in a given discipline, between, say, Stanford and Berkeley, Duke and the University of North Carolina at Chapel Hill, and arguably, Washington State University and Oregon State University. But once below the top few dozen or, at most, the top one hundred departments in a discipline, it is very hard to differentiate among departments on the basis of their faculty's research reputations, which are often slender or nonexistent.

Another criticism often levelled against reputational rankings is that they are subject to "halo effects" — that is, that the overall reputation of an institution may influence, for better or worse, raters' assessment of the particular department they are being asked to rank. The ranking of five universities without business programs among schools with the best undergraduate business programs is powerful evidence that the halo effect influences rankings. But substantial evidence also points *against* the halo effect. In numerous instances individual departments in reputational rankings are ranked far higher or lower than their university as a whole, or even of any other department in the school. For example, in Roose and Andersen's reputational ranking, the New York University art history department was ranked first in the United States, the University of Pittsburgh philosophy department fourth, the University of Arizona astronomy department seventh, and the University of Delaware chemical engineering department tenth. All these rankings are far higher than would be that of the institution as a whole if its departmental rankings were averaged.

Moreover, it is not uncommon for individual departments to be ranked far *lower* than their institution as a whole. In the Roose/Andersen study, the University of Michigan's English department was tied for 17th in the U.S., as was Stanford's Spanish department. Harvard's civil engineering department was ranked 18th, Yale's sociology department was tied for 13th, and the psychology departments at Columbia and Princeton were tied for 27th, as were these universities' physiology departments. So the halo effect may exist, especially in studies in which those doing the rating are not well informed, but in reputational rankings like the Roose/Andersen study, where the rankers are experts in their field, it is still common for departments to greatly exceed or fall short of their institution's overall reputation.

Another criticism often made of reputational rankings is that they lag several years behind "reality." This argument was first made by Raymond Hughes in his 1925 reputational ranking,[5] and even today it is made from time to time. It was probably more true in 1925 than now. Today, with *Change* magazine and the *Chronicle of Higher Education,* among other publications, serving as widely read sources of information about higher education, and with most disciplines having one or more journals and newsletters containing news of faculty appointments and departures, the time lag before word of senior faculty appointments at major universities gets around can probably be measured in months, rather than years. When Erving Goffman left Berkeley for the University of Pennsylvania or Seymour Martin Lipset left Harvard for Stanford, the news got around very quickly, at least to the well-connected people who are often used as raters for reputational rankings. Even today, though, there is certainly a time lag at the junior faculty level, and if a department were to appoint two or three members just out of graduate school whose abilities greatly exceeded or fell short of those of the older members of the department, it would undoubtedly take time for these appointments to be reflected in the department's standing in reputational rankings.

Still another criticism often made about reputational rankings, and probably a valid one, is that scholars from the nation's leading universities serve in disproportionately large numbers as raters, and they tend to rank high those departments of the same type, and with the same emphases, as their own universities. Consequently, so this argument goes, innovative or "different" departments, such as the University of California at Davis's relatively nonquantitative and "humanistic" sociology department and UC/Irvine's department of English and comparative literature, which emphasizes critical theory more than do most of the nation's top-ranked English departments, may be rated lower than they deserve to be. (Still, some departments manage to buck the norms of their discipline and still be rated high, as, for example, the University of

Chicago's English department which, despite using, more than any other leading English department, an Aristotelian approach to the study of literature, has consistently been rated very high in reputational rankings. The University of Iowa's English department, which over the years has devoted far more of its resources to creative writing than do most highly ranked English departments, even accepting "imaginative writing" as Ph.D. dissertations, has also fared well in reputational rankings.)

Faculty Awards, Honors, and Prizes

Some have argued that reputational rankings are based on people's subjective opinions and are little more than compendia of rumor, hearsay, and gossip. They reject them and seek to rank institutions and departments on the basis of objective data, often espousing a second type of quality ranking based on faculty accomplishments, such as awards, honors, prizes, and memberships in honorific organizations. The major advantage often claimed for such rankings is that they are "objective," not "subjective" like reputational rankings. But, as Allan Cartter pointed out, these are not really the objective rankings their proponents claim, but rather subjective rankings once removed. The awards, honors, and prizes that those who do this type of study tally so ardently in their pursuit of an "objective" ranking were themselves conferred largely on the basis of subjective judgments.

In addition, these studies, like reputational rankings, are useful only for ranking the best or better institutions or departments. Faculty earn few such accolades for their research at the vast majority of American colleges. To attempt to distinguish among, say, such New Jersey colleges as Rider, Monmouth, Upsala, and St. Peter's on the basis of how many Nobel prizes or Guggenheim fellowships their faculty members have won would scarcely work, and doing so would certainly not be fair to these institutions, which have many virtues not "captured" by counting, say, the number of their faculty members who have been elected to the National Academy of Sciences.

Another disadvantage of rankings that tabulate faculty prizes and awards is that they may be years behind, or ahead of, reality. In the 1960s, the University of Chicago English department would probably have ranked very high in such studies, based partly on the presence there of two eminent scholars, R. S. Crane and George Williamson. Both were then very advanced in years, and the accolades they had earned, over their distinguished careers, probably overstated their research and teaching contributions to Chicago's English department *at that time.* Similarly, tallies of prizes and awards may understate the quality of departments that have several junior people doing important work for which they will earn prizes and honors in years to come.

For many years, until the recent glut of Ph.D.s in the academic labor market meant that almost any department that wished to could be chock full of professors with earned doctorates, one frequently used "objective" measure of ranking institutions and individual departments was by the percentage of their faculty, or their senior faculty, who possessed Ph.D.s. Around 1970, one well-known department would have ranked quite low in such a quality ranking—fully three of its senior professors had no Ph.D. One had a law degree, one had only an M.Ed., and the third had only a B.A. Yet these three members of Harvard's social relations department—David Riesman, Christopher Jencks, and Erik Erikson— might possibly have been better scholars and teachers than some professors who *did* possess earned doctorates. Rankings of institutions and individual departments, then, based on so-called "objective" measures of faculty achievement, have serious flaws.

Realizing this, some researchers have sought to rank order departments on still another measure of faculty research accomplishment, one that avoids many of the faults of reputational rankings and those based on faculty honors and awards. This methodology ranks departments by the number of citations their faculty members earn, over a period of time, in "citation indexes."

Citations in Citation Indexes

Citation indexes are published annually and list each citation of a scholar's work appearing in journals and periodicals covered by that index in a particular year. If, for instance, Smith published an article in 1984 and Jones cited it in 1985 in a source covered by the *Social Sciences Citation Index,* then the edition of *SSCI* covering 1985 will duly list Smith's article and the journal in which Jones cited it. Many researchers, in recent years, have tabulated the citations of professors in leading departments in a discipline over a period of time, and sometimes using aggregate and sometimes *per capita* citations, have rank ordered departments based on the number of citations of their faculty members' work.

Rankings done by counting citations have several obvious virtues.

First, they are useful in assessing the influence and importance—if, for argument's sake, one agrees that often cited articles are, as a group, more influential and important than seldom cited ones—of faculty members' publications, and not just their sheer volume. The researcher who runs up the numbers with many mediocre publications is not likely to be cited very often.

Second, they show the present—or, at least, the very recent—influence of a department's publications. The professor who did seminal work twenty years ago but has published little since then may help his department's standing in reputational studies and add to its list of awards and honors but is unlikely to have a great many recent citations.

For research universities, at least, such rankings reflect the achievements of all, or at least most, of a department's faculty members, not just a few of them. Even the most distinguished chemistry department will have only a tiny percentage of its members who have won a Nobel prize; in even the most distinguished English department, only a fraction of the faculty are likely to be members of the American Academy of Arts and Sciences. To know which departments rank highest in the number or percentage of faculty members who have achieved such honors is to know nothing about the contributions of the majority of members of the department. But since at many universities most of the faculty publishes and thus has publications available to be cited, citation indexes reflect the achievements of most of a department's faculty, not just its stars.

But quality rankings based on citation indexes have many disadvantages, too. First, they are obviously greatly influenced by how many scholars are currently publishing in a field. If a scholar is publishing in a popular area such as educational equity or evaluation, he is likely to garner, all things being equal, more citations than if he were working in a less popular area. The historian Martin Duberman's brilliant *Black Mountain: An Exploration in Community*[6] has never been heavily cited. Its subject was a tiny institution in an obscure setting that existed for a relatively short time and had closed forever when Duberman's work was published.

Second, the number of citations of a scholar's work is strongly influenced by whether, in the years after he writes, his field expands or contracts. The explosion of certain fields like black studies in the 1960s and women's studies in the 1970s meant that scholars who published a reasonably good book or article before or just after the explosion began would, all things being equal, be cited more often than those whose fields did not expand. Even within disciplines there can be sharp increases and decreases in the rate of scholarly publication over time. For example, probably a greater proportion of scholarship on the English Romantic and pre-Romantic writers is published today about Blake, and less about Shelley, than was the case a generation ago, and although thirty years is quite a long time between publication and citation, even for the humanities, those who did important work on Blake in the 1950s probably get more citations than those who did equally important work on Shelley.

A third disadvantage of rankings based on citation indexes is that these indexes do not distinguish in any way among "good," "neutral," or "bad" citations. If an author writes that "the best book ever published in this field was by Murphy; Schwartz has also published in this field; and by far the worst piece of nonsense ever written on this subject was by Adams," then Murphy, Schwartz, and Adams are each duly credited with one citation.

Another shortcoming of such rankings is that those who produce them have so far failed to take account of who is doing the citing. It could be argued, for example, that in the social sciences a citation by Robert Merton, Clifford Geertz, or Michael Walzer may be worth more than a citation by one's graduate students.

Still another fault of quality rankings based on citations is that citation counts are easily susceptible to manipulation. While some figures—in the social sciences, people like Freud, Marx, Weber, and Piaget—are cited hundreds of times every year, the average scholar is cited far less. In fact, in the social sciences an article's modal number of citations per year is zero. That is, if Smith published an article in 1984, the most likely number of times it will be listed in the *SSCI* covering 1985, or covering any subsequent year, is none. With the average article being cited so seldom, it is relatively easy to increase one's standing in the citation indexes. If, for example, a scholar published an article in 1984 and in 1985 published another one, citing his earlier study, and if he managed to persuade one of his colleagues and one of his graduate students to do likewise, that article already has three citations in one year. The scholar is still hardly a threat to Marx and Freud, but his article now has more citations than the great majority of social science articles receive in a year, and his standing and that of his department will consequently be higher than they should be.

The three most frequently used methodologies for ranking institutions and individual departments based on their faculty's research accomplishments—those based on the faculty's scholarly "reputation," their awards and honors, and on citations to their publications—clearly all have serious shortcomings.

Many researchers, though, have attempted to rank colleges and universities not according to faculty achievements but to those of students. These rankings have chiefly been of two kinds, one based on how successful the graduates of a college or university are in later life, the other on how well they achieve on standardized tests, such as the Scholastic Aptitude Test (SAT), the American College Test (ACT), and the National Merit Scholarship Qualifying Test (NMSQT) shortly before they enter college. Although it might seem more logical to rank institutions based on how much their students learn while they are *there*, rather than on how well they achieve after they leave or before they arrive, strangely enough almost no academic quality rankings have been based on the "value added" that institutions confer upon their students while they are in attendance.

RANKINGS BASED ON STUDENTS' ACHIEVEMENTS

Students' Achievements in Later Life

The older of the two types of student achievement rankings is based on student accomplishment in later life. Cattell published several quality rankings based on how many distinguished scientists colleges and universities "produced," and "distinguished alumni" studies were by far the most frequently published type of academic quality ranking from 1910 until the early 1960s, when they were largely discredited as measures of academic quality. Even today they still continue to appear, though in diminished numbers.

One obvious advantage of such rankings is that while only a small percentage of colleges and universities have faculties that produce or even aspire to produce much research, almost all of them attempt to prepare their students for rewarding careers in later life. This generalization is at least as true for small liberal arts colleges as for multiversities, and while it would make no sense to compare, say, Michigan's Adrian College, Albion College, Hillsdale College, and Olivet College with the University of Michigan based on their faculties' research accomplishments, it is eminently possible to rank all these institutions based on the percentage of their graduates who later become scientists, scholars, physicians, corporation executives, or are listed in *Who's Who in America.*

Despite this great advantage—that "achievement of graduates" rankings enable one effectively to rank all colleges and universities, not just research universities—such a method has disadvantages as well. One serious flaw is that the rankings are inevitably thirty years or more behind the times, since it takes at least that long for most of the graduates eventually to be listed in *Who's Who in America* or *American Men & Women of Science.*

A second disadvantage is that the achievements of a college's graduates depend much more on the ability of the students it attracts in the first place than on the quality of the institution itself. Colleges and universities that for whatever reasons attract superior freshmen succeed, almost invariably, in "producing" high-achieving graduates.

Students' Scores on Standardized Tests

The other commonly used method of ranking institutions on their students' achievements relies on students' scores on standardized tests. One advantage of such a measure is that the data are easy to obtain. Scores on the SAT and ACT are readily available, requiring no massive data collection effort such as searching through *Who's Who in America* and counting how many times each college is represented in it. These rankings also show the academic ability of the students a college is attracting currently, not of those it was attracting thirty years ago. Moreover, such rankings are a measure on which a great many institutions—all those recording standardized test scores for most or all of their entering students—can be ranked, and not one, like reputational rankings, on which only research universities can be effectively compared. The ranking is based on the achievements of most, or even all, of a school's entering students, whereas "alumni achievement" rankings, like most rankings based on faculty awards, honors, and prizes, are based on the achievements of only a few outstanding people.

These are powerful advantages. However, such rankings have a number of serious disadvantages, too. First, they are based on the academic abilities of students before they enter a college, and they utterly fail to consider anything that these institutions do to *educate* their students once they enroll. This method is thus comparable to ranking professional football teams not by how many games they win and lose during the season but by how many early round draft choices they manage to sign.

Second, a school's admissions policies play a large role in determining its students' scores on standardized tests. A school that weighs scores on standardized tests very heavily in its admissions decisions will, all things being equal, enroll more high-scoring students than will an institution like the University of California, which emphasizes high school grades, not test scores, in its admissions practices.

Third, schools with very small enrollments—that is, whose applicants are competing for very few places—may well tend to be rated higher than they deserve to be, based on other commonly used criteria for ranking colleges and universities. In fall, 1982, for example, freshmen at tiny Harvey Mudd College in California (1310), Webb Institute of Naval Architecture in New York (1290), and St. John's College in Maryland (1240), all had combined SAT scores far higher than did freshmen at UC/Berkeley (1125).[7] Similarly, hundreds of American colleges and universities attracted freshmen whose SAT scores were higher than those of freshmen at UCLA (1042), including such small schools as Whitman College in Washington (1135), Wheaton College in Illinois (1126), Agnes Scott College in Georgia (1110), Colorado College (1099), and Ursinus College in Pennsylvania (1089).[8] Based on some other criteria that have been used to rank institutions according to their "quality," though, like faculty research and publication achievements, many of these schools would doubtless be ranked lower than UCLA.

RANKINGS BASED ON INSTITUTIONAL ACADEMIC RESOURCES

Finally, we come to the sixth commonly used method of ranking colleges and universities, one based on the resources they can offer to their students, either in aggregate or on a *per capita* student basis. Among the institutional resources that have been used in quality rankings are educational expenditures per student, faculty-student ratios, and the number of volumes in the library. This method has several advantages. It is one by which all colleges and universities, not just some of them, can be compared with each other. Furthermore, as in the case of student scores on standardized tests, it is relatively easy to obtain data on many kinds of institutional resources. Unlike rankings based on graduates' achievements in later life, those based on institutional resources show what is happening at an institution now, not thirty years ago. Such a method appears intuitively to have an advantage over some other methods of ranking colleges, since it appears to provide information about what students are actually experiencing on their campus, not just about students before they enter college or after they leave.

But rankings based on institutional resources have at least one severe disadvantage. That is, although they measure what resources students have available, as they are currently done they offer little or no information about how often and how beneficially students *use* these resources. To know an institution's faculty-student ratio and how much its faculty is paid is not the same as knowing how well its faculty teaches and how much its students learn. Knowing how many books an institution has in its library and how many it has per student is not the same as knowing how often students read these books and how much they learn from them. In the future, researchers who do academic quality rankings based on institutional resources would be wise to measure not just what resources institutions possess, but how much their students *benefit* from these resources.

Chapter Seventeen

REQUIREMENTS FOR THE IDEAL ACADEMIC QUALITY RANKING

To belabor the obvious, the ideal academic quality ranking has not yet been done. Such a ranking should possess at least seven qualities. First, it should be multidimensional—that is, it should be based not simply on one aspect of colleges and universities, but on many. There is room for debate about exactly what criteria should be used and whether or not they should be weighted, but at the very least, multiple criteria should be used.

Second, the measures employed in such a multidimensional ranking should be based on the achievements of most or all of a department's or university's faculty, students, and alumni, not just a few outstanding ones.

Third, any study should be based on *per capita*, rather than aggregate figures. Few would claim that East Los Angeles is a richer community than, say, San Marino, California, because the hundreds of thousands of people who live there have more aggregate wealth than the 13,000 who live in San Marino. Astonishingly enough, however, aggregate figures *are* often used in ranking colleges and universities with, for example, the number of students winning prestigious graduate fellowships used as a measure of quality without any correction for the size of the senior classes from which they came.

Fourth, the ideal quality ranking should not only rank departments or institutions, as ratings now do, but it should also show how they compare with some external standard of quality. It should not only list the top 20 or 40 psychology departments or law schools, but it should show how many of them, if any, are excellent ones.

Fifth, it should rank not only departments as a whole, as current quality rankings do, but also the important fields of study within departments, what David Riesman has called their "microclimates." For a prospective graduate student in history who wishes to concentrate in

153

American history, a history department's quality in that area, for example, may well be more important than its overall standing.

Sixth, the ideal ranking should take into consideration the contributions of ancillary departments. These may often be quite substantial. For instance, in 1977 Cox and Catt ranked psychology departments according to how many articles their faculty members had authored in the thirteen journals published by the American Psychological Association. They ranked the University of Wisconsin at Madison's psychology department first.[1]

Soon afterwards, however, others demonstrated that about 40% of the authors of those articles had been situated elsewhere at the university — in the sociology department and the schools of agriculture, business, education, and law, among other places.[2] If scholars housed elsewhere than the psychology department published fully 40% of the articles in these psychology journals, then certainly they might well have been able to provide a substantial amount of instruction and guidance to psychology students. So the ideal quality ranking should also consider the resources of ancillary departments.

Finally, since virtually all colleges, universities, and departments at them, whatever other goals they aspire towards, consider the education of students one of their primary missions, it is remarkable how few academic quality rankings have been based on how much students learn. While there are serious difficulties involved in measuring what students studying a great many different subjects learn during their years of college or graduate school, the education of students is so important a goal of such an overwhelmingly large proportion of American colleges and universities that the ideal academic quality ranking, whatever other criteria it uses, should be based partly on how much students learn.

NOTES

CHAPTER ONE

[1]Arthur Steven Higgins, "The Rating of Selected Fields of Doctoral Study in the Graduate Schools of Education: An Opinion Survey," Columbia University Teachers College Ed.D. dissertation, 1968.

[2]Raymond M. Hughes, *A Study of the Graduate Schools of America* (Oxford, Ohio: Miami University Press), 1925.

[3]Higgins polishes off the work of Cattell in part of one sentence, as follows. "By this time James McKeen Cattell, a pioneer in the field of measurement, had written a series of articles in *Science* magazine on distinguished American men of science (and their university affiliations). . . . " (p. 11).

[4]Allan M. Cartter, *An Assessment of Quality in Graduate Education* (Washington, D.C.: American Council on Education), 1966.

[5]Richard Smith and Fred E. Fiedler, "The Measurement of Scholarly Work: A Critical Review of the Literature," *Educational Record,* vol. 52, no. 3, summer, 1971, pp. 225–232.

[6]Robert T. Blackburn and Paul E. Lingenfelter, *Assessing Quality in Doctoral Programs: Criteria and Correlates of Excellence* (Ann Arbor, Mich.: Center for the Study of Higher Education), 1973.

[7]Wilbur J. Cohen, preface to Blackburn and Lingenfelter, *ibid.,* p. i.

[8]Judith K. Lawrence and Kenneth C. Green, *A Question of Quality: The Higher Education Ratings Game,* American Association for Higher Education—ERIC Research Report no. 5 (Washington, D.C.: American Association for Higher Education), 1980.

[9]Thus Smith and Fiedler write, "The earliest significant attempts to measure the performance of academic departments were undertaken by R.M. Hughes" (*ibid.,* p. 225). Blackburn and Lingenfelter write, "The most widely known, heralded, and criticized evaluations of doctoral programs have been the reputational studies. Hughes (1925) conducted the first of these in the 20's" (*ibid.,* p. 3). Lawrence and Green refer to "Hughes' pioneering rating study in 1925. . . . " (*ibid.,* p. 2). They refer again to his "pioneering reputational study of graduate programs" (*ibid.,* p. 4).

[10]Logan Wilson, foreword to Cartter, *ibid.,* p. vii.

[11]W. Patrick Dolan, *The Ranking Game: The Power of the Academic Elite* (Lincoln: University of Nebraska Printing and Duplicating Service), 1976.

[12]Arthur Levine, "Quality in Higher Education: Who Protects the Consumer?," *Chronicle of Higher Education,* vol. 21, no. 3, September 8, 1980, p. 48.

[13]"Search Reopened, Director of Public Relations," *Chronicle of Higher Education*, vol. 21, no. 15, December 1, 1980, p. 51.

[14]"The College of Idaho," *Chronicle of Higher Education*, vol. 21, no. 23, February 17, 1981, p. 33.

[15]"These Faces Are the Key to Your Future," *Chronicle of Higher Education*, vol. 21, no. 7, October 6, 1980, p. 9.

[16]"In Time, Every Great City Has a Great University," *U.S. News and World Report*, January 21, 1980, un-numbered page.

[17]"Slippery Rock State College," *Chronicle of Higher Education*, vol. 22, no. 12, May 11, 1981, p. 33.

[18]Dick Pothier, "Community College Gets a Real Campus," *Philadelphia Inquirer*, July 20, 1982, p. 4BW.

[19]"Rutgers Subsidizes Prof's Condo," University of Pennsylvania *Daily Pennsylvanian*, April 23, 1984, p. 2.

[20]Cartter, *ibid.*, p. 22.

[21]Kenneth D. Roose and Charles J. Andersen, *A Rating of Graduate Programs* (Washington, D.C.: American Council on Education), 1970, p. 40.

[22]See Malcolm G. Scully, "The Well-Known Universities Lead in Rating of Faculties' Reputations," *Chronicle of Higher Education*, vol. 19, no. 17, January 15, 1979, p. 6.

[23]Lyle V. Jones, Gardner Lindzey, and Porter E. Coggeshall (ed. by), *An Assessment of Research-Doctorate Programs in the United States: Humanities* (Washington, D.C.: National Academy Press), 1982, pp. 70–71.

[24]Dick Pothier, "President-elect is Banking on Temple's Strengths," *Philadelphia Inquirer*, December 19, 1981, p. 11A.

[25]William Trombley, "New USC President Wants the Power at the Top," *Los Angeles Times*, pt. 2, February 17, 1981, p. 3.

[26]David S. Webster, "America's Highest Ranked Graduate Schools, 1925–1982," *Change*, vol. 15, no. 4, May/June, 1983, p. 25.

[27]Charles Hillinger, "Howard University: Seedbed of Black Leadership," *Los Angeles Times*, pt. 1A, March 16, 1980, p. 7.

[28]Jonathan R. Cole and James A. Lipton, "The Reputations of American Medical Schools," *Social Forces*, vol. 55, no. 3, March, 1977, pp. 669–671.

CHAPTER TWO

[1]That is when Hayward Keniston published his reputational ranking as part of *Graduate Study and Research in the Arts and Sciences at the University of Pennsylvania* (Philadelphia: University of Pennsylvania Press), 1959.

[2]For a discussion of the role played by *American Men of Science* in the origins of academic quality rankings, see David S. Webster, "A Note on a Very Early Academic Quality Ranking by James McKeen Cattell," *Journal of the History of the Behavioral Sciences*, vol. 20, no. 2, April, 1984, pp. 180–183.

[3]There are, of course, many legitimate reasons for criticizing quality rankings

independent of how well one's own institution is rated by them. For a discussion of some of these reasons, see David S. Webster, "Advantages and Disadvantages of Methods of Assessing Quality," *Change*, vol. 13, no. 7, October, 1981, pp. 20–24.

[4]Claude Welch, *Graduate Education in Religion: A Critical Appraisal* (Missoula: University of Montana Press), 1971.

[5]There have been at least two modern attempts to stratify historically black colleges into three or four levels according to their academic quality, although in both of them the information about which colleges were assigned to which levels has not been made public. See A. J. Jaffe, Walter Adams, and Sandra G. Meyers, *Negro Higher Education in the 1960's* (New York: Praeger), 1968, pp. 233–242.

[6]One recent attempt to rank colleges by type was reported by Lucia Solorzano with Barbara E. Quick in "Rating the Colleges," *U.S. News and World Report*, November 28, 1983, pp. 41–46; 48. Still, this rating could not have been very useful to students wishing to select a college because the categories into which it grouped institutions differed so widely from the categories in which students normally think of colleges. The magazine's categories were as follows: national universities, national liberal arts colleges, regional liberal arts colleges, comprehensive universities, and smaller comprehensive universities. Very few students, however, decide to choose a college from among only, for example, "comprehensive universities" or "smaller comprehensive universities." This ranking's usefulness was also limited by its strange assignment of institutions to categories. Many of its "regional liberal arts colleges" were universities, including San Diego State University, which enrolls more than 30,000 students, of whom more than 6,000 are graduate students; many of its "comprehensive universities" and almost all its "smaller comprehensive universities" were liberal arts colleges.

[7]Lyle V. Jones, Gardner Lindzey, and Porter E. Coggeshall (ed. by), *An Assessment of Research-Doctorate Programs in the United States*, 5 vols. (Washington, D.C.: National Academy Press), 1982.

[8]For a discussion of stability and change in the reputation of American Ph.D.-granting universities since 1925, see David S. Webster, "America's Highest Ranked Graduate Schools, 1925–1982," *Change*, vol. 15, no. 4, May/June, 1983, pp. 14–24.

[9]Since very few modern academic quality rankings have rated either undergraduate departments or "whole" institutions, either on the graduate or undergraduate level, scholars have sometimes fallen back on the quality rankings published by Jack Gourman, some of which do purport to rate undergraduate education and "whole" institutions. The many bizarre features of Gourman's rankings, though, only one of which is his stout refusal to say how he arrives at them, make them of little or no use as measures of academic quality.

[10]Stephen Sargent Visher, *Scientists Starred, 1903-1943, in "American Men of Science"* (Baltimore: Johns Hopkins University Press), 1947.

[11]Robert H. Knapp and Hubert B. Goodrick, *Origins of American Scientists* (New York: Russell and Russell), 1952.

[12]Robert H. Knapp and Joseph J. Greenbaum, *The Younger American Scholar: His Collegiate Origins* (Chicago: University of Chicago Press), 1953.

[13]Robert H. Knapp, *The Origins of American Humanistic Scholars* (Englewood Cliffs, N.J.: Prentice-Hall), 1964.

[14]Raymond M. Hughes, *A Study of the Graduate Schools of America* (Oxford, Ohio: Miami University Press), 1925 and "Report of the Committee on Graduate Instruction," *Educational Record,* vol. 15, no. 2, April, 1934, pp. 192–234.

[15]Keniston, *ibid.*

[16]Allan M. Cartter, *An Assessment of Quality in Graduate Education* (Washington, D.C.: American Council on Education), 1966.

[17]Kenneth D. Roose and Charles J. Andersen, *A Rating of Graduate Programs* (Washington, D.C.: American Council on Education), 1970.

[18]Rebecca Zames Margulies and Peter M. Blau, "America's Leading Professional Schools," *Change,* vol. 5, no. 9, November, 1973, pp. 21–27 and Blau and Margulies, "The Reputations of American Professional Schools," *Change,* vol. 6, no. 10, December/January, 1974–'75, pp. 42–47.

[19]Ladd and Lipset's ranking is displayed in Malcolm G. Scully's "The Well-Known Universities Lead in Rating of Faculties' Reputations," *Chronicle of Higher Education,* vol. 19, no. 17, January 15, 1979, pp. 6–7.

[20]Jones, Lindzey, and Coggeshall (ed. by), *ibid.*

CHAPTER THREE

[1]Most of these studies included a small number of women, with some exceptions like Galton's *English Men of Science* and Maclean's *Where We Get Our Best Men,* which were based entirely on eminent males, yet their authors commonly referred, even in studies based partly upon women subjects, to "men of genius," "men of science," or whatever. Galton, for example, who in *Hereditary Genius* did discuss a small number of eminent women, including the authors Maria Edgeworth, Charlotte Brontë, Madame de Sévigné, and Madame de Staël, nevertheless referred throughout this book to his subjects as "eminent men" (p. 2), "men of eminence" (p. 3), and so on. Since both men and women of exceptional ability were included in most of these studies, their titles and their authors' frequent references to their subjects as men notwithstanding, reference will be made, throughout, to the subjects of those studies that were based upon both sexes as studies of "men and women."

[2]Following the usage of Francis Galton in his *Hereditary Genius,* prefatory chapter to the edition of 1892 (London: Watts and Co.), 1950, the contributors to this debate used the word "genius" not necessarily to describe someone of great intellectual powers, but rather anyone with "an ability that was exceptionally high, and at the same time inborn" (p. viii), "an equivalent for natural ability" (p. ix). Under such a broad definition, Galton included judges, military officers, clergymen, and even outstanding oarsmen and wrestlers among his people of "genius." Though later authors contributing to this debate did not generally go as far as Galton in including military officers and athletes in their studies of "genius," they did include many people of ability, talent, and learning whom today would scarcely be considered geniuses. Galton himself admitted that the title of his book "seems apt to mislead,

and if it could be altered now, it should appear as *Hereditary Ability*" (*ibid.*, p. ix).

[3]Candolle was the famous son of an even more famous father, Augustin Pyrame de Candolle (1778–1841). He eventually succeeded his father in the chair of natural history at the University of Geneva, and even, with *his* own son, labored to complete one of his father's unfinished botanical works. It is not clear whether the close parallel between the botanical careers of Candolle *père et fils* should be attributed to the influence of heredity, environment, or both.

[4]Both quotations are from Candolle, *Histoire des Sciences et des Savants depuis Deux Siècles* (Geneva: H. Georg), 1873, pp. 196–197. (Translated by David S. Webster).

[5]*National Union Catalog, Pre-1956 Imprints*, vol. 426 (London: Mansell Information/Publishing), 1976, p. 567.

[6]Alfred Odin, *Genèse des Grands Hommes: Gens de Lettres Francais Modernes*, vol. 1 (Paris: H. Welter), 1895, p. 527, (Translated by David S. Webster).

[7]Lester F. Ward, *Applied Sociology* (Boston: Ginn and Co.), 1906, p. 229.

[8]*Ibid.*, p. 250.

[9]Ward, whose *Applied Sociology* contains an extended and, for the most part, judicious discussion of some of the leading participants in the debate, although he tends towards the panegyrical in his discussion of Odin, wrote in that book that "there is an almost universal belief that education has no influence in the production of genius or even of success" (p. 215).

[10]Francis Galton, "Hereditary Talent and Character," *MacMillan's Magazine*, vol. 12, no. 68, June, 1865, pp. 157–166; "Hereditary Talent and Character," Second Paper, *MacMillan's Magazine*, vol. 12, no. 70, August, 1865, pp. 318–327.

[11]Galton's definition of the terms was as follows. "Nature is all that a man brings with himself into the world; nurture is every influence from without that affects him after birth." See Galton, *English Men of Science: Their Nature and Nurture* (London: Frank Cass and Co.), 1960, p. 12.

[12]Victor L. Hilts, *A Guide to Francis Galton's English Men of Science*, Transactions of the American Philosophical Society, New Series, vol. 65, pt. 5 (Philadelphia: American Philosophical Society), 1975, p. 3.

[13]Galton, *English Men of Science, ibid.*, p. 1.

[14]*Ibid.*, p. 236.

[15]*National Union Catalog, Pre-1956 Imprints*, vol. 492 (London: Mansell Information/Publishing), 1977, pp. 263–272.

[16]Théodule Ribot, *L'Hérédité Psychologique*, 2nd ed. (Paris: Germer Ballière), 1882. Quoted by Ward in *Applied Sociology, ibid.*, pp. 215–216. (The emphases appear to be Ribot's.)

[17]Galton, *Hereditary Genius, ibid.*, p. 14.

[18]"Senior Wranglers," *Cornhill Magazine*, vol. 45, 1882, p. 233.

[19]James Sully, "The Education of Genius," *English Illustrated Magazine*, vol. 8, January, 1891, p. 321.

[20]Havelock Ellis, *A Study of British Genius* (London: Hurst and Blackett), 1904, pp. 145–146.

[21]Walter G. Bowerman, *Studies in Genius* (New York: Philosophical Library), 1947, p. 87.

[22]Alick Henry Herbert Maclean, *Where We Get Our Best Men* (London: Simpkin, Marshall, Hamilton, Kent and Co.), 1900.

[23]*Ibid.*, p. 44. These figures add up to 1230, because when a man had attended more than one university, Maclean counted both or all these universities.

[24]Today, when it is nearly universally agreed that both nature and nurture are vitally important in forming people of exceptional abilities and nearly everyone else, it seems odd that most of the early participants in the debate—until about 1910—believed that one or the other was almost entirely responsible. By World War I, though, most sociologists had concluded that both nature and nurture were important in "producing" geniuses, as Edwin Leavitt Clarke pointed out in *American Men of Letters: Their Nature and Nurture,* Columbia Studies in History, Economics and Public Law, vol. 168, no. 1 (New York: Columbia University Press), 1916, pp. 18–19.

[25]It is probably not a coincidence that in turn-of-the-century America, under the strong influence of social Darwinism, many of the forerunners of today's academic quality rankings ranked *all* the schools in a discipline, even (especially?) the worst ones. For example, the American Medical Association's Council on Medical Education and several accrediting organizations for professional schools often rated all the schools in their respective fields A, B, C, and so on, based upon their purported quality. Indeed, their keenest interest was, if anything, in the lowest-rated schools in each field. The professional associations and accrediting organizations generally wanted these low-ranking schools either to evolve into fitter institutions or to "die."

Today, by contrast, accrediting organizations, both those responsible for professional fields and those responsible for all colleges and universities in a geographical region, almost invariably publish only a single list of "approved" schools and do not publicly stratify or classify the schools they are accrediting. Though they do sometimes place schools on probation, accredit them on "condition," or serve notice that the school will be reevaluated, because of its shortcomings, after a shorter period of time has elapsed than customary, all these sanctions are generally placed on the school privately, not in published lists of accredited schools. So the worst schools on contemporary lists of accredited institutions are not generally singled out for obloquy, as they were on earlier lists published by accrediting agencies. On rare occasions, though, when a school is considered to be particularly inadequate or especially refractory in its dealings with an accrediting agency, it still may be publicly censured. Thus, in 1963 the North Central Association placed Iowa's Parsons College, which had ignored many of the Association's previous requests for major changes, on "public probation." See James D. Koerner, *The Parsons College Bubble: A Tale of Higher Education in America* (New York: Basic Books), 1970, p. 173.

Similarly, modern academic quality rankings generally rank only the best, or at least the better schools in an academic discipline. The most recently published multidisciplinary ranking was unusual in listing almost all the doctoral-granting programs in each of 32 disciplines. However, as if to atone for this indiscretion, its compilers listed departments in each field in alphabetical order, not by "quality," making it extremely difficult for readers to ascertain where any department ranked. See Lyle V. Jones, Gardner Lindzey, and Porter E. Coggeshall (ed. by), *An Assess-*

ment of Research-Doctorate Programs in the United States, 5 vols. (Washington, D.C.: National Academy Press), 1982.

[26]The cities are listed in Ward, *ibid.,* p. 212.

[27]*Report of the Commissioner of Education for the Year 1899–1900,* vol. 1 (Washington, D.C.: Government Printing Office), 1901, table 1, p. 1168.

[28]Friedrich Paulsen, *The German Universities and University Study,* translated by Frank Thilly, appendix (London: Longmans, Green and Co.), 1906, p. 443.

[29]*Report of the Commissioner of Education for the Year 1900–1901,* vol. 2 (Washington, D.C.: Government Printing Office), 1902, p. 1611. Of course, France had, in addition to its universities, institutions such as the *Ecole Pratique des Hautes Etudes,* the *Ecole Polytechnique,* and the *Ecole Normale Superieure.* Great Britain had some technical institutions and also colleges for women, art schools, training colleges for elementary school teachers, and others. Germany had, *c.* 1910, in addition to its universities, several other types of institutions, including ten technical schools and special schools for the study of mining, forestry, agriculture, and commerce, plus schools for the study of veterinary and military science.

[30]Fritz Ringer, professor of history at Boston University, pointed this out in a personal communication.

[31]Abraham Flexner, *Medical Education in the United States and Canada: A Report to the Carnegie Foundation for the Advancement of Teaching,* Bulletin no. 4 (New York: Carnegie Foundation for the Advancement of Teaching), 1910, p. 158.

[32]Abraham Flexner, *Medical Education in Europe: A Report to the Carnegie Foundation for the Advancement of Teaching,* Bulletin no. 6 (New York: Carnegie Foundation for the Advancement of Teaching), 1912, pp. 308–309.

[33]Fritz Ringer made this observation in a personal communication. For the same reason, today American professors of English, history, philosophy, and other disciplines in which there are no standardized licensing examinations are probably judged more—five, ten, or even twenty years after receiving their Ph.D.—by the quality of the institutions from which they earned it than are, say, lawyers, doctors, and dentists judged by where they received their law, medical, and dentistry degrees.

[34]For example, to illustrate this point with an example from the area of graduate education, a 1902 study commissioned by the Association of American Universities compared students at American universities who had received their Ph.D.'s from 1896–1901 with those at German universities who had received doctoral degrees in the same period. It found that "about two-thirds of the German doctors of Philosophy have studied at more than one university, while in America less than one-third have migrated." See E.A. Birge, "Report on Statistics Concerning the Migration of Graduate Students," Association of American Universities, *Journal of Proceedings and Addresses of the Third Annual Conference* (Chicago: Association of American Universities), 1902, p. 45.

CHAPTER FOUR

[1]*Report of the Commissioner of Education for the Year 1871* (Washington, D.C.: Government Printing Office), 1872, table 9, pp. 638–649.

[2]*Ibid.*, table 10, pp. 650–653.

[3]Samuel P. Capen, "College 'Lists' and Surveys Published by the Bureau of Education," *School and Society*, vol. 6, July 14, 1917, p. 37.

[4]*Report of the Commissioner of Education for the Year 1885-'86* (Washington, D.C.: Government Printing Office), 1888, tables 33–35, pp. 462–464.

[5]*Report of the Commissioner of Education for the Year 1886-87* (Washington, D.C.: Government Printing Office), table 43, pp. 658–659.

[6]*Ibid.*, table 44, pp. 660–661.

[7]*Ibid.*, p. 656.

[8]*Report of the Commissioner of Education for the Year 1888-89*, vol. 2 (Washington, D.C.: Government Printing Office), 1891, pp. 1090–1091.

[9]*Report of the Commissioner of Education for the Year 1889-90*, vol. 2 (Washington, D.C.: Government Printing Office), 1893, table 8, pp. 788–789.

[10]Up to and including the 1889–90 *Report*, the reports also listed the nation's state universities separately from all the other colleges and universities. But state universities were all grouped together in a single list, alphabetically by state, and the *Report* made no attempt to distinguish among them by quality or to compare them in quality with the leading private comprehensive institutions.

[11]*Report of the Commissioner of Education for the Year 1886-87, ibid.*, p. 642.

[12]*Ibid.*, p. 642.

[13]This institution no longer exists.

[14]For the list, see the *Report of the Commissioner of Education for the Year 1886-87, ibid.*, table 42, Division A, p. 645.

[15]*Report of the Commissioner of Education for the Year 1888-89*, vol. 2, *ibid.*, 1891, p. 1070.

[16]*Report of the Commissioner of Education for the Year 1890-'91*, vol. 2, (Washington, D.C.: Government Printing Office), 1894, p. 831.

[17]*Report of the Commissioner of Education for the Year 1889-90*, vol. 2, *ibid.*, table 1, pp. 1572–73.

[18]*Report of the Commissioner of Education for the Year Ended June 30, 1909*, vol. 2 (Washington, D.C.: Government Printing Office), 1910, table 71, pp. 978–979.

[19]Capen, *ibid.*, p. 37.

[20]The last tables listing them were published in the *Report of the Commissioner of Education for the Year Ended June 30, 1910*, vol. 2 (Washington, D.C.: Government Printing Office), 1911, table 60, pp. 962–963 and table 61, pp. 964–965. After that year, the names of exclusively women's colleges and other colleges and universities were published together in a single, undifferentiated list, without any attempt to stratify them by quality.

[21]In 1886–87, for example, only seven of the 159 women's colleges listed, or 4%, were placed in Division A. See the *Report of the Commissioner of Education for the Year 1886-87, ibid.*, table 42, Division A, p. 645 and table 2, Division B, pp. 646–655. By the

Report for 1909–10, many women's colleges had closed, and some had been elevated to Division A, but still only 16 of the 108 women's colleges (15%) were placed in Division A. This was much more conservative "grading" than that of the professional associations like the American Medical Association's Council on Medical Education, which over the years tended to classify increasingly larger percentages of schools as "A" schools to the point where nearly every single school was rated "A."

[22]*Report of the Commissioner of Education for the Year Ended June 30, 1911,* vol. 2 (Washington, D.C.: Government Printing Office), 1912, p. 884.

[23]*Ibid.,* p. 884.

[24]After this episode agencies of the federal government very seldom sought to accredit institutions and to publish multilevel stratifications of institutions of higher learning. An exception, though, was the United States Department of Agriculture's long-lasting practice of accrediting both American and foreign veterinary schools. This custom began in 1908 because the Department of Agriculture was then the major employer of veterinarians and so was naturally concerned with the quality of their veterinary education. Soon the Department of Agriculture was classifying veterinary schools, as other accrediting organizations did in that era, into three classes of quality, labelled A, B, and C, and it continued to accredit veterinary schools until 1961. Today, in deciding which schools to certify as eligible to participate in programs involving veterans' allowances, federally insured student loans, and other public programs, the federal government generally refrains from making its own lists of accredited institutions and depends mostly on the lists formulated by other agencies.

[25]P. P. Claxton, "An Explanatory Statement in Regard to 'A Classification of Universities and Colleges with Reference to Bachelor's Degrees,'" (Washington, D.C.: U.S. Bureau of Education), no. 501, 1912. It is reprinted in Richard Wayne Lykes, *Higher Education and the United States Office of Education (1867–1953)* (Washington, D.C.: U.S. Office of Education), 1975, pp. 227–237. For a discussion of why the deans wanted an outsider to conduct the survey, see p. 229. Their reasoning was similar to that employed by the officers of the Carnegie Foundation for the Advancement of Teaching in 1908 when they engaged Abraham Flexner, who was not a physician and had no medical school training, to study medical schools in America, Canada, and Newfoundland.

[26]Fred J. Kelly *et al., Collegiate Accreditation by Agencies within States,* Bulletin 1940, no. 3 (Washington, D.C.: Government Printing Office), 1940, p. 17.

[27]Kendric Charles Babcock, "Higher Education in the United States," *Report of the Commissioner of Education for the Year Ended June 30, 1911,* vol. 2, *ibid.,* pp. 43–44.

[28]Babcock, "A Classification of Universities and Colleges with Reference to Bachelor's Degrees" (Washington, D.C.: Government Printing Office), 1911, in Lykes, *ibid.,* p. 214.

[29]*Ibid.,* p. 216.

[30]*Ibid.,* p. 216.

[31]*Ibid.,* p. 216.

[32]*Ibid.,* p. 216.

[33]In addition to his overall four or five part stratification system, Babcock often

limited the rating given a school either to only some of its programs or to its recent degrees. So, for example, in the case of more than 40 schools he placed in class II and two schools in class III, Babcock noted that since they "do their soundest and most efficient work in classical lines . . . ," they should be regarded as belonging in class II only for their "traditional classical or distinctively arts course" (*ibid.*, p. 215).

Babcock made similar limitations in classifying some science and engineering schools. While he placed Yale in class I, he put its Sheffield Scientific School in class II, without even a star. Similarly, Babcock placed Purdue in class I, but only for science and engineering; he placed Rensselaer Polytechnic Institute in class I for civil engineering only and Stevens Institute of Technology in class I for mechanical engineering only. (In the case of these three institutions, unlike that of Yale and its Sheffield Scientific School, Babcock did not indicate what class the "rest" of the institution belonged in.) Babcock also placed some schools in a classification with the warning that this classification pertained only for their recent degree recipients. So, for example, in placing Mills College (California) and Monmouth College (Illinois) in class II, Babcock said that this rating applied only for these schools' "recent degrees." Sometimes he was more specific than that. He placed the Normal College of the City of New York and the New York State Normal College in class II only for students who had received degrees since 1905, and he placed Ohio Northern University in class III only for those who had received degrees from it since 1910. Interestingly, Babcock did not place any school in a class with the proviso that the institution belonged in that high class only for alumni who had graduated *before* a certain date.

[34]George F. Zook and M. E. Haggerty, *The Evaluation of Higher Institutions, I. Principles of Accrediting Higher Institutions* (Chicago: University of Chicago Press), 1936, p. 21.

[35]Claxton, "An Explanatory Statement . . . ," in Lykes, *ibid.*, pp. 232–233.

[36]*Ibid.*, p. 50. Lykes has pointed out in correspondence with the author that Hardy, although he professed "sympathy with the great work of the U.S. Department of Education," was unable to get the name of that organization straight. Since 1870, it had been called the United States *Bureau* of Education.

[37]Claxton, "An Explanatory Statement . . . ," in Lykes, *ibid.*, pp. 48–49.

[38]*Ibid.*, p. 233.

[39]*Ibid.*, p. 231. At least, this was Claxton's public posture. In notes that he prepared many years later for a biographer's use, he wrote about the uproar caused by this classification, "the trouble was that it was too nearly correct." See Charles Lee Lewis, *Philander Priestley Claxton: Crusader for Public Education* (Knoxville: University of Tennessee Press), 1948, p. 173.

[40]Quoted in Lykes, *ibid.*, p. 234.

[41]*Ibid.*, p. 233.

[42]*Ibid.*, p. 233.

[43]*Ibid.*, p. 235.

[44]Personal correspondence from Frank G. Dickey to the author.

[45]Lykes, *ibid.*, p. 51.

[46]Jennings B. Saunders, "The United States Office of Education and Accreditation,"

in Lloyd E. Blauch (ed. by), *Accreditation in Higher Education* (Washington, D.C.: Government Printing Office), 1959, p. 18.

[47]Capen, "College 'Lists' . . . ," *ibid.*, p. 39.

[48]William Craig Smyser, "Our First Fifty Years," in Clifford L. Constance (comp. by), *Historical Review of the Association* (n.p.: American Association of Collegiate Registrars and Admissions Officers), 1972, p. 11.

[49]Allan Cartter, quoted in W. Patrick Dolan, *The Ranking Game: The Power of the Academic Elite* (Lincoln: University of Nebraska Printing and Duplicating Service), 1976, p. 26.

[50]Babcock, "A Classification . . . ," in Lykes, *ibid.*, p. 216.

CHAPTER FIVE

[1]The Council on Medical Education's early work has been discussed by Arthur Dean Bevan, its first chairman, in "Cooperation in Medical Education and Medical Service," *Journal of the American Medical Association*, vol. 90, no. 15, April 14, 1928, pp. 1173–1177. Victor Johnson traced its history from 1904 to 1947 in "The Council on Medical Education and Hospitals" in Morris Fishbein (ed. by), *A History of the American Medical Association, 1847 to 1947* (Philadelphia: W.B. Saunders Co.), 1947, pp. 887–922. In 1959, Herman G. Weiskotten extended the history of the Council to 1959. See Victor Johnson and Herman G. Weiskotten, *A History of the Council on Medical Education and Hospitals of the American Medical Association* (Chicago: Council on Medical Education and Hospitals), 1960?

[2]Interestingly, Northwestern, whose graduates had the second highest pass rate of the 42 medical schools, did not especially impress Abraham Flexner when he visited it five years later. While praising a few of its features, he lamented that it lacked adequate pedagogical control over some of its clinical facilities, that its admissions requirements were "more or less nominal," with advanced standing being granted "to students from decidedly inferior schools, some of them among the worst institutions in the country," and that its pharmacology and chemistry laboratories were "mediocre." See Flexner, *Medical Education in the United States and Canada: A Report to the Carnegie Foundation for the Advancement of Teaching*, Bulletin no. 4 (New York: Carnegie Foundation for the Advancement of Teaching), 1910, pp. 208–209.

Of course, because the licensing board examinations differed in difficulty from state to state, the outstanding performance of Northwestern's graduates may well have been because many of them took the exams in states with low flunk rates. It is likely that many of them took the exam in Illinois, where Northwestern is located, and, indeed, of the eleven states in which 100 or more candidates took the exam in 1904, the state of Illinois had the third highest pass rate. (See "State Board Examinations During 1904," *Journal of the American Medical Association*, vol. 44, no. 18, May 6, 1905, p. 1454.) It could be argued that the reason why some states had higher pass rates than others was not because their examinations were easier but because those who sat for the examination in those states were better prepared.

This argument is not convincing, though, as an explanation of Illinois' exceptionally high pass rate. In 1910, six years after the 1904 state licensing exams, Flexner listed all 18 of Illinois' medical schools as located in Chicago (Flexner, *ibid.*, pp. 207–216). He went on to state that "the city of Chicago is in respect to medical education the plague spot of the country") and that of Chicago's fourteen under-graduate medical schools, "the majority exist and prepare candidates for the Illinois state board examinations in unmistakable contravention of law and state board rules." Since every one of Illinois' medical schools was located in Chicago, Flexner's "plague spot of the country" in medical education, and since many of these schools' graduates undoubtedly took the examination in Illinois, the state where they had attended medical school, the great success rate of the candidates taking the Illinois licensing exam clearly seems to be due more to the Illinois' medical examiners' lax standards than to the exam takers' superb medical education.

[3]"State Board Examinations During 1904," *ibid.*, p. 1455.

[4]N. P. Colwell, "Council on Medical Education of the American Medical Association," *Journal of the American Medical Association*, vol. 48, no. 20, May 18, 1907, p. 1702.

[5]*Ibid.*, pp. 1704–1705.

[6]*Ibid.*, p. 1704.

[7]*Ibid.*, p. 1702.

[8]Johnson and Weiskotten, *ibid.*, p. 9.

[9]Henry S. Pritchett, "The Classification of American Medical Schools," *Proceedings of the Association of American Medical Schools*, vol. 25, 1915, p. 14.

[10]*Ibid.*, p. 13.

[11]*Ibid.*, p. 17.

[12]*Ibid.*, p. 18.

[13]Fred J. Kelly *et al.*, *Collegiate Accreditation by Agencies within States*, Bulletin 1940 (Washington, D.C.: Government Printing Office), 1940, p. 89.

[14]*Laws (Abstract) and Board Rulings Regulating the Practice of Medicine in the United States and Elsewhere*, 19th ed. (Chicago: American Medical Association), 1912, pp. 168–175.

[15]*Laws (Abstract) and Board Rulings Regulating the Practice of Medicine in the United States and Elsewhere*, 20th ed. (Chicago: American Medical Association), 1913, pp. 175–181.

[16]Pritchett, *ibid.*, p. 15.

[17]*Ibid.*, p. 15.

[18]Bevan, *ibid.*, p. 1176.

[19]See "Medical Education in the United States," *Journal of the American Medical Association*, vol. 97, no. 9, August 29, 1931, table 1, "Statistics of Medical Colleges in the United States and Canada," pp. 618–619.

[20]William J. Gies, *Dental Education in the United States and Canada: A Report to the Carnegie Foundation for the Advancement of Teaching*, Bulletin no. 19 (New York: Carnegie Foundation for the Advancement of Teaching), 1926. For a discussion of the Council's early work in classifying dental schools, see pp. 104–111.

[21]*Ibid.*, pp. 109–110.

[22]John G. Hervey, "Legal Education: I. Accreditation by the American Bar

Association," in Lloyd E. Blauch (ed. by), *Accreditation in Higher Education* (Washington, D.C.: Government Printing Office), 1959, p. 133.

[23]William Greenspon, "Optometric Education," in Blauch, *ibid.,* p. 169.

[24]W. Earl Armstrong, "Teacher Education," in Blauch, *ibid.,* pp. 203–204.

[25]Kelly *et al., ibid.,* p. 89.

[26]As Dr. Colwell, Secretary of the Council on Medical Education, said in 1915, "when all medical schools become high grade it will not be necessary to classify them" (N. P. Colwell, "Discussion," in Pritchett, *ibid.,* p. 22.)

[27]A parallel situation is that of some regulatory agencies which, originally established to protect the general public from the abuses of an industry, wind up protecting the industry from the wrath of the general public.

[28]North Central Association of Colleges and Secondary Schools, "Statement of Policy Relative to the Accrediting of Institutions of Higher Education," in George F. Zook and M. E. Haggerty, *The Evaluation of Higher Institutions I. Principles of Accrediting Higher Institutions* (Chicago: University of Chicago Press), 1936, pp. 149; 151.

CHAPTER SIX

[1]Most material for this section is based on the Carnegie Foundation for the Advancement of Teaching's *Third Annual Report of the President and Treasurer* (New York: Carnegie Foundation for the Advancement of Teaching), 1908, pp. 172–177.

[2]The states under the auspices of the Methodist Episcopal Church, South ranged as far north as Virginia, as far south as Florida, and as far west as Texas and Oklahoma.

[3]Units of the Carnegie Foundation were those in certain specified subjects recommended by that organization as useful preparation, compared to other subjects taught in secondary schools, for college work.

[4]A "conditioned" student was one admitted to college "conditionally" because he or she had not met the college's entrance requirements in one or more areas. Students were generally "conditioned" because either they had not completed a full high school course of 14–16 units or they had finished such a course but had not completed all the specific subjects a particular college required for admission.

[5]Most material for this section is based on the Carnegie Foundation for the Advancement of Teaching's *Third Annual Report.....* *ibid.,* pp. 100–101.

[6]*Ibid.,* pp. 100–101.

[7]*Patterson's College and School Directory of the United States and Canada,* comp. and ed. by Homer L. Patterson (Chicago: American Educational Company), 1910, pp. 484–485.

[8]CFAT, *Fourth Annual Report of the President and of the Treasurer* (New York: Carnegie Foundation for the Advancement of Teaching), 1909, p. 177.

[9]A good early source for the history of state accreditation organizations is Fred J. Kelly *et al., Collegiate Accreditation by Agencies within States,* U. S. Office of Education Bulletin 1940, no. 3 (Washington, D. C.: Government Printing Office), 1940. A short

overview is provided by Theresa Birch Wilkins, "Accreditation in the States," in Lloyd E. Blauch (ed. by), *Accreditation in Higher Education* (Washington, D.C.: Government Printing Office), 1959, pp. 31–41.

[10]Wilkins in Blauch, *ibid.,* p. 31.

[11]*Ibid.,* pp. 31–39.

[12]*Ibid.,* p. 31.

[13]*Ibid.,* p. 178.

[14]*Ibid.,* p. 178.

[15]*Ibid.,* p. 178.

[16]*Ibid.,* p. 180.

[17]*Ibid.,* p. 34.

[18]*Ibid.,* p. 34.

[19]*Ibid.,* p. 34.

CHAPTER SEVEN

[1]For a detailed history of Phi Beta Kappa, especially in its first century, 1776–1876, see Oscar M. Voorhees, *The History of Phi Beta Kappa* (New York: Crown Publishers), 1945. This book largely ignores the impact Phi Beta Kappa had on American life and culture, concentrating instead on the minutiae of the early history of Phi Beta Kappa's various chapters. For a very brief recent description and history of Phi Beta Kappa, see *Baird's Manual of American College Fraternities* (ed. by John Robson), 19th ed. (Menasha, Wis.: Baird's Manual Foundation), 1977, pp. 5; 698–703.

[2]Voorhees, *The History of Phi Beta Kappa, ibid.,* p. 56.

[3]*Ibid.,* p. 256.

[4]*Baird's Manual of American College Fraternities, ibid.,* p. 698.

[5]*Ibid.,* p. 5.

[6]Voorhees, *The History of Phi Beta Kappa, ibid.,* p. 232.

[7]*Ibid.,* p. 700.

[8]*Ibid.,* p. 700.

CHAPTER EIGHT

[1]The main source for this chapter is Marion Talbot and Lois Kimball Mathews Rosenberry, *The History of the American Association of University Women, 1881–1931* (Boston: Houghton Mifflin Co.), 1931, especially chapter 6, "Expansion by the Admission of Institutions," pp. 63–94.

[2]They were Boston University, Cornell University, the University of Michigan, Oberlin College, Smith College, Vassar College, Wellesley College, and the University of Wisconsin.

[3]John F. Nevins, *A Study of the Organization and Operation of Voluntary Accrediting Agencies,* Catholic University of America Educational Research Monographs, vol. 22, no. 3, May, 1959, p. 13.

[4]Talbot and Rosenberry, *ibid.,* p. 71.

[5]*Ibid.*, p. 71.

[6]*Ibid.*, p. 72.

[7]*Ibid.*, pp. 75–77.

[8]*Ibid.*, p. 76.

[9]*Ibid.*, p. 76.

[10]*Ibid.*, p. 76.

[11]Fred J. Kelly *et al., Collegiate Accreditation by Agencies within States,* Bulletin 1940, no. 3 (Washington, D.C.: Government Printing Office), 1940, p. 11.

[12]*Ibid.*, pp. 11–12.

CHAPTER NINE

[1]For a good description of the early years of the General Education Board's benefactions to colleges and universities, see [Abraham Flexner], *The General Education Board: An Account of its Activities, 1902–1914* (New York: General Education Board), 1915. Though the book bears no author's name, it was written by Abraham Flexner, then the Board's Assistant Secretary (see Flexner, *An Autobiography* [New York: Simon and Schuster], 1960, pp. 135–136). For a later account, bringing the history of the Board's benefactions to colleges and universities up to about 1960, see Raymond B. Fosdick, *Adventure in Giving: The Story of the General Education Board* (New York: Harper and Row), 1962. A slightly later work giving a final summary of the Board's activities, written by its Vice-President from 1961–1964, is [Flora M. Rhind], *General Education Board: A Review and Final Report, 1902–1964* (New York: General Education Board), 1964.

[2]The General Education Board still exists today, but it is inactive.

[3]Fosdick, *ibid.*, p. 127.

[4][Flexner], *ibid.*, p. 139.

[5]*Ibid.*, "Subscriptions to Colleges by Sections," pp. 156–159.

[6]*Ibid.*, p. 133. In later years, though, the Board came to consider mostly the promise of individual institutions, instead of their geographical location. (See Fosdick, *ibid.*, p. 133.)

[7]Daniel Coit Gilman, *University Problems in the United States* (New York: Century Co.), 1898, pp. 280–281.

[8]John Corbin, *Which College for the Boy?* (Boston: Houghton, Mifflin and Co.), 1908, p. 4.

[9]*Ibid.*, p. 163.

[10]Fosdick, *ibid.*, p. 130.

[11][Flexner], *ibid.*, "Subscriptions to Colleges by Sections," pp. 156–159.

[12]Fosdick, *ibid.*, p. 131.

[13]*Ibid.*, p. 135.

CHAPTER TEN

[1]For information on the CFAT's criteria for accepting institutions for its pension plan, see its annual reports, especially volumes 1–5, which devote more attention to the Foundation's criteria and standards for admission than do most of the later volumes. Beginning with volume 2, these reports contain brief historical sketches of the institutions admitted during the previous year. These sketches provide much revealing information about what criteria the CFAT applied in deciding what schools to accept. For a brief overview of CFAT criteria, in its first few years, concerning what schools to "accept," see Howard J. Savage, *Fruit of an Impulse: Forty-Five Years of the Carnegie Foundation, 1905–1950* (New York: Harcourt, Brace and Co.), 1953, pp. 71–79. Savage, who had been Secretary of the CFAT from 1931–49, is very sympathetic to its trustees' motivations. For an account of the early years of the CFAT considerably less sympathetic to the motives and intentions of its trustees, one that concentrates on the efforts of American state universities to persuade the CFAT trustees to make their professors eligible for Carnegie pensions, see Theron F. Schlabach, *Pensions for Professors* (Madison: The State Historical Society of Wisconsin for the Department of History, University of Wisconsin), 1963.

[2]Carnegie Foundation for the Advancement of Teaching, *First Annual Report of the President and Treasurer* (New York: Carnegie Foundation for the Advancement of Teaching), 1906, p. 7.

[3]Schlabach, *ibid.*, p. 19.

[4]CFAT, *First Annual Report, ibid.*, p. 8.

[5]Schlabach argues that Carnegie actually refused to give money to sectarian schools for a different reason. He writes, "[Carnegie] declined to give to sectarian schools, but that decision probably stemmed less from the fact that sectarian schools drew support from religious bodies than from his dislike of sectarian education. . . . he had a profound distrust of theological dogmas and systems and believed that sectarian ideas interfered with the search for truth" (p. 24).

[6]CFAT, *First Annual Report, ibid.*, p. 79.

[7]*Ibid.*, p. 79.

[8]Schlabach, *ibid.*, p. 10.

[9]*Ibid.*, p. 16.

[10]This point was made by Ellen Condliffe Lagemann of Columbia University Teachers College in personal correspondence to the author.

[11]CFAT, *First Annual Report, ibid.*, p. 10.

[12]*Ibid.*, p. 11.

[13]These schools are listed in the CFAT's *First Annual Report, ibid.*, pp. 21–22. In addition, the Foundation granted pensions—and continued to do so until 1931—to a number of professors and administrators who, although not employed by any of the accepted colleges and universities, had performed "distinguished and unusual service" to higher education.

[14]Schlabach, *ibid.*, pp. 30–31.

[15]*Ibid.*, p. 30.

[16]Deciding what constituted a "denominational" college was no easy task, and the

CFAT trustees spent much time wrestling with this problem. Many of the schools ultimately accepted by the CFAT had strong historic ties with a church, but not ties that the CFAT considered to be "controlling." One unintended effect of the CFAT pension program was to cause many institutions to loosen their church ties just enough to be considered acceptable for the CFAT pension program.

[17]Interestingly, in accepting four of these five publicly-controlled institutions, the CFAT refused to accept certain parts of them. It specifically excluded the departments and schools of agriculture at Wisconsin, Minnesota, and Missouri, even while acknowledging that "the college of agriculture of the University of Wisconsin has been one of the most effective agriculture schools in the country." See the CFAT, *Fourth Annual Report of the President and of the Treasurer* (New York: Carnegie Foundation for the Advancement of Teaching), 1909, p. 101. It did so because of what it called "the lack of a consistent educational ideal among the colleges of agriculture and mechanic arts or of any well sustained effort to articulate with the general system of their states" (p. 97). The CFAT did not exclude any other departments of these universities which may have lacked consistent educational ideas and failed to articulate with the general system of education of their states at least equally much as did agricultural departments. In admitting the University of Toronto, the CFAT did not accept that university's "affiliated denominational colleges" (Savage, *ibid.*, p. 77) like Trinity University and St. Michael's College (*ibid.*, p. 32). So, unlike most of the other organizations discussed here, which either admitted or rejected entire institutions, the CFAT on occasion, especially when dealing with publicly-controlled institutions, sometimes excluded *parts* of a school.

[18]See the CFAT, *Fourth Annual Report, ibid.*, pp. 41–45. In dropping some members, the CFAT acted differently from many other organizations, like the Association of American Universities, which, once they admitted an institution to membership, stayed with it forever, even if these institutions' reputations subsequently declined, even sharply, relative to those of the other member institutions.

[19]Despite Carnegie's strong preference for aiding less than flourishing institutions, the CFAT trustees had thus accepted, as they had done with private nondenominational universities, by and large the nation's most affluent state universities (the University of Alabama being an exception), exactly those institutions whose states could most easily have funded their pension programs.

[20]For these 73 institutions, see the CFAT, *Rules for the Admission of Institutions and for the Granting of Retiring Allowances* (New York: Carnegie Foundation for the Advancement of Teaching), 1913, pp. 9–10.

[21]*Fourth Annual Report, ibid.*, pp. 86–88.

[22]*Ibid.*, p. 89.

[23]CFAT, *Fifth Annual Report of the President and of the Treasurer* (New York: Carnegie Foundation for the Advancement of Teaching), 1910, p. 17.

[24]*Ibid.*, p. 18.

[25]*Ibid.*, p. 18. The CFAT's fears that Galesburg could not support two colleges were soon realized. In 1930 Knox and Lombard merged, retaining Knox's name and campus.

CHAPTER ELEVEN

[1]Association of American Universities, *Journal of Proceedings and Addresses of the First and Second Annual Conferences* (Chicago: University of Chicago Press), 1901, p. 11.

[2]For brief overviews of the Association of American Universities' efforts to evaluate the quality of colleges and universities, see Fred J. Kelly *et al., Collegiate Accreditation by Agencies within States,* Bulletin 1940, no. 3 (Washington, D. C.: Government Printing Office), 1940, pp. 13–15; William K. Selden, "The AAU and Accreditation," *Graduate Journal,* vol. 2, no. 2, fall, 1959, pp. 325–333; and George F. Zook and M. E. Haggerty, *The Evaluation of Higher Institutions, I. Principles of Accrediting Higher Institutions* (Chicago: University of Chicago Press), 1936, pp. 33–38.

[3]C. W. Eliot *et al.,* "Report of the Special Committee on Aim and Scope of the Association," Association of American Universities, *Journal of Proceedings and Addresses of the Ninth Annual Conference* (Chicago: University of Chicago Press), 1908, p. 76.

[4]AAU, *Fourteenth Annual Conference,* 1912, p. 14.

[5]AAU, *Fifteenth Annual Conference,* 1913, p. 58.

[6]*Ibid.,* pp. 58–59.

[7]*Ibid.,* p. 59.

[8]For the complete list, see the AAU, *Fifteenth Annual Conference, ibid.,* pp. 60–62.

[9]*Ibid.,* p. 19.

[10]AAU, *Sixteenth Annual Conference,* 1914, p. 18.

[11]Richard Wayne Lykes, *Higher Education and the United States Office of Education (1867-1953)* (Washington, D. C.: U. S. Office of Education), 1975, p. 216.

[12]*Ibid.,* p. 216.

[13]AAU, *Sixteenth Annual Conference, ibid.,* p. 18.

[14]*Ibid.,* p. 18.

[15]Lykes, *ibid.,* p. 216.

[16]AAU, *Sixteenth Annual Conference, ibid.,* p. 18.

[17]Lykes, *ibid.,* p. 216.

[18]AAU, *Nineteenth Annual Conference,* 1917, pp. 102–103. In 1922, the AAU began to differentiate among the colleges and universities on its approved list according to their *type.* In that year, it divided the schools into three groups, as follows: "Universities of Complex Organization, Usually with Graduate Schools and Certain Professional and Technological Schools; Technical Institutions; Colleges Primarily Organized with Undergraduate Curricula Leading to the B.A. or B.S., in Some Cases with Strong Technological Divisions, and Occasionally a Strong Professional School" (AAU, *Twenty-fourth Annual Conference,* 1922, pp. 24–26).

[19]AAU, *Twenty-sixth Annual Conference,* 1924, p. 31.

[20]*Ibid.,* pp. 33–34.

[21]*Ibid.,* p. 32. This was not just an idle threat. In 1927, for example, the Committee on Classification of Universities and Colleges, after reviewing 19 schools already approved, recommended that Clarkson Institute of Technology (New York) and Centre College (Kentucky) be dropped from the approved list and that five other schools be warned about certain weak points. (AAU, *Twenty-ninth Annual Conference,* 1927, pp. 26–27). Despite these reexaminations of schools on its approved list, the

AAU has never removed any institution from the ranks of its own members. Charter institutions Catholic University and Clark University, for example, continue to be members to this day, even though they have declined in academic reputation relative to other AAU members and have long since been surpassed in research and graduate work, according to almost all commonly used criteria, by some institutions that are not AAU members.

[22]AAU, *Twenty-sixth Annual Conference, ibid.,* p. 33.

[23]Among the more influential of these studies were two conducted by the Carnegie Foundation for the Advancement of Teaching in the 1930s which concluded that "the data did not indicate that entrants from colleges accredited by the Association of American Universities had been more successful in graduate study than students received from other institutions...." For a discussion of these studies, see Marcia Edwards, *Studies in American Graduate Education* (New York: Carnegie Foundation for the Advancement of Teaching), 1944, pp. 1–8. (The passage quoted appears on p. 8.)

[24]Selden, *ibid.,* p. 331.

[25]For the discussion preceding the AAU's decision to end its accreditation of undergraduate programs, see AAU, *Forty-ninth Annual Conference,* 1948, pp. 13–14; 29–42.

CHAPTER TWELVE

[1]For brief overviews of the early history of the regional accrediting associations, see George F. Zook and M. E. Haggerty, *The Evaluation of Higher Institutions, I. Principles of Accrediting Higher Institutions* (Chicago: U. of Chicago Press), 1936, pp. 26–33; Fred J. Kelly *et al., Collegiate Accreditation by Agencies within States,* Bulletin 1940, pp. 20–23; and the six brief chapters, one on each regional accrediting agency, in Lloyd E. Blauch (ed. by), *Accreditation in Higher Education* (Washington, D.C.: Government Printing Office), 1959, pp. 42–73.

[2]Allan O. Pfnister, "Accreditation in the North Central Region," in Blauch, *ibid.,* p. 53.

[3]Zook and Haggerty, *ibid.,* p. 32.

CHAPTER THIRTEEN

[1]Abraham Flexner, *Medical Education in the United States and Canada: A Report to the Carnegie Foundation for the Advancement of Teaching,* Bulletin no. 4 (New York: Carnegie Foundation for the Advancement of Teaching), 1910.

[2]For some opinions along these lines, see those quoted in H. David Banta, "Abraham Flexner—a Reappraisal," *Social Science & Medicine,* vol. 5, no. 6, December, 1971, p. 655 and in Howard S. Berliner, "A Larger Perspective on the Flexner Report," *International Journal of Health Services,* vol. 5, no. 4, winter, 1975, pp. 573–574.

[3]For a good, concise summary of these pre-Flexnerian reforms of American medical education, see Saul Jarcho, "Medical Education in the United States—

1910–1956," *Journal of the Mount Sinai Hospital,* vol. 26, no. 4, July–August, 1959, pp. 339–340.

[4]Flexner, *ibid.,* pp. 11–12.

[5]E. Richard Brown, *Rockefeller Medicine Men: Medicine and Capitalism in American* (Berkeley: University of California Press), 1979, p. 154.

[6]Berliner, *ibid.,* p. 589. This article was unfair to Flexner in implying that he wished to restrict medical school entry only to those "who could afford" college and medical school. The *Flexner Report* of 1910 made it clear that Flexner wanted medical school admission to be based on intellectual ability, not affluence.

[7]Reuben A. Kessel, "Price Discrimination in Medicine," in R.H. Coase and Merton H. Miller (ed. by), *Essays in Applied Price Theory by Reuben A. Kessel* (Chicago: University of Chicago Press), 1980, p. 11. It is sometimes argued that the *Flexner Report,* influential as it undoubtedly was, has received too much credit for changing the shape of American medical education, and that the work of the American Medical Association's Council on Medical Education, which for more than 80 years has painstakingly studied and issued reports on American medical education, has received too little. There is some merit in this argument. No professional association connected with any professional field or arts and sciences discipline has done as much work, or has served to upgrade the quality of education in its field so much, as has the Council on Medical Education. Perhaps one reason why its cumulative work has received less credit than the *Flexner Report* is that, although the Council on Medical Education has issued large numbers of reports over the years, not one of them was so influential, by itself, as the *Flexner Report.* Another is that the *Flexner Report,* unlike most of the work of the Council of Medical Education, was intended for the general public and was widely discussed, after it was published, on the front pages and in the editorial sections of the nation's newspapers, (Some of the material in this note was provided by Professor William P. Longmire, Jr., Professor of Surgery, UCLA School of Medicine, in a personal communication.)

[8]Flexner himself told the story in his autobiography, *I Remember* (New York: Simon and Schuster), 1940, pp. 113–132 and then again, in almost exactly the same words, in the expanded and slightly revised version of his autobiography published 20 years later, *An Autobiography* (New York: Simon and Schuster), 1960, pp. 73–88. A good, though now dated, study of the *Flexner Report* and its influence is by Saul Jarcho, *ibid.,* pp. 339–385, especially pp. 339–352. Good, more recent treatments of the *Flexner Report* and its influence are Carleton B. Chapman, "*The Flexner Report* by Abraham Flexner," *Daedalus,* vol. 103, no. 1, winter, 1963, pp. 105–117; Martin Kaufman, *American Medical Education: The Formative Years, 1765–1910* (Westport, Conn.: Greenwood Press), 1976, pp. 167–175; and Ellen Condliffe Lagemann, *Private Power for the Public Good: A History of the Carnegie Foundation for the Advancement of Teaching* (Middletown, Conn.: Wesleyan University Press), 1983, pp. 66–74. For a feminist critique of the *Flexner Report* and its influence, see Barbara Ehrenreich and Deirdre English, *For Her Own Good: 150 Years of the Experts' Advice to Women* (Garden City, N.Y.: Doubleday), 1978, pp. 86–91.

[9]Berliner, *ibid.,* p. 587.

[10]"It will, however, be urged by weak schools that the fact that an institution is ill

manned and poorly equipped is inconclusive; that in the time devoted to the examination of a single school it is impossible to do it justice. . . . In my opinion the objection is without force. A trained observer of wide experience can go directly to the heart of a problem of this character. The spirit, ideals, and facilities of a professional or technical school can be quickly grasped" (Pritchett, "Introduction" to the *Flexner Report* of 1910, *ibid.,* p. xiii).

[11]In selecting some of the subjects he covered in this essay Flexner was influenced by Theodor Billroth's classic work on medical education in Germany, . . . *Lehren und Lernen der medicinischen Wissenschaften* . . . (Vienna: Carl Gerold's Sohn), 1876. Years later, the General Education Board financed its translation into English, and it was published as *The Medical Sciences in the German Universities* (New York: Macmillan Co.), 1924.

[12]True B. Eveleth, "Osteopathic Education," in Lloyd E. Blauch (ed. by), *Accreditation in Higher Education* (Washington, D.C.: Government Printing Office), 1959, p. 174.

[13]Work on the quality of medical schools has probably included every American medical school, or at least a large proportion of them, more often than the studies of any other professional field or academic discipline have included most or all of the schools in their discipline. In addition to the *Flexner Report* and the early work of the Council on Medical Education, a modern study which ranked every medical school that had been approved by the American Medical Association a few years earlier was Jonathan R. Cole and James A. Lipton's "Reputations of American Medical Schools," *Social Forces,* vol. 55, no. 3, March, 1977, pp. 662–684. Perhaps the reason why rankings of medical schools include most or all of them more than rankings of other fields cover the schools in their discipline is because there are fewer medical schools, and it is thus easier to include all of them. In 1984, for example, there were only about 140 American medical schools, fewer than the number of law, business, and education schools and fewer than the number of Ph.D.-granting departments in many arts and science disciplines. (In 1910, though, when Flexner's *Report* was published, there were 147 medical schools in America, far more than the number of Ph.D.-granting departments in any arts and science discipline at the time.) Perhaps it is because more seems to be at stake in medical education than in any other field. Incompetent doctors and inadequate medical schools can probably cause far more serious damage than incompetent historians or philosophers and inadequate history or philosophy departments. Consequently, it seems important not just to rank the most-esteemed departments but to identify the worst ones. Possibly it is because doctors are often "employed" by patients, while most historians and philosophers with doctorates are employed by college and university history and philosophy departments. Because those who often "employ" doctors are frequently less knowledgeable, less able to protect themselves, than the employers of historians or philosophers, special protection must be given to them. One way to do this is through the identification of the poorest medical schools so that patients can be cautious about being treated by physicians who have attended these schools.

[14]Flexner, I *Remember, ibid.,* p. 120.

[15]Ironically, Flexner, who excoriated the faculty members at many of the medical

schools he visited for not possessing the proper formal qualifications for their positions, scarcely had any formal qualifications for *his* task as assessor of American and Canadian medical schools when he was appointed to do his study. As Kessel has pointed out, "Flexner was neither a physician nor a scientist, and had no qualifications as a medical educator. He had an undergraduate degree in arts from Johns Hopkins and had operated a small, private, and apparently profitable preparatory school in Louisville for fifteen years. It is unlikely, if not inconceivable, that he would have been accepted in a court of law as an expert witness in the field of medical education before he undertook his study." See Reuben A. Kessel, "The A.M.A. and the Supply of Physicians," in R. H. Coase and Merton H. Miller (ed. by), *ibid.*, p. 39.

[16]Flexner, *I Remember, ibid.*, p. 121.

[17]*Ibid.*, p. 218.

[18]The CFAT also placed much emphasis on entrance requirements in its work on deciding which colleges and universities to accept into its pension program. One may wonder why medical school officials so readily made information available to Flexner about their nominal and actual entrance requirements and their financial status, since they were under no obligation to do so. One reason is because many of them believed that since Andrew Carnegie had once made a gift to a medical school in Atlanta, when their own school's inadequacies were revealed, the CFAT might give them a huge grant to set things right. See Flexner, *ibid.*, pp. 121–122.

[19]*Ibid.*, p. 120.

[20]About Johns Hopkins, for example, Flexner's consideration of faculty research was limited to the following: "all the laboratory teaching is conducted by instructors who give their entire time to teaching and research...." (*Medical Education in the United States and Canada, ibid.*, p. 234). On research at Western Reserve, he referred only to the school's "excellent laboratories, in which teaching and research are both vigorously prosecuted...." (p. 285).

[21]This point has been made by Kessel. Describing Flexner's *Report* of 1910, he wrote, "there was no attempt to evaluate the outputs of medical schools; there was no investigation of what their graduates could or could not do." (See Kessel, "The A.M.A. and the Supply of Physicians," *ibid.*, pp. 38–39). One of the major difficulties of academic quality ranking studies or of studies like Flexner's which seek to assess the quality of schools, even though they do not stratify or "rank" them, is that one of the best ways to determine the quality of any teaching institution is probably to measure how much it teaches its students and how well, using the knowledge they have learned there, they fare in later life. But these "output" measures, as they are called today, require years or decades before the necessary data are available. Someone doing a report, as Flexner did, in about two years' time, clearly could not collect his own information on "output" measures such as how much the schools' graduates knew about medicine five years after they had graduated or about the quality of medical treatment they provided, as physicians, in later life. If the schools had collected their own information on this subject, Flexner could have used that, but collecting detailed information on alumni was not something that schools in that

era, especially the marginal schools that Flexner was most eager to close, were likely to do.

[22]Flexner, *Medical Education in the United States and Canada, ibid.*, p. 256.

[23]Jarcho, *ibid.*, un-numbered footnote, p. 342.

[24]Flexner, *Medical Education in the United States and Canada, ibid.*, p. 223.

[25]*Ibid.*, p. 190.

[26]*Ibid.*, p. 229.

[27]*Ibid.*, p. 230. In light of Flexner's long career as a severe critic of American colleges, universities, and medical schools, a story he chose to tell almost at the beginning of his autobiography is worth retelling. Flexner, when in high school, had complained to his father of the injustice of one of his teachers. The next day his father accompanied him to school, went with the young Flexner to the office of the principal, and said to the principal in Flexner's presence, "My son has complained to me of what he regards as the injustice of one of his teachers. I should like you and all his teachers to know that if any question arises between my son and his teachers I shall always regard his teachers as being in the right." Flexner recounted this incident in later life with the obvious approval of his father's behavior, writing that "it shows a strain of common sense capable of very wide application." (See *I Remember, ibid.*, pp. 7–8). Coming from the pen of a man who for decades sharply criticized American institutions of higher learning and who invariably regarded himself, not the instructors or administrators of these schools, as being "in the right," it is a remarkable anecdote virtually to lead off Flexner's autobiography.

[28]Flexner, *Medical Education in the United States and Canada, ibid.*, p. 240.

[29]*Ibid.*, p. 268.

[30]Quoted in Howard S. Berliner, "New Light on the Flexner Report: Notes on the AMA-Carnegie Foundation Background," *Bulletin of the History of Medicine,* vol. 51, no. 4, winter, 1977, p. 608.

[31]*Ibid.*, p. 608.

[32]As he wrote in his autobiography concerning his visit to Johns Hopkins before beginning to write his *Report,* it was "a small but ideal medical school embodying in a novel way, adapted to American conditions, the best features of medical education in England, France, and Germany. Without this pattern in the back of my mind, I could have accomplished little" (*I Remember, ibid.*, p. 115). Interestingly enough, although he wanted to impose the Johns Hopkins model on American medical schools and to close down most of them—he recommended that the 155 medical schools in the United States and Canada be reduced to 31—he was much more pluralistic and *laissez-faire*, at least in later life, about America's small colleges, not wanting to impose any particular model upon them. In his autobiography, he wrote that "a country as large and varied as the United States, whose colleges were mainly local in their appeal—and still are—requires a very large number of small institutions quite as much as it requires a relatively small number of large ones.... It would be a great pity to standardize the small colleges for needs and opportunities vary" (*ibid.*, pp. 236–237). This statement was at odds with the philosophy of both the General Education Board and the CFAT, two organizations for which Flexner

worked, both of which were reluctant to aid America's small colleges before they met fairly stringent educational and financial standards.

[33]Abraham Flexner, *Universities: American, English, German* (New York: Oxford University Press), 1968.

[34]See Clark Kerr's introductory essay, "Remembering Flexner," in Flexner's *Universities: American, English, German, ibid.,* pp. xvii–xviii. It has been argued that Flexner's devotion to the model of Johns Hopkins Medical School resulted in a medical school curriculum based almost exclusively on the scientific disciplines, to the neglect of the social sciences, community medicine, family care, and what is sometimes called "holistic medicine."

[35]Flexner, *Universities . . . , ibid., fn.* 29, p. 348.

[36]William J. Gies, *Dental Education in the United States and Canada: A Report to the Carnegie Foundation for the Advancement of Teaching,* Bulletin no. 19 (New York: Carnegie Foundation for the Advancement of Teaching), 1926.

[37]Pritchett, preface to Gies, *ibid.,* p. xv.

[38]Gies, *ibid.,* pp. 310–311.

[39]Alfred Zantzinger Reed, *Present-Day Law Schools in the United States and Canada,* Carnegie Foundation for the Advancement of Teaching, Bulletin no. 21 (New York: Carnegie Foundation for the Advancement of Teaching), 1928.

[40]Henry S. Pritchett, preface to Reed, *ibid.,* p. xii.

[41]United States Bureau of Education, *Negro Education: A Study of the Private and Higher Schools for Colored People in the United States,* 2 vols., Bulletin 1916, nos. 38 and 39 (Washington: Government Printing Office), 1917.

[42]*Ibid.,* vol. II, p. 2. One reason why the report "covered" all private elementary schools and not all public ones was, of course, that there were far fewer private elementary schools. Another reason was that a major purpose of this study was to inform would-be philanthropists, both individuals and organizations, about which private southern schools for blacks, of the many then actively soliciting contributions, were worthy of their contributions.

[43]*Ibid.,* vol. II, p. 2.

[44]P. P. Claxton, "Letter of Transmittal," *ibid.,* vol. I, p. ix.

CHAPTER FOURTEEN

[1]The rank orders of the most eminent people in each of the twelve disciplines "covered" in the various editions of *American Men of Science,* although they were collected in 1903, were not published until 1933. The reason is because Cattell had assured his panels when he asked for their rankings that the information would not be made public for at least twenty years. The rank orders were finally published in J. M. Cattell, "Leading Men of Science in the United States in 1903 Arranged in the Order of Distinction in Each Science," in J. McKeen Cattell and Jaques Cattell (ed. by), *American Men of Science,* 5th ed. (New York: Science Press), 1933, pp. 1269–1278. For the ranking of the leading psychologists, see pp. 1277–1278.

[2]Nathan Reingold, entry on Cattell in the *Dictionary of Scientific Biography* (ed. by Charles Coulston Gillispie), vol. 3 (New York: Charles Scribner's Sons), 1971, p. 130.

[3]The following materials, though, are among the best of the small amount available. Some of Cattell's most important writings can be found in *James McKeen Cattell: Man of Science, 1860–1944*, ed. by A. T. Poffenberger, 2 vols. (Lancaster, Pa: Science Press), 1947. Volume I of this collection contains 29 of Cattell's most important psychological publications and also a nearly complete bibliography of his published writings. Volume II contains a few more of Cattell's scientific articles and also some of his addresses, many of them on the administration of universities and the role of science in American life.

Unlike his near contemporary, Abraham Flexner, who published an autobiography and 20 years later issued a revised version of it bringing it up to date, Cattell published little about his own life and work. A very short, uncompleted autobiographical manuscript, written about seven years before he died but unpublished in Cattell's lifetime, was finally published in 1971; it had notes and commentary by the Cattell scholar, Michael Sokal, but this fragment runs to only about five pages in journal form. See Michael M. Sokal, "The Unpublished Autobiography of James McKeen Cattell," *American Psychologist*, vol. 26, no. 7, July, 1971, pp. 626–635.

The most complete account of the first half of Cattell's life, the years when he did most of his important psychological research, has not been published. It is Sokal, "The Education and Psychological Career of James McKeen Cattell, 1860–1944," a Ph.D. dissertation at Case Western Reserve University, 1972. A published work that does cover Cattell's early years is Sokal (ed. by), *An Education in Psychology: James McKeen Cattell's Journal and Letters from Germany and England, 1880–1888* (Cambridge, Mass.: MIT Press), 1981.

Of the many brief published summaries of Cattell's life and work, perhaps the best is Dorothy Ross' biographical sketch in the *Dictionary of American Biography, Supplement Three, 1941–1945*, edited by Edward T. James (New York: Charles Scribner's Sons), 1973, pp. 148–151. Another satisfactory short account is W. B. Pillsbury's "James McKeen Cattell, 1860–1944," in *Biographical Memoirs*, vol. 25 (Washington, D.C.: National Academy of Sciences), 1949, pp. 1–9.

[4]Ross, *ibid.*, p. 149.

[5]Carol S. Gruber, "Academic Freedom at Columbia University, 1917–1918: The Case of James McKeen Cattell, 1917–1918," *AAUP Bulletin*, vol. 58, no. 3, autumn, 1972, p. 300. For additional discussion of Cattell's personality and temperament and his relations with his faculty colleagues and the administrative officers at Columbia, see this entire article (pp. 297–305) and also Carol S. Gruber, *Mars and Minerva: World War I and the Uses of the Higher Learning in America* (Baton Rouge: Louisiana State University Press), 1975, pp. 187–206. It is ironic that Cattell, who quarreled bitterly not only with his Columbia colleagues and administrators but also with many psychologists and other scientists in his lifetime, gave these scientists more fame than most of them otherwise would have achieved by publishing brief biographies of them, over many years, in his *American Men of Science*.

[6]Ross, *ibid.*, p. 151.

[7]For a fine discussion of Cattell's dismissal from Columbia and the events leading up to it, see Gruber, *ibid.,* pp. 297–305.

[8]In the *Psychological Review,* vol. 2, no. 2, March, 1895, pp. 155–156.

[9]Cattell, "A Statistical Study of Eminent Men," *Popular Science Monthly,* vol. 62, February, 1903, pp. 359–377. It is reprinted in Poffenberger (ed. by), *James McKeen Cattell: Man of Science,* vol. II, *ibid.,* pp. 165–184.

[10]For an English translation, see Lambert A. J. Quetelet, *A Treatise on Man and the Development of his Faculties* (Gainesville, Fla.: Scholars' Facsimiles & Reprints), 1969.

[11]E. L. Thorndike, "Professor Cattell's Relation to the Study of Individual Differences," *The Psychological Researches of James McKeen Cattell: A Review by Some of his Pupils* (ed. by R. S. Woodworth), *Archives of Psychology,* no. 30 (New York: Science Press), April, 1914, p. 92.

[12]One example of this line of work is the article Cattell wrote with Livingston Farrand (Cattell was senior author). It was published in 1896 in the *Psychological Review* and is most accessible today in Poffenberger's collection of Cattell's writings. See "Physical and Mental Measurements of the Students of Columbia University," in A. T. Poffenberger (ed. by), *James McKeen Cattell: Man of Science,* vol. I, *ibid.,* pp. 305–330.

[13]Michael M. Sokal, "The Unpublished Autobiography of James McKeen Cattell," *ibid.,* p. 634. Sokal adds that he believes Cattell was "probably overstating" the importance that his interest in sports and games had in fostering his interest in the study of individual differences, arguing that while [Cattell] did " . . . measure rates of reading from the start of his career as a psychologist, he did not explicitly compare these rates to illustrate individual differences until after he had worked with Galton" (*ibid.,* p. 634).

[14]James McKeen Cattell and George Stuart Fullerton, "On the Perception of Small Differences," in *James McKeen Cattell: Man of Science,* vol. I, *ibid.,* pp. 142–251.

[15]In the *Psychological Review, ibid.*

[16]"The Time of Perception as a Measure of Differences in Intensity," in *James McKeen Cattell: Man of Science,* vol. I, *ibid.,* pp. 355–359.

[17]J. McKeen Cattell (ed. by), *American Men of Science: A Biographical Dictionary* (New York: Science Press), 1906, p. v.

[18]*Ibid.,* p. vi.

[19]*Ibid.,* p. v.

[20]*Ibid.,* p. vii.

[21]Cattell, "A Statistical Study of American Men of Science," in *James McKeen Cattell: Man of Science,* vol. I, *ibid.,* p. 391.

[22]*Ibid.,* p. 391.

[23]Stephen Sargent Visher, "J. McKeen Cattell and American Science," *School and Society,* vol. 66, December 13, 1947, p. 452. Another useful article, in which Visher discussed Cattell's method of choosing scientists to be "starred" and suggested changes for "starring" procedures in future editions of *American Men of Science* was Visher, "Starring in *American Men of Science," Science,* vol. 106, October 17, 1947, pp. 359–361.

[24]*American Men & Women of Science* (ed. by Jaques Cattell Press), 15th ed., 8 vols. (New York: R.R. Bowker Co.), 1982.

[25]"Statistics of American Psychologists," in *James McKeen Cattell: Man of Science*, vol. I, *ibid.*, pp. 360–375. (In this early study, Cattell presented data on all 200 psychologists listed in *American Men of Science*, not just the 50 of them who were "starred".)

[26]Cattell, "Statistics of American Psychologists," *ibid.*, p. 373.

[27]Cattell, "A Statistical Study of American Men of Science," *ibid.*, p. 417.

[28]*Ibid.*, p. 424.

[29]*Ibid.*, table IV, p. 423.

[30]Cattell, "A Further Statistical Study of American Men of Science," in *James McKeen Cattell: Man of Science*, vol. I, *ibid.*, p. 439.

[31]From Cattell, "A Further Statistical Study of American Men of Science," *ibid.*, table XI, p. 468.

[32]Some of Astin's studies published before the mid-1960s that supported this position were as follows: "A Reexamination of College Productivity," *Journal of Educational Psychology*, vol. 52, no. 3, June, 1961, pp. 173–178; "'Productivity' of Undergraduate Institutions," *Science*, vol. 36, April 13, 1962, pp. 129–135; and "Differential Effects on the Motivation of Talented Students to Obtain the Ph.D.," *Journal of Educational Psychology*, vol. 54, no. 1, February, 1963, pp. 63–71.

[33]Allan M. Cartter, *An Assessment of Quality in Graduate Education* (Washington, D.C.: American Council on Education), 1966.

[34]George W. Pierson, *The Education of American Leaders: Comparative Contributions of U.S. Colleges and Universities* (New York: Praeger), 1969. Though this book is a gold mine of data on the academic origins of eminent people in dozens of fields and endeavors, and though its compiler was scarcely an obscure figure—he was Larned Professor of History and Director of the Division of the Humanities at Yale—this work is almost never cited and deserves to be much more widely known and used than it is. Perhaps the incredibly heterogeneous nature of the material in this book is partly responsible for its obscurity. In one place Pierson published a table ranking colleges and universities according to how many students who had earned their baccalaureate degree at each over a period of almost 60 years went on to earn Ph.D.'s in science or to be starred in *American Men of Science* (p. 149). In another, he solemnly ranked colleges and universities based upon their production of a group of "eighty volunteer Red Feather Campaign Chairmen . . ." (p. 131). Perhaps it is because Pierson, though he presented a vast amount of data in approximately 100 tables and discussed, sometimes extensively, each of them, provided very little, other than a few pages on *per capita* productivity, in the way of overall conclusions.

CHAPTER FIFTEEN

[1]Kenneth D. Roose and Charles J. Andersen, *A Rating of Graduate Programs* (Washington, D.C.: American Council on Education), 1970.

[2]Lyle V. Jones, Gardner Lindzey, and Porter E. Coggeshall (ed. by), *An Assess-*

ment of Research-Doctorate Programs in the United States, 5 vols. (Washington, D.C.: National Academy Press), 1982.

[3]Rebecca Zames Margulies and Peter M. Blau, "America's Leading Professional Schools," *Change,* vol. 5, no. 9, November, 1973, pp. 21–27 and Peter M. Blau and Rebecca Zames Margulies, "The Reputations of American Professional Schools," *Change,* vol. 6, no. 10, December/January, 1974–'75, pp. 42–47.

[4]Raymond M. Hughes, *A Study of the Graduate Schools of America* (Oxford, Ohio: Miami University Press), 1925.

[5]Raymond M. Hughes, "Report of the Committee on Graduate Instruction," *Educational Record,* vol. 15, no. 2, April, 1934, pp. 192–234.

[6]Hayward Keniston, *Graduate Study and Research in the Arts and Sciences at the University of Pennsylvania* (Philadelphia: University of Pennsylvania Press), 1959.

[7]Allan M. Cartter, *An Assessment of Quality in Graduate Education* (Washington, D.C.: American Council on Education), 1966.

[8]Raymond H. Ewell, "A Quantified Summary of the American Council on Education Report, *An Assessment of Quality in Graduate Education,*" mimeographed (Buffalo: State University of New York at Buffalo), 1966.

[9]Roose and Andersen, *ibid.*

[10]For this ranking, see Malcolm G. Scully, "The Well-Known Universities Lead in Rating of Faculties' Reputations," *Chronicle of Higher Education,* vol. 19, no. 17, January 15, 1979, pp. 6–7.

[11]George H. Callcott, "The Costs of Excellence," University of Maryland Graduate School *Chronicle,* vol. 13, no. 3, April, 1980, pp. 2–9.

[12]See *College-Rater: A Composite Index of 700 Numerically Ranked Colleges and Universities* (Allentown, Pa.: College-Rater), 1967 and *Where the Colleges Rank* (Allentown, Pa.: College-Rater), 1973.

[13]Jon M. Nicholson, "A Guide to the College Guides," *Change,* vol. 15, no. 1, January/February, 1983, pp. 16–21; 46–50.

CHAPTER SIXTEEN

[1]W. Miles Cox and Viola Catt, "Productivity Ratings of Graduate Programs in Psychology Based on Publication in the Journals of the American Psychological Association," *American Psychologist,* vol. 32, no. 10, October, 1977, pp. 793–813.

[2]John S. Robey, "Political Science Departments: Reputations Versus Productivity," *PS,* vol. 12, no. 2, spring, 1979, pp. 202–209.

[3]J. David Hunger and Thomas L. Wheelen, "A Performance Appraisal of Undergraduate Business Education," *Human Resource Management,* vol. 19, no. 1, spring, 1980, pp. 24–31.

[4]James McKeen Cattell, "A Further Statistical Study of American Men of Science," *Science,* vol. 32, November 4, 1910, pp. 672–688.

[5]Raymond M. Hughes, *A Study of the Graduate Schools of America* (Oxford, Ohio: Miami University Press), 1925, p. 4.

[6]Martin Duberman, *Black Mountain: An Exploration in Community* (New York: Dutton), 1972.

[7]James Cass and Max Birnbaum, *Comparative Guide to American Colleges*, 11th ed. (New York: Harper and Row), 1983.

[8]*Ibid.*

CHAPTER SEVENTEEN

[1]W. Miles Cox and Viola Catt, "Productivity Ratings of Graduate Programs in Psychology Based on Publication in the Journals of the American Psychological Association," *American Psychologist*, vol. 32, no. 10, October, 1977, pp. 793–813.

[2]Joel R. Levin *et al.,* "University Productivity Rankings: A Psychologist by any Other Name," *American Psychologist*, vol. 33, no. 7, July, 1978, pp. 694–695.

BIBLIOGRAPHY

American Men & Women of Science (ed. by Jaques Cattell Press). 15th ed., 8 vols. (New York: R.R. Bowker Co.), 1982.

Association of American Universities. *Journal of Proceedings and Addresses of the Annual Conference* (Chicago: University of Chicago Press), 1901–.

Astin, Alexander W. "A Re-examination of College Productivity," *Journal of Educational Psychology,* vol. 52, no. 3, June, 1961, pp. 173–178.

_____. "Differential College Effects on the Motivation of Talented Students to Obtain the Ph.D.," *Journal of Educational Psychology,* vol. 54, no. 1, February, 1963, pp. 63–71.

_____. " 'Productivity' of Undergraduate Institutions," *Science,* vol. 136, April 13, 1962, pp. 129–135.

Babcock, Kendric Charles. "Higher Education in the United States," *Report of the Commissioner of Education for the Year Ended June 30, 1911,* vol. 1 (Washington, D.C.: Government Printing Office), pp. 37–65.

Baird's Manual of American College Fraternities (ed. by John Robson). 19th ed. (Menasha, Wis.: Baird's Manual Foundation), 1977.

Banta, H. David. "Abraham Flexner—a Reappraisal," *Social Science & Medicine,* vol. 5, no. 6, December, 1971, pp. 655–661.

Berliner, Howard S. "A Larger Perspective on the Flexner Report," *International Journal of Health Services,* vol. 5, no. 4, winter, 1975, pp. 573–592.

_____. "New Light on the Flexner Report: Notes on the AMA–Carnegie Foundation Background," *Bulletin of the History of Medicine,* vol. 51, no. 4, winter, 1977, pp. 603–609.

Bevan, Arthur Dean. "Cooperation in Medical Education and Medical Service," *Journal of the American Medical Association,* vol. 90, no. 15, April 14, 1928, pp. 1173–1177.

Billroth, Theodor. *The Medical Sciences in the German Universities* (New York: Macmillan Co.), 1924.

_____. *Über das Lehren und Lernen der medicinischen Wissenschaften an den Universitäten der deutschen Nation nebst allgemeinen Bemerkungen über Universitäten; eine culturhistorische Studie* (Vienna: Carl Gerold's Sohn), 1876.

Birge, E. A. "Report on Statistics Concerning the Migration of Graduate Students," Association of American Universities, *Journal of Proceedings and Addresses of the Third Annual Conference* (Chicago: Association of American Universities), 1902, pp. 37–45.

Blackburn, Robert T. and Paul E. Lingenfelter. *Assessing Quality in Doctoral Programs:*

Criteria and Correlates of Excellence (Ann Arbor, Mich.: Center for the Study of Higher Education), 1973.

Blau, Peter M. and Rebecca Zames Margulies. "The Reputations of American Professional Schools," *Change*, vol. 6, no. 10, December/January, 1974–'75, pp. 42–47.

Blauch, Lloyd E. (ed. by). *Accreditation in Higher Education* (Washington, D. C.: Government Printing Office), 1959.

Bowerman, Walter G. *Studies in Genius* (New York: Philosophical Library), 1947.

Brown, E. Richard. *Rockefeller Medicine Men: Medicine and Capitalism in America* (Berkeley: University of California Press), 1979.

Callcott, George H. "The Costs of Excellence," University of Maryland Graduate School *Chronicle*, vol. 13, no. 3, April, 1980, pp. 2–9.

Candolle, Alphonse de. *Histoire des Sciences et des Savants depuis Deux Siècles* (Geneva: H. Georg), 1873.

Capen, Samuel P. "College 'Lists' and Surveys Published by the Bureau of Education," *School and Society*, vol. 6, July 14, 1917, pp. 35–41.

Carnegie Foundation for the Advancement of Teaching. *Annual Reports of the President and Treasurer* [titles vary slightly], (New York: Carnegie Foundation for the Advancement of Teaching), 1906–.

––––––––––. *Rules for the Admission of Institutions and for the Granting of Retiring Allowances* (New York: Carnegie Foundation for the Advancement of Teaching), 1913.

Cartter, Allan M. *An Assessment of Quality in Graduate Education* (Washington, D.C.: American Council on Education), 1966.

Cass, James and Max Birnbaum. *Comparative Guide to American Colleges*, 11th ed. (New York: Harper and Row), 1983.

Cattell, James McKeen. "A Further Statistical Study of American Men of Science," James McKeen Cattell (ed. by), *American Men of Science*, 2nd ed. (New York: Science Press), 1910, pp. 564–596.

––––––––––. "A Further Statistical Study of American Men of Science," *Science*, vol. 32, November 4, 1910, pp. 633–648 and *Science*, vol. 32, November 11, 1910, pp. 672–688.

––––––––––. *American Men of Science: A Biographical Dictionary* (New York: Science Press), 1906.

––––––––––. "A Statistical Study of American Men of Science," in James McKeen Cattell (ed. by), *American Men of Science*, 2nd ed. (New York: Science Press), 1910, pp. 537–563.

––––––––––. "A Statistical Study of Eminent Men," *Popular Science Monthly*, vol. 62, February, 1903, pp. 359–377.

––––––––––. *James McKeen Cattell: Man of Science, 1860–1944*, ed. by A.T. Poffenberger, 2 vols. (Lancaster, Pa.: Science Press), 1947.

––––––––––. "Leading Men of Science in the United States in 1903 Arranged in the Order of Distinction of Each Science," in J. McKeen Cattell and Jaques Cattell (ed. by), *American Men of Science*, 5th ed. (New York: Science Press), 1933, pp. 1269–1278.

_____. "On the Distribution of Exceptional Ability," *Psychological Review*, vol. 2, no. 2, March, 1895, pp. 155–156.

Chapman, Carleton B. "*The Flexner Report* by Abraham Flexner," *Daedalus*, vol. 103, no. 1, winter, 1963, pp. 105–117.

Clarke, Edwin Leavitt. *American Men of Letters: Their Nature and Nurture*, Columbia Studies in History, Economics and Public Law, vol. 168, no. 1 (New York: Columbia University Press), 1916.

Coase, R. H. and Merton H. Miller (ed. by). *Essays in Applied Price Theory by Reuben A. Kessel* (Chicago: University of Chicago Press), 1980.

Cole, Jonathan R. and James A. Lipton. "The Reputations of American Medical Schools," *Social Forces*, vol. 55, no. 3, March, 1977, pp. 662–684.

College-Rater: A Composite Index of 700 Numerically Ranked Colleges and Universities (Allentown, Pa.: College-Rater), 1967.

Colwell, N. P. "Council on Medical Education of the American Medical Association," *Journal of the American Medical Association*, vol. 48, no. 20, May 18, 1907, pp. 1701–1707.

Corbin, John. *Which College for the Boy?* (Boston: Houghton, Mifflin and Co.), 1908.

Cox, W. Miles and Viola Catt. "Productivity Ratings of Graduate Programs in Psychology Based on Publication in the Journals of the American Psychological Association," *American Psychologist*, vol. 32, no. 10, October, 1977, pp. 793–813.

Dolan, W. Patrick. *The Ranking Game: The Power of the Academic Elite* (Lincoln: University of Nebraska Printing and Duplicating Service), 1976.

Duberman, Martin. *Black Mountain: An Exploration in Community* (New York: Dutton), 1972.

Ehrenreich, Barbara and Deirdre English. *For Her Own Good: 150 Years of the Experts' Advice to Women* (Garden City, N. Y.: Doubleday), 1978.

Eliot, C. W., J. G. Schurman, C. R. Van Hise, J. H. Penniman, and Munroe Smith. "Report of the Special Committee on Aim and Scope of the Association," Association of American Universities, *Journal of Proceedings and Addresses of the Ninth Annual Conference* (Chicago: University of Chicago Press), 1908, pp. 74–76.

Ellis, Havelock. *A Study of British Genius* (London: Hurst and Blackett), 1904.

Ewell, Raymond H. "A Quantified Summary of the American Council on Education Report, *An Assessment of Quality in Graduate Education*." Mimeographed (Buffalo: State University of New York at Buffalo), 1966.

Flexner, Abraham. *An Autobiography* (New York: Simon and Schuster), 1960.

_____. *I Remember* (New York: Simon and Schuster), 1940.

_____. *Medical Education in Europe: A Report to the Carnegie Foundation for the Advancement of Teaching*, Bulletin no. 6 (New York: Carnegie Foundation for the Advancement of Teaching), 1912.

_____. *Medical Education in the United States and Canada: A Report to the Carnegie Foundation for the Advancement of Teaching*, Bulletin no. 4 (New York: Carnegie Foundation for the Advancement of Teaching), 1910.

_____. *The American College: A Criticism* (New York: Century Co.), 1908.

[_____]. *The General Education Board: An Account of its Activities, 1902–1914* (New York: General Education Board), 1915.

——————. *Universities: American, English, German* (New York: Oxford University Press), 1968.

Fosdick, Raymond B. *Adventure in Giving: The Story of the General Education Board* (New York: Harper and Row), 1962.

Galton, Francis. *English Men of Science: Their Nature and Nurture* (London: Frank Cass and Co.), 1960.

——————. *Hereditary Genius* (London: Watts and Co.), 1950.

——————. "Hereditary Talent and Character," *MacMillan's Magazine*, vol. 12, no. 68, June, 1865, pp. 157–166.

——————. "Hereditary Talent and Character," Second Paper, *MacMillan's Magazine*, vol. 12, no. 70, August, 1865, pp. 318–327.

Gies, William J. *Dental Education in the United States and Canada: A Report to the Carnegie Foundation for the Advancement of Teaching*, Bulletin no. 19 (New York: Carnegie Foundation for the Advancement of Teaching), 1926.

Gilman, Daniel Coit. *University Problems in the United States* (New York: Century Co.), 1898.

Gruber, Carol S. "Academic Freedom at Columbia University, 1917–1918: The Case of James McKeen Cattell," *AAUP Bulletin*, vol. 58, no. 3, autumn, 1972, pp. 297–305.

——————. *Mars and Minerva: World War I and the Uses of the Higher Learning in America* (Baton Rouge: Louisiana State University Press), 1975.

Higgins, Arthur Steven. "The Rating of Selected Fields of Doctoral Study in the Graduate Schools of Education: An Opinion Survey," Columbia University Teachers College Ed.D. dissertation, 1968.

Hillinger, Charles. "Howard University: Seedbed of Black Leadership," *Los Angeles Times*, pt. 1a, March 16, 1980, pp. 6–7.

Hilts, Victor L. *A Guide to Francis Galton's "English Men of Science,"* Transactions of the American Philosophical Society, New Series, vol. 65, pt. 5 (Philadelphia: American Philosophical Society), 1975.

Hughes, Raymond M. *A Study of the Graduate Schools of America* (Oxford, Ohio: Miami University Press), 1925.

——————. "Report of the Committee on Graduate Instruction," *Educational Record*, vol. 15, no. 2, April, 1934, pp. 192–234.

Hunger, J. David and Thomas L. Wheelen. "A Performance Appraisal of Undergraduate Business Education," *Human Resource Management*, vol. 19, no. 1, spring, 1980, pp. 24–31.

"In Time, Every Great City Has a Great University," *U. S. News and World Report*, January 21, 1980, un-numbered page.

Jaffe, A. J., Walter Adams, and Sandra G. Meyers, *Negro Higher Education in the 1960's* (New York: Praeger), 1968, pp. 233–242.

Jarcho, Saul. "Medical Education in the United States—1910–1956," *Journal of the Mount Sinai Hospital*, vol. 26, no. 4, July–August, 1959, pp. 339–385.

Johnson, Victor. "The Council on Medical Education and Hospitals," in Morris Fishbein (ed. by), *A History of the American Medical Association, 1847 to 1947* (Philadelphia: W. B. Saunders Co.), 1947, pp. 887–922.

Johnson, Victor and Herman G. Weiskotten, *A History of the Council on Medical Education and Hospitals of the American Medical Association* (Chicago: Council on Medical Education and Hospitals), 1960?

Jones, Lyle V., Gardner Lindzey, and Porter E. Coggeshall (ed. by). *An Assessment of Research-Doctorate Programs in the United States*, 5 vols. (Washington, D.C.: National Academy Press), 1982.

Kaufman, Martin. *American Medical Education: The Formative Years, 1765-1910* (Westport, Conn.: Greenwood Press), 1976.

Kelly, Fred J., Benjamin W. Frazier, John H. McNeely, and Ella B. Ratcliffe. *Collegiate Accreditation by Agencies within States*, Bulletin 1940, no. 3 (Washington, D. C.: Government Printing Office), 1940.

Keniston, Hayward. *Graduate Study and Research in the Arts and Sciences at the University of Pennsylvania* (Philadelphia: University of Pennsylvania Press), 1959.

Knapp, Robert H. *The Origins of American Humanistic Scholars* (Englewood Cliffs, N. J.: Prentice-Hall), 1964.

Knapp, Robert H. and Hubert B. Goodrich. *Origins of American Scientists* (New York: Russell and Russell), 1952.

Knapp, Robert H. and Joseph J. Greenbaum. *The Younger American Scholar: His Collegiate Origins* (Chicago: University of Chicago Press), 1953.

Koerner, James D. *The Parsons College Bubble: A Tale of Higher Education in America* (New York: Basic Books), 1970.

Lagemann, Ellen Condliffe. *Private Power for the Public Good: A History of the Carnegie Foundation for the Advancement of Teaching* (Middletown, Conn.: Wesleyan University Press), 1983.

Lawrence, Judith K. and Kenneth C. Green. *A Question of Quality: The Higher Education Ratings Game*, American Association for Higher Education—ERIC Research Report no. 5 (Washington, D.C.: American Association for Higher Education), 1980.

Laws (Abstract) and Board Rulings Regulating the Practice of Medicine in the United States and Elsewhere. 19th ed. (Chicago: American Medical Association), 1912.

Laws (Abstract) and Board Rulings Regulating the Practice of Medicine in the United States and Elsewhere. 20th ed. (Chicago: American Medical Association), 1913.

Levin, Joel R., *et al.* "University Productivity Ratings: A Psychologist by any Other Name," *American Psychologist*, vol. 33, no. 7, July, 1978, pp. 694-695.

Levine, Arthur. "Quality in Higher Education: Who Protects the Consumer?", *Chronicle of Higher Education*, vol. 21, no. 3, September 8, 1980, p. 48.

Lewis, Charles Lee. *Philander Priestley Claxton: Crusader for Public Education* (Knoxville: University of Tennessee Press), 1948.

Lykes, Richard Wayne. *Higher Education and the United States Office of Education (1867-1953)* (Washington, D.C.: U.S. Office of Education), 1975.

Maclean, Alick Henry Herbert. *Where We Get Our Best Men* (London: Simpkin, Marshall, Hamilton, Kent, and Co.), 1900.

Margulies, Rebecca Zames and Peter M. Blau. "America's Leading Professional Schools," *Change*, vol. 5, no. 9, November, 1973, pp. 21-27.

"Medical Education in the United States." *Journal of the American Medical Association*, vol. 97, no. 9, August 29, 1931, pp. 611–628.

Nevins, John F. *A Study of the Organization and Operation of Voluntary Accrediting Agencies*, Catholic University of America Educational Research Monographs, vol. 22, no. 3, May, 1959.

Nicholson, Jon M. "A Guide to the College Guides," *Change*, vol. 15, no. 1, January/February, 1983, pp. 16–21; 46–50.

Odin, Alfred. [A listing of his published works], *National Union Catalog, Pre-1956 Imprints*, vol. 426 (London: Mansell Information/Publishing), 1976, p. 567.

_____. *Genèse des Grands Hommes: Gens de Lettres Francais Modernes*, vol. 1 (Paris: H. Welter), 1895.

Patterson's College and School Directory of the United States and Canada. Comp. and ed. by Homer L. Patterson (Chicago: American Educational Company), 1910.

Paulsen, Friedrich. *The German Universities and University Study.* Translated by Frank Thilly (London: Longmans, Green and Co.), 1906.

Pierson, George W. *The Education of American Leaders: Comparative Contributions of U.S. Colleges and Universities* (New York: Praeger), 1969.

Pillsbury, W. B. "James McKeen Cattell, 1860–1944," *Biographical Memoirs*, vol. 25 (Washington, D.C.: National Academy of Sciences), 1949, pp. 1–9.

Pothier, Dick. "Community College Gets a Real Campus," *Philadelphia Inquirer*, July 20, 1982, p. 4BW.

_____. "President-elect is Banking on Temple's Strengths," *Philadelphia Inquirer*, December 19, 1981, pp. 11A–12A.

Pritchett, Henry S. "The Classification of American Medical Schools," *Proceedings of the Association of American Medical Schools*, vol. 25, 1915, pp. 11–29.

Quetelet, Lambert A. J. *A Treatise on Man and the Development of his Faculties* (Gainesville, Fla.: Scholars' Facsimiles & Reprints), 1969.

Reed, Alfred Zantzinger. *Present-Day Law Schools in the United States and Canada*, Carnegie Foundation for the Advancement of Teaching, Bulletin no. 21 (New York: Carnegie Foundation for the Advancement of Teaching), 1928.

Reingold, Nathan. Entry on James McKeen Cattell in the *Dictionary of Scientific Biography* (ed. by Charles Coulston Gillispie), vol. 3 (New York: Charles Scribner's Sons), 1971, pp. 130–131.

Reports of the Commissioner of Education [titles vary slightly], (Washington, D.C.: Government Printing Office), issued annually, 1872–.

[Rhind, Flora M.]. *General Education Board: Review and Final Report, 1902–1964* (New York: General Education Board), 1964.

Ribot, Théodule. [A listing of his published works]. *National Union Catalog, Pre-1956 Imprints*, vol. 492 (London: Mansell Information/Publishing), 1977, pp. 263–272.

_____. *L'Hérédité Psychologique*, 2nd ed. (Paris: Germer Ballière), 1882.

Robey, John S. "Political Science Departments: Reputations Versus Productivity," *PS*, vol. 12, no. 2, spring, 1979, pp. 202–209.

Roose, Kenneth D. and Charles J. Andersen. *A Rating of Graduate Programs* (Washington, D.C.: American Council on Education), 1970.

Ross, Dorothy. Entry on James McKeen Cattell in Edward T. James (ed. by),

Dictionary of American Biography, Supplement Three, 1941–1945 (New York: Charles Scribner's Sons), 1973, pp. 148–151.

"Rutgers Subsidizes Prof's Condo." University of Pennsylvania *Daily Pennsylvanian*, April 23, 1984, p. 2.

Savage, Howard J. *Fruit of an Impulse: Forty-Five Years of the Carnegie Foundation, 1905–1950* (New York: Harcourt, Brace and Co.), 1953.

Schlabach, Theron F. *Pensions for Professors* (Madison: The State Historical Society of Wisconsin for the Department of History, University of Wisconsin), 1963.

Scully, Malcolm G. "The Well-Known Universities Lead in Rating of Faculties' Reputations," *Chronicle of Higher Education*, vol. 19, no. 17, January 15, 1979, pp. 6–7.

"Search Reopened, Director of Public Relations." *Chronicle of Higher Education*, vol. 21, no. 15, December 1, 1980, p. 51.

Selden, William K. "The AAU and Accreditation," *Graduate Journal*, vol. 2, no. 2, fall, 1959, pp. 325–333.

"Senior Wranglers." *Cornhill Magazine*, vol. 45, 1882, pp. 225–234.

"Slippery Rock State College." *Chronicle of Higher Education*, vol. 22, no. 12, May 11, 1981, p. 33.

Smith, Richard and Fred E. Fiedler. "The Measurement of Scholarly Work: A Critical Review of the Literature," *Educational Record*, vol 52, no. 3, summer, 1971, pp. 225–232.

Smyser, William Craig. "Our First Fifty Years," in Clifford L. Constance (comp. by), *Historical Review of the Association* (n.p.: American Association of Collegiate Registrars and Admissions Officers), 1972, pp. 10–23.

Sokal, Michael M. (ed. by). *An Education in Psychology: James McKeen Cattell's Journal and Letters from Germany and England, 1880–1888* (Cambridge, Mass.: MIT Press), 1981.

_____. "The Education and Psychological Career of James McKeen Cattell, 1860–1904," Ph.D. dissertation, Case Western Reserve University, 1972.

_____. "The Unpublished Autobiography of James McKeen Cattell," *American Psychologist*, vol. 26, no. 7, July, 1971, pp. 626–635.

Solorzano, Lucia with Barbara E. Quick. "Rating the Colleges," *U. S. News and World Report*, November 28, 1983, pp. 41–46; 48.

"State Board Examinations During 1904." *Journal of the American Medical Association*, vol. 44, no. 18, May 6, 1905, pp. 1454–1456.

Sully, James. "The Education of Genius," *English Illustrated Magazine*, vol. 8, January, 1891, pp. 316–322.

Talbot, Marion and Lois Kimball Mathews Rosenberry. *The History of the American Association of University Women, 1881–1931* (Boston: Houghton Mifflin Co.), 1931.

"The College of Idaho." *Chronicle of Higher Education*, vol. 21, no. 23, February 17, 1981, p. 33.

"These Faces Are the Key to Your Future." *Chronicle of Higher Education*, vol. 21, no. 7, October 6, 1980, p. 9.

Thorndike, E. L. "Professor Cattell's Relation to the Study of Individual Differences," *The Psychological Researches of James McKeen Cattell: A Review by Some of His*

Pupils (ed. by R.S. Woodworth), *Archives of Psychology*, no. 30 (New York: Science Press), April, 1914, pp. 92–101.

Trombley, William. "New USC President Wants the Power at the Top," *Los Angeles Times*, pt. 2, February 17, 1981, pp. 1–3.

United States Bureau of Education. *Negro Education: A Study of the Private and Higher Schools for Colored People in the United States*, 2 vols, Bulletin 1916, nos. 38 and 39 (Washington, D. C.: Government Printing Office), 1917.

Visher, Stephen Sargent. "J. McKeen Cattell and American Science," *School and Society*, vol. 66, December 13, 1947, pp. 449–452.

——————. *Scientists Starred, 1903-1943, in "American Men of Science"* (Baltimore: Johns Hopkins University Press), 1947.

——————. "Starring in *American Men of Science*," *Science*, vol. 106, October 17, 1947, pp. 359–361.

Voorhees, Oscar M. *The History of Phi Beta Kappa* (New York: Crown Publishers), 1945.

Ward, Lester F. *Applied Sociology.* (Boston: Ginn and Co.), 1906.

Webster, David S. "Advantages and Disadvantages of Methods of Assessing Quality," *Change*, vol 13, no. 7, October, 1981, pp. 20–24.

——————. "America's Highest Ranked Graduate Schools, 1925–1982," *Change*, vol. 15, no. 4, May/June, 1983, pp. 14–24.

——————. "A Note on a Very Early Academic Quality Ranking by James McKeen Cattell," *Journal of the History of the Behavioral Sciences*, vol. 20, no. 2, April, 1984, pp. 180–183.

Welch, Claude. *Graduate Education in Religion: A Critical Appraisal* (Missoula: University of Montana Press), 1971.

Where the Colleges Rank (Allentown, Pa.: College-Rater), 1973.

Zook, George F. and M. E. Haggerty. *The Evaluation of Higher Institutions, I. Principles of Accrediting Higher Institutions* (Chicago: University of Chicago Press), 1936.

NAME INDEX

SUBJECT INDEX

A

Aberdeen University, 22, 24
Abilene Christian University, 12
Academic quality, quotations regarding, vii–xi
Academic quality rankings
  advantage ranking institutions by graduates
    produced, 118
  ascent "academic origins" studies, 17–18
    basis studies of, 17–18
    inventor of (*see* Cattell, James McKeen)
  ascent reputational rankings, 18
  basis of
    citations in citation indexes, 146–149
    faculty accomplishments, 142–146
    faculty awards, honors, prizes, 145–149
    institutional academic resources, 151–152
    number scientists and scholars produced, 18
    reputational rankings of faculty, 142–145
    students' achievements in later life, 149–150
    students' scores on standardized tests, 150–151
  by Methodist Episcopal Church, South (*see*
    Methodist Episcopal Church, South)
  by state organizations (*see* Iowa Board of
    General Examiners)
  comparison American and German doctoral
    degreed, 161
  comparison early and modern (*see* Comparison
    early and modern academic quality
    ratings)
  contemporary methods of, 141–152 (*see also*
    Contemporary methods assessing college
    and university quality)
  decline in use of, 118–119
  definition of, 5–6, 155
    criteria for, 5
  disadvantage of time lag of studies, 118
  earliest attempts, 155
  emphasis on research to obtain research funds,
    17
  first academic quality ranking, 115–117
    development weighting system for, 116
    differences from 1903 list, 115
    importance of, 116

measurement quality university science
  departments, 115
ratio starred faculty to total faculty, 115–116
research method used, 115
tables displayed, 115
for black colleges, 13, 157
ideal, 153–154, 183
influences available general reference works on,
  11
invention by Cattrell (*see* Cattrell, James
  McKeen)
James McKeen Cattell and, 107–119 (*see also*
  Cattell, James McKeen)
lasting influence of Cattrell, 117–119
lists with potential for
  Babcock's classification, 33–43 (*see also*
    Babcock's classification)
  backgrounds eminent people, European
    studeis, 19–28 (*see also* Backgrounds
    eminent people, European studies)
  by American Association of University
    Women, 65–69 (*see* Association of
    Collegiate Alumnae)
  by Iowa Board of General Examiners, 53–57
    (*see also* Iowa Board of General
    Examiners)
  by Methodist Episcopal Church, South,
    53–55 (*see also* Methodist Episcopal
    Church, South)
  by Phi Beta Kappa, 61–64 (*see also* Phi Beta
    Kappa)
  classification efforts (*see* Classification efforts)
  early versus modern academic quality
    rankings, 11–18
  Maclean's rank order, 23–25 (*see also*
    Maclean's rank order)
  *Medical Education in the United States and
    Canada*, 95–106 (*see also Flexner Report*)
  medical school ratings, 45–49
  of Association of American Universities (*see*
    Association of American Universities)
  of Carnegie Foundation for Advancement of
    Teaching (*see* Carnegie Foundation
    for Advancement of Teaching)

July 28, 1986

Dear Martha,

Thanks very much for your help with this book.

Best

Dave